225

HILLSIDE
HOME PLANS

**Designs
& Ideas
for Homes on
Sloping Lots**

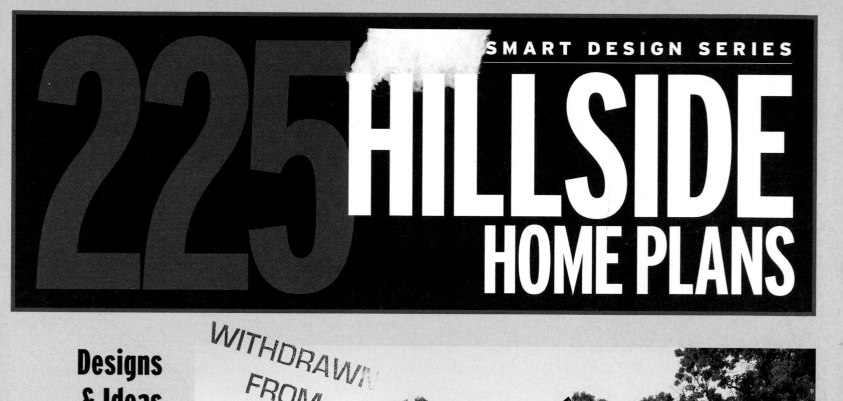

329/342 ·

Published by Hanley Wood
One Thomas Circle, NW, Suite 600
Washington, DC 20005

Distribution Center
29333 Lorie Lane
Wixom, Michigan 48393

Group Publisher, Andrew Schultz
Associate Publisher, Editorial Development, Jennifer Pearce
Senior Editor, Nate Ewell
Associate Editor, Simon Hyoun
Senior Plan Merchandiser, Morenci C. Clark
Plan Merchandiser, Nicole Phipps
Proofreader/Copywriter, Dyana Weis
Graphic Artist, Joong Min
Plan Data Team Leader, Susan Jasmin
Production Manager, Brenda McClary

Vice President, Retail Sales, Scott Hill
National Sales Manager, Bruce Holmes
Director, Plan Products, Matt Higgins

Most Hanley Wood titles are available at quantity discounts with bulk purchases for educational,
business, or sales promotional use. For information, please contact Bruce Holmes at bholmes@hanleywood.com.

BIG DESIGNS, INC.
President, Creative Director, Anthony D'Elia
Vice President, Business Manager, Megan D'Elia
Vice President, Design Director, Chris Bonavita
Editorial Director, John Roach
Assistant Editor, Patricia Starkey
Senior Art Director, Stephen Reinfurt
Production Director, David Barbella
Photo Editor, Christine DiVuolo
Art Director, Jacque Young
Graphic Designer, Billy Doremus
Graphic Designer, Frank Augugliaro
Assistant Production Manager, Rich Fuentes

PHOTO CREDITS
Front Cover and Page 1: Photo courtesy of Stephen Fuller, Inc. See page 77 for details.
Back Cover Left: Photo by Donna L. Ahmann. See page 176 for details.
Back Cover Right: Photography by Exposures Unlimited, Ron & Donna Kolb. See page 71 for details.
Facing Page Top: Photo by Ahmann Design, Inc.
Facing Page Bottom: Photo courtesy of Alan Mascord Design Associates, Inc. Photograph by Bob Greenspan.

10 9 8 7 6 5 4 3 2 1

Printed in the United States of America

Library of Congress Control Number: 2005927715

ISBN-13: 9781931131438
ISBN-10: 1-931131-44-9

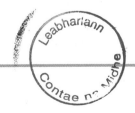

Contents

ONLINE EXTRA!

Hanley Wood Passageway

The Hanley Wood Passageway is an online search tool for your home plan needs! Discover even more useful information about building your new home, search additional new home plans, access online ordering, and more at www.hanleywood books.com/hillsidehomeplans

hanley▪wood

Downhill From Here

The opportunities presented by a sloped lot outweigh the challenges

You might think most home designs begin with a blank slate. But some—including some of the most ingenious and some of the most livable—begin on a hillside.

As America's housing boom continues, there's a dwindling availability of land for new homes. As a result, more and more lots include slopes that can present a challenge to architects and builders. The designers and architects presented in these pages have cer-

tainly risen to that challenge.

With innovative approaches to foundations and floor plans, these designers demonstrate the opportunities available to homeowners looking to build on a hillside lot. The setting can be spectacular—many sloped lots feature terrific views or lakefront locations—and the homes themselves don't sacrifice anything in the design just because they aren't on a perfectly flat lot.

Look inside and see the different ways you can take full advantage of a sloped lot:

Bargain Basements

The chance to incorporate a finished basement is one of the biggest positives of building a hillside home. Chances are you can incorporate a basement into the terrain, allowing light into what may be a dark space on a flat lot. It adds living space—at a fraction of the cost of an additional aboveground story—and can be the perfect location for a number of in-demand amenities, like a home theater.

Natural Choices

The best new homes fit in perfectly with their surroundings, whether it's the prevailing architectural style of the neighborhood, or the use of natural materials that meshes with the local environment. With some of the best homes designed for sloping lots, you'll find designs that fit naturally within your land's topography as well.

Flexibility

Most of the foundations showcased in these pages provide flexibility for use in a variety of lots. A raised foundation, for example, can

Luxury and convenience converge in this contemporary design (page 18), which incorporates a drive-under three-car garage.

Living Spaces

As important as it is to consider your lot while searching for a home plan, don't lose sight of where you'll spend your time—inside, as the floor plan comes to life. Among these beautiful hillside homes you'll find an assortment of open, flowing floor plans that create seamless living spaces the whole family can enjoy. The best of these will connect to outdoor spaces and showcase the tremendous views that many hillside lots offer. Meanwhile, keep an eye out for the personal spaces as well—locations like the master suite where you can get away from it all. ■

Left: A raised foundation accommodates a basement game room and helps this farmhouse design fit the landscape perfectly. See page 237 for details. Below: This gorgeous French Country manor, found on page 205, incorporates a walkout basement to fit its lot, which slopes to the rear.

work just as easily on a flat beachfront property as it would on a front- or side-sloping lot. Many of the home plans featured in these pages are also available with more than one possible foundation, or they can be customized to meet your needs. Consider all your options before you decide on your new home.

Auto Access

Consider where you'll park as you plan your hillside home. Can you incorporate a drive-under, side-loading, or rear-loading garage? These are popular options whether a lot slopes from back to front or toward one of its sides. They can minimize what can often seem like an overbearing presence of your garage doors in the view of a home from the street—ot help the garage vanish from sight.

Selecting a Site

Finding the right place to call home is as important as selecting your home plan

The home-building process is different for everyone, and that's true right from the get-go. You may have picked up this book because you have a plot of land waiting for a new home. Or you're dreaming about the finished product before you have a place to begin digging the foundation. There's no wrong stage in the process to begin thinking about your dream home, but if you haven't purchased land yet, there are some crucial considerations you will want to keep in mind.

Before buying anything—certainly before finalizing any house plans—familiarize yourself with all aspects of your prospective property. Remember that physical, environmental, and aesthetic factors, as well as local codes, can have a profound effect on the design of a house in relation to its site.

Above: Don't let a site limit your imagination. Here, modern design conforms to a sloping lot and meets the needs of the entire family (page 12). Opposite page top: Perched on a hill with windows across the back, this plan (page 15) takes advantage of its beautiful views.

LIVING CONCEPTS

STUDY THE SITE

Spend time at the location. With a compass, camera, notepad, graph paper, and tape measure, record precise data as well as personal impressions to help shape what you build.

Examine physical characteristics. Note the overall dimensions of the site and its topographical features. For example, is it near a lake, a river, or the ocean? Is any portion unsuitable for building, such as a pond? Check the grade, or slope, as well as the compass orientation. Study the soil composition: Does it consist of sand? Clay? Rocks? All of these factors will affect the excavation, bearing capacity, and the type of foundation. Also find out if any of the property is on landfill.

Take note of environmental factors. Consider the climate in terms of typical temperature, temperature extremes, cloudiness, humidity, and breezes. Can the structure be oriented on a south-facing slope to optimize ventilation and solar benefits? Is the property in a flood plain? Building codes may require the floor to be as much as 10 to 12 feet above the mean high-water level.

Research legal requirements. Check zoning laws concerning building height, size, materials, and distance from property lines. If you're building in an historic area, regulations regarding the exterior of the house might be quite extensive.

Analyze your aesthetic desires. Select the views you want to see out of your windows—and those you don't. Then think about what view of your house you want the neighbors, your guests, and passersby to see.

BLEND SITE AND HOUSE

After making sure the site is large enough for your needs and can accommodate future expansion should you want it, review all of the characteristics of your lot—including local regulations—with your builder. Keeping these considerations in mind, use the following tips to analyze how the house you wish to build can be designed to blend naturally with the site.

Work with the existing contours. Take advantage of any natural slope or obstruction rather than trying to fight it. It can be less expensive and easier to incorporate a huge boulder into the foundation, for example, than to blast it out of the way. A rocky hillside can be overcome with a creative design, and may even be better than flat land for maximizing or minimizing views.

Incorporate existing vegetation. Trees and plantings can have a big impact on how you situate your house and on how it will look once it's built. The challenge of building a house in the woods, for example, can be met without completely clearing the trees, the very element that endows the landscape with character and beauty. Pastureland, however, is like a blank slate that gives you much freedom in choosing a design for your home.

Choose styles and materials suited to the region. Various architectural styles function differently: In exposed, windy areas like the Great Plains, for instance, houses tend to be low to the ground, set on basements, and protected by cultivated tree breaks. Also try to use indigenous building materials—tile roofing in the Southwest, for example. Of course, technology has made it possible to build any house style, with any number of materials, in any part of the country. But for economic as well as functional and aesthetic reasons, it's wiser to take a cue from your surroundings. ■

LIVING CONCEPTS

All-Inclusive

Find everything you could want in this distinctive four-bedroom layout

Above: The kitchen, which showcases a marble-topped island, boasts a stunning view of the rear property. **Right:** A copper-crowned bay window and warm wood tones add welcoming touches to this home's distinguished stone exterior.

From its three full-bath bedroom suites to its generous outdoor living spaces, the floor plans of this gorgeous home read like a must-have list of today's most popular home-building trends. No detail is missed, from a convenient and spacious laundry room to plentiful storage, including a butler's pantry and smart built-in cabinets and shelves throughout.

The open floor plan on the main level creates a comfortable atmosphere, but with places for privacy as well. Double doors separate both the den, located at the front of the home, and the master suite, located at the back right. The master suite is packed with intelligent features, from the deck access to the large walk-in closet, which fea-

tures immediate access to the laundry room.

The wonders continue in the lower level, where three bedrooms each have bathrooms, walk-in closets, and access to the outdoors. A large sunken games room is sure to be a favorite spot in the home for young and old, and features a corner fireplace with a built-in entertainment center along one wall. ■

SMART DESIGN
Placing the family bedrooms downstairs, in the basement, gives the master suite added privacy.

Far Left: The butler's pantry, with plenty of cabinets for storage, overlooks the kitchen and dining room. **Middle:** A fireplace set into a striking surround serves as the focal point of the great room. **Above:** The tray-ceilinged master bedroom receives natural light from a bay window.

THIS HOME, AS SHOWN IN THE PHOTOGRAPH, MAY DIFFER FROM THE ACTUAL BLUEPRINTS. FOR MORE DETAILED INFORMATION, PLEASE CHECK THE FLOOR PLANS CAREFULLY.

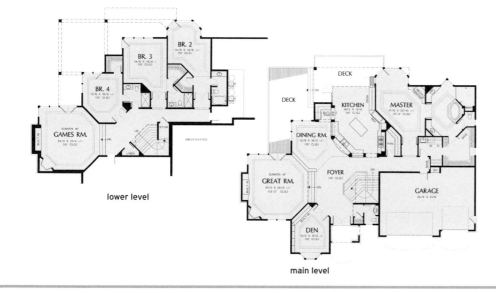

lower level

main level

PLAN: HPK1400006

STYLE: EUROPEAN COTTAGE	
MAIN LEVEL: 2,792 SQ. FT.	
LOWER LEVEL: 2,016 SQ. FT.	
TOTAL: 4,808 SQ. FT.	
BEDROOMS: 4	
BATHROOMS: 4½	
WIDTH: 81' - 0"	
DEPTH: 66' - 0"	
FOUNDATION: FINISHED WALKOUT BASEMENT	

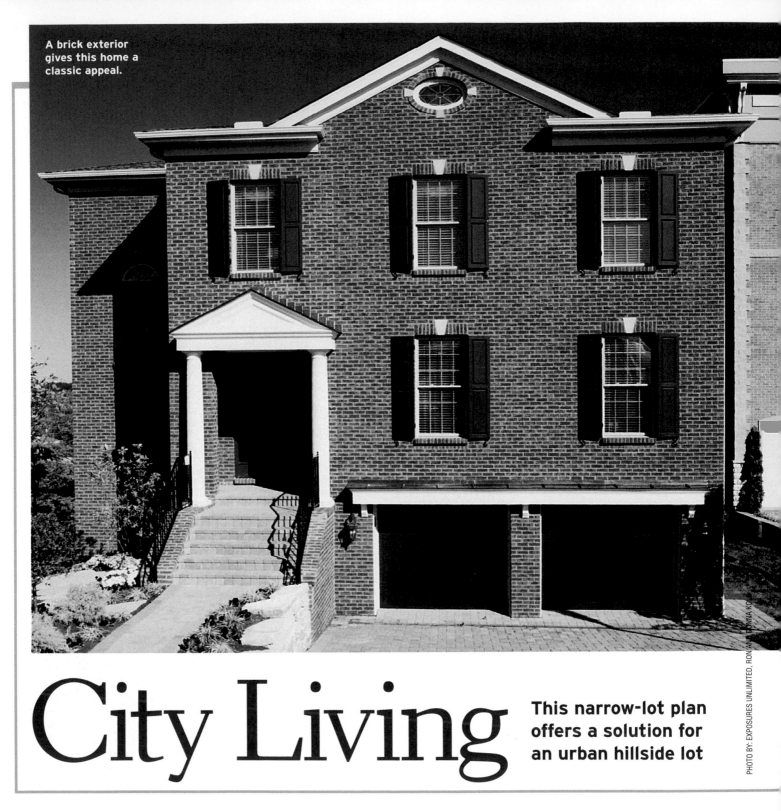

A brick exterior gives this home a classic appeal.

City Living

This narrow-lot plan offers a solution for an urban hillside lot

PHOTO BY: EXPOSURES UNLIMITED, RON AND DONNA KOL

At two stories and just under 42 feet wide, this Colonial Revival design includes a lot of luxury in a relatively small footprint. It's the ideal design for a narrow hillside lot, one that can present a lot of challenges without the proper foresight.

This plan, however, approaches those challenges as opportunities. The drive-under garage answers what could have been a tricky parking situation and fits nicely into the lot's slope. The Colonial design fits well with other urban architecture, and a screened porch, deck, and balcony in back extend the living space and allow homeowners to enjoy the view.

The island kitchen is well positioned to enjoy the view as well, and opens easily to the dining room and great room. Upstairs, the master suite comes with all the finest accoutrements—fireplace, whirlpool tub, separate shower, walk-in closet, etc.—with a couple of handy extras nearby: a laundry room, connected to the walk-in closet, and an office. ■

SMART DESIGN *A drive-under garage offers convenience, and preserves the architectural integrity of the facade.*

PLAN: HPK1400007

STYLE: COLONIAL

FIRST FLOOR: 1,442 SQ. FT.

SECOND FLOOR: 1,456 SQ. FT.

TOTAL: 2,898 SQ. FT.

BEDROOMS: 3

BATHROOMS: 3

WIDTH: 41' - 8"

DEPTH: 53' - 0"

FOUNDATION: FINISHED BASEMENT

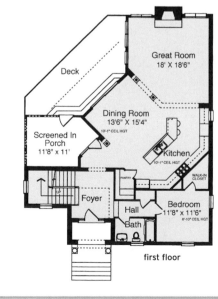

first floor

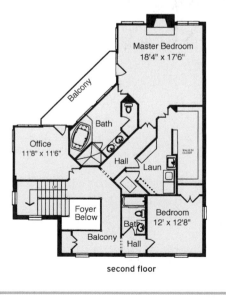

second floor

THIS HOME, AS SHOWN IN THE PHOTOGRAPH, MAY DIFFER FROM THE ACTUAL BLUEPRINTS. FOR MORE DETAILED INFORMATION, PLEASE CHECK THE FLOOR PLANS CAREFULLY. PHOTO BY LIVING CONCEPTS.

PLAN: HPK1400008

STYLE: CONTEMPORARY

MAIN LEVEL: 2,347 SQ. FT.

SECOND LEVEL: 1,800 SQ. FT.

THIRD LEVEL: 1,182 SQ. FT.

TOTAL: 5,329 SQ. FT.

BASEMENT: 1,688 SQ. FT.

BEDROOMS: 4

BATHROOMS: 5½

WIDTH: 75' - 5"

DEPTH: 76' - 4"

FOUNDATION: FINISHED WALKOUT BASEMENT

■ A level for everyone! On the first floor, there's a study with a full bath, a formal dining room, a grand room with a fireplace, and a fabulous kitchen with an adjacent morning room. The second floor contains three suites—each with a walk-in closet—two full baths, a loft, and a reading nook. A lavish master suite on the third floor is full of amenities, including His and Hers walk-in closets, a huge private bath, and a balcony. In the basement, casual entertaining takes off with a large gathering room, a home theater, and a spacious game room.

rear exterior

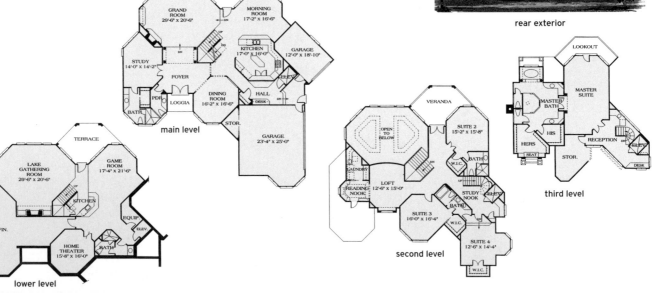

main level

lower level

second level

third level

PLAN: HPK1400009

STYLE: SANTA FE

FIRST FLOOR: 2,024 SQ. FT.

SECOND FLOOR: 800 SQ. FT.

TOTAL: 2,824 SQ. FT.

BEDROOMS: 4

BATHROOMS: 3½

WIDTH: 80' - 10"

DEPTH: 54' - 0"

FOUNDATION: SLAB

L

QUOTE ONE®

■ Tame the Wild West with this handsome adobe-style home. Suitable for side-sloping lots, it contains a wealth of livability. An abundance of windows and a raised stucco hearth with a long window-seat bench or banco graces the living room. The formal dining room is nearby, creating a lovely space for entertaining. All will enjoy the family room with adjacent gourmet kitchen and breakfast nook. Split styling puts the master bedroom suite on the right side of the plan. Here, a walk-in closet, whirlpool tub, and curved shower bring a touch of luxury. A private den/sitting room is located within the master bedroom suite. Three upstairs bedrooms share two hall baths.

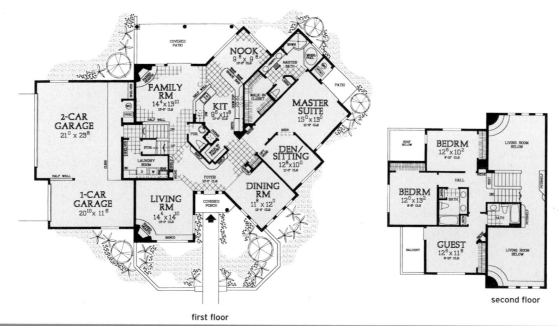

first floor

second floor

PLAN: HPK1400010

STYLE: EUROPEAN COTTAGE

FIRST FLOOR: 1,592 SQ. FT.

SECOND FLOOR: 1,259 SQ. FT.

TOTAL: 2,851 SQ. FT.

BEDROOMS: 4

BATHROOMS: 3

WIDTH: 56' - 0"

DEPTH: 53' - 6"

FOUNDATION: UNFINISHED BASEMENT

■ A combination of architectural details makes this home elegant: keystone arches, shuttered windows, a two-story bay with a copper roof, and a recessed entry. A formal living room with a fireplace and a dining room with a bay window flank the vaulted foyer. The hearth-warmed family room sits to the rear near the island kitchen and breakfast bay. Double doors lead from the bay to a deck. A den—or guest room—with a tray ceiling has the use of a full bath. Look for the master suite on the second floor, just off a skylit hall. It features a walk-in closet and private bath with a separate tub and shower. The other three bedrooms share the use of a hall bath. A full basement could be finished later for additional space.

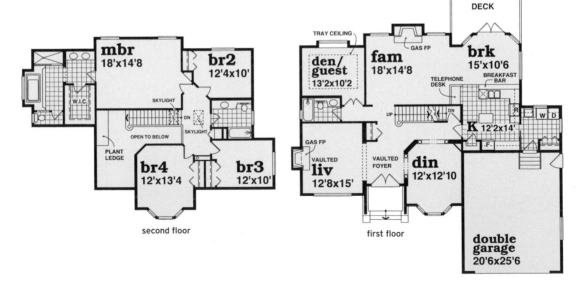

second floor

first floor

PLAN: HPK1400011

STYLE: MEDITERRANEAN

MAIN LEVEL: 2,391 SQ. FT.

UPPER LEVEL: 922 SQ. FT.

LOWER LEVEL: 1,964 SQ. FT.

TOTAL: 5,277 SQ. FT.

BONUS SPACE: 400 SQ. FT.

BEDROOMS: 4

BATHROOMS: 4½

WIDTH: 63' - 10"

DEPTH: 85' - 6"

FOUNDATION: FINISHED WALKOUT BASEMENT

rear exterior

■ Here's an upscale multilevel plan with expansive rear views. The first floor provides an open living and dining area, defined by decorative columns and enhanced by natural light from tall windows. A breakfast area with a lovely triple window opens to a sunroom, which allows light to pour into the gourmet kitchen. The master wing features a tray ceiling in the bedroom, two walk-in closets, and an elegant private vestibule leading to a lavish bath. Upstairs, a reading loft overlooks the great room and leads to a sleeping area with two suites. A recreation room, exercise room, office, guest suite, and additional storage are available in the finished basement.

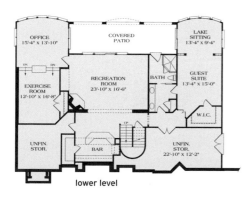

lower level

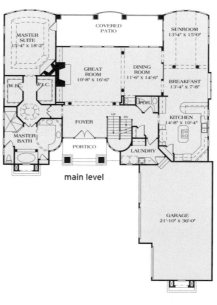

main level

upper level

PLAN: HPK1400012

STYLE: TRADITIONAL

FIRST FLOOR: 1,563 SQ. FT.

SECOND FLOOR: 772 SQ. FT.

TOTAL: 2,335 SQ. FT.

BEDROOMS: 3

BATHROOMS: 2½

WIDTH: 45' - 0"

DEPTH: 55' - 8"

FOUNDATION: CRAWLSPACE

■ Graceful, elegant living takes place in this charming cottage, which showcases a stone-and-stucco facade. Inside, the formal dining room features a columned entrance and a tray ceiling; nearby, the kitchen boasts a central island and a bay window. The expansive gathering room includes a fireplace and opens to the covered rear veranda, which extends to a side deck. The master suite, also with a tray ceiling, offers a walk-in closet and lavish private bath. Upstairs, two family bedrooms—both with walk-in closets—share a full bath and the captain's quarters, which opens to a deck.

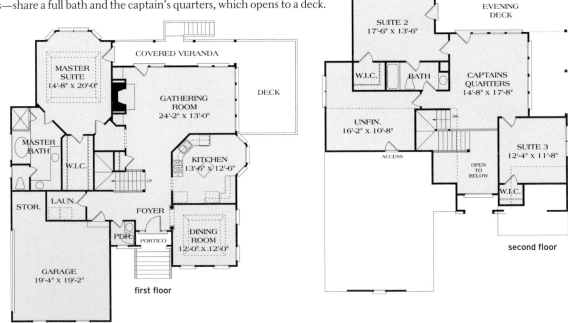

first floor

second floor

PLAN: HPK1400013

STYLE: EUROPEAN COTTAGE

FIRST FLOOR: 2,403 SQ. FT.

SECOND FLOOR: 2,328 SQ. FT.

TOTAL: 4,731 SQ. FT.

BONUS SPACE: 644 SQ. FT.

BEDROOMS: 4

BATHROOMS: 4½

WIDTH: 77' - 10"

DEPTH: 55' - 8"

FOUNDATION: CRAWLSPACE, UNFINISHED BASEMENT

rear exterior

■ Finished in stucco with an elegant entry, this dramatic two-story home is the essence of luxury. Double doors open to a foyer with a sunken living room on the right and a den on the left. An archway leads to the formal dining room, mirroring the curved window in the living room and the bowed window in the dining room. The den and nearby computer room have use of a full bath—making them handy as extra guest rooms when needed. The family room, like the living room, is sunken down and warmed by a hearth, but also has built-in bookcases. A snack-bar counter separates the U-shaped kitchen from the light-filled breakfast room. The second floor can be configured in two ways. Both allow for a gigantic master suite with His and Hers vanities, an oversized shower, a walk-in closet, and a sitting area.

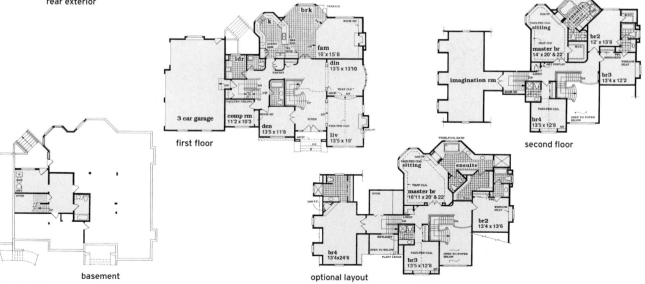

basement

first floor

second floor

optional layout

PLAN: HPK1400014

STYLE: NW CONTEMPORARY

MAIN LEVEL: 1,989 SQ. FT.

UPPER LEVEL: 1,349 SQ. FT.

LOWER LEVEL: 105 SQ. FT.

TOTAL: 3,443 SQ. FT.

BONUS SPACE: 487 SQ. FT.

BEDROOMS: 3

BATHROOMS: 2½

WIDTH: 63' - 0"

DEPTH: 48' - 0"

FOUNDATION: FINISHED WALKOUT BASEMENT

■ Dramatic balconies and spectacular window treatments enhance this stunning luxury home. Inside, a through-fireplace warms the formal living room and a restful den. Both living spaces open to a balcony that invites quiet reflection on starry nights. The banquet-sized dining room is easily served from the adjacent kitchen. Here, space is shared with an eating nook that provides access to the rear grounds and a family room with a corner fireplace—perfect for casual gatherings. The upper level contains two family bedrooms and a luxurious master suite that enjoys its own private balcony. The basement accommodates a shop and a bonus room for future development.

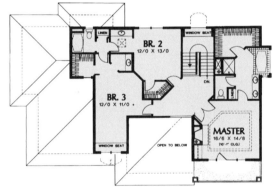

upper level

lower level

main level

PLAN: HPK1400015

STYLE: NW CONTEMPORARY

SQUARE FOOTAGE: 2,412

BEDROOMS: 3

BATHROOMS: 2½

WIDTH: 60' - 0"

DEPTH: 59' - 0"

FOUNDATION: SLAB

■ This gorgeous design would easily accommodate a sloping lot. With windows and glass panels to take in the view, this design would make an exquisite seaside resort. A grand great room sets the tone inside, with an elegant tray ceiling and French doors to a private front balcony. The formal dining room is off the center of the plan for quiet elegance and is served by a nearby gourmet kitchen. Three steps up from the foyer, the sleeping level includes a spacious master suite with a sizable private bath. The two additional bedrooms access a shared bath with two vanities.

PLAN: HPK1400016

STYLE: TUDOR

FIRST FLOOR: 1,484 SQ. FT.

SECOND FLOOR: 1,402 SQ. FT.

TOTAL: 2,886 SQ. FT.

BONUS SPACE: 430 SQ. FT.

BEDROOMS: 4

BATHROOMS: 2½

WIDTH: 63' - 0"

DEPTH: 51' - 0"

FOUNDATION: CRAWLSPACE

L

■ This impressive Tudor is designed for lots that slope up slightly from the street—the garage is five feet below the main level. Just to the right of the entry, the den is arranged to work well as an office. Formal living areas include a living room with a fireplace and an elegant dining room. The family room also offers a fireplace and is close to the bumped-out nook. On the upper level, all the bedrooms are generously sized, and the master suite features a tray ceiling and a huge walk-in closet. A large vaulted bonus room is provided with convenient access from both the family room and the garage. Three family bedrooms and a full bath complete the upper level.

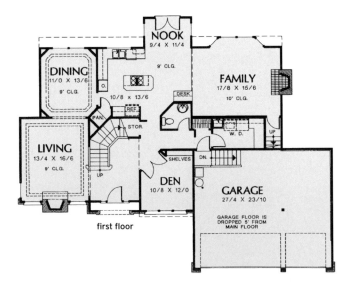

first floor

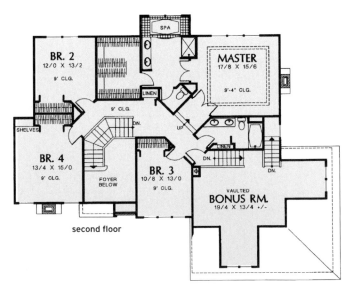

second floor

PLAN: HPK1400017

STYLE: COUNTRY COTTAGE

SQUARE FOOTAGE: 1,756

BEDROOMS: 3

BATHROOMS: 2

WIDTH: 52' - 6"

DEPTH: 51' - 6"

FOUNDATION: CRAWLSPACE, UNFINISHED WALKOUT BASEMENT

■ This sweet ranch-style home uses chic ceiling treatments to adorn its creative floor plan. With lots of focal-point wallspace, this home is perfect for the aspiring art collector—or artist! The angled foyer directs you to the vaulted great room, where built-in bookshelves and an extended-hearth fireplace enjoy natural light through radius windows. Toward the front of the home reside two family bedrooms. In the opposite corner, the master suite revels in privacy and grandeur.

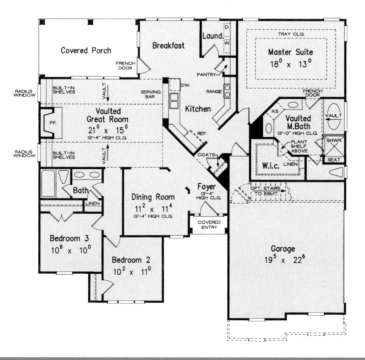

PLAN: HPK1400018

STYLE: SW CONTEMPORARY

SQUARE FOOTAGE: 2,572

BONUS SPACE: 1,607 SQ. FT.

BEDROOMS: 3

BATHROOMS: 2½

WIDTH: 76' - 0"

DEPTH: 63' - 4"

FOUNDATION: UNFINISHED
WALKOUT BASEMENT

■ The lower level of this magnificent home includes unfinished space that could have a future as a den and a family room with a fireplace. This level could also house extra bedrooms or an in-law suite. On the main level, the foyer spills into a tray-ceilinged living room with a fireplace and an arched, floor-to-ceiling window wall. Up from the foyer, a hall introduces a vaulted family room with a built-in media center and French doors that open to an expansive railed deck. Featured in the gourmet kitchen are a preparation island with a salad sink, double-door pantry, corner-window sink and breakfast bay. The vaulted master bedroom opens to the deck, and the deluxe bath offers a raised whirlpool spa and a double-bowl vanity under a skylight. Two family bedrooms share a compartmented bath.

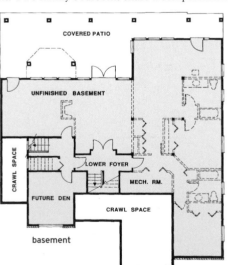

basement

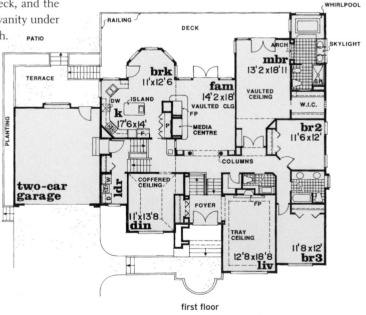

first floor

PLAN: HPK1400019

STYLE: EUROPEAN COTTAGE

FIRST FLOOR: 2,596 SQ. FT.

SECOND FLOOR: 2,233 SQ. FT.

TOTAL: 4,829 SQ. FT.

BEDROOMS: 4

BATHROOMS: 3½ + ½

WIDTH: 81' - 0"

DEPTH: 61' - 0"

FOUNDATION: UNFINISHED BASEMENT

■ This grand, two-story European home is adorned with a facade of stucco and brick, meticulously appointed with details for gracious living. Guests enter through a portico to find a stately two-story foyer. The formal living room features a tray ceiling and a fireplace and is joined by a charming dining room with a large bay window. A butler's pantry joins the dining room to the gourmet kitchen, which holds a separate work kitchen, an island work center, and a breakfast room with double doors leading to the rear patio. The nearby family room enjoys a built-in aquarium, media center, and fireplace. A den with a tray ceiling, window seat, and built-in computer center is tucked in a corner for privacy. Served by two separate staircases, the second floor features a spectacular master suite with a separate sitting room, an oversized closet, and a bath with a spa tub.

basement

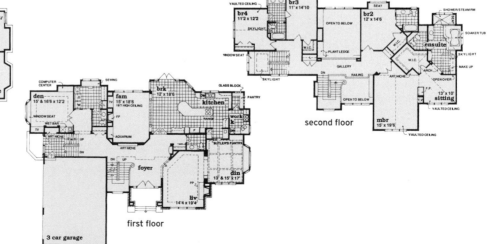

first floor

second floor

PHOTO BY: STEVE RILEY, COURTESY OF SELECT HOME DESIGNS. THIS HOME, AS SHOWN IN THE PHOTOGRAPH, MAY DIFFER FROM THE ACTUAL BLUEPRINTS. FOR MORE DETAILED INFORMATION, PLEASE CHECK THE FLOOR PLANS CAREFULLY.

PLAN: HPK1400020

STYLE:	EUROPEAN COTTAGE
FIRST FLOOR:	1,664 SQ. FT.
SECOND FLOOR:	1,404 SQ. FT.
TOTAL:	3,068 SQ. FT.
BEDROOMS:	4
BATHROOMS:	2½
WIDTH:	42' - 4"
DEPTH:	50' - 4"
FOUNDATION:	UNFINISHED BASEMENT

■ This spacious four-bedroom design offers plenty of extras. Open living and dining areas boast distinctive styling, including the lovely archways from the foyer. Among the extras in the dining area are a serving bar and built-in space for a buffet. The large kitchen offers ample counter space and opens to the breakfast area with a telephone desk, pantry, and double French doors to the patio. The family room features a TV alcove over the gas fireplace. The study, accessed from the front foyer, overlooks the front yard. The luxurious master bedroom boasts its own separate sitting room with a vaulted ceiling.

first floor

second floor

PLAN: HPK1400021

STYLE: TRADITIONAL

FIRST FLOOR: 1,266 SQ. FT.

SECOND FLOOR: 856 SQ. FT.

TOTAL: 2,122 SQ. FT.

BONUS SPACE: 301 SQ. FT.

BEDROOMS: 4

BATHROOMS: 2½

WIDTH: 40' - 0"

DEPTH: 52' - 10"

FOUNDATION: UNFINISHED
WALKOUT BASEMENT

■ This bright and airy home will surely make your time at home the best part of your day. Light streams into the living and dining rooms through a wall of three tall windows. A fireplace offers cheery nights, and a rear door opens to a porch. The family room, host to a second fireplace, and the multiwindowed breakfast area work well as a unit. A den—or make it a spare bedroom—and a sunny bonus room round out the main level. Sure to bring pleasure, the luxurious master suite enjoys a front-facing box bay with three big windows. Two other bedrooms share a bath with a skylight; one of the rooms boasts corner windows. The plan comes with a two-car garage.

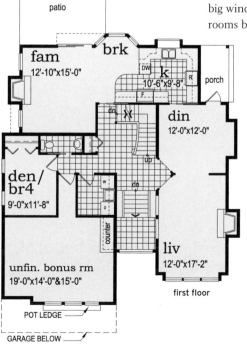

first floor

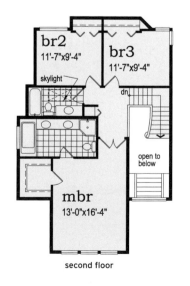

second floor

PLAN: HPK1400022

STYLE: NW CONTEMPORARY

FIRST FLOOR: 1,022 SQ. FT.

SECOND FLOOR: 813 SQ. FT.

TOTAL: 1,835 SQ. FT.

BEDROOMS: 3

BATHROOMS: 2½

WIDTH: 36' - 0"

DEPTH: 33' - 0"

FOUNDATION: SLAB

L

■ This home is quite a "looker" with its steeply sloping rooflines and large sunburst and multipane windows. This plan not only accommodates a narrow lot, but it also fits a sloping site. The angled corner entry gives way to a two-story living room with a tiled hearth. The dining room shares an interesting angled space with this area and enjoys easy service from the efficient kitchen. The family room offers double doors to a refreshing balcony. A powder room and laundry room complete the main level. Upstairs, a vaulted master bedroom enjoys a private bath; two other bedrooms share a bath.

first floor

second floor

PLAN: HPK1400023

STYLE: CRAFTSMAN

FIRST FLOOR: 1,501 SQ. FT.

SECOND FLOOR: 921 SQ. FT.

TOTAL: 2,422 SQ. FT.

BEDROOMS: 3

BATHROOMS: 2½

WIDTH: 52' - 0"

DEPTH: 36' - 0"

FOUNDATION: UNFINISHED
WALKOUT BASEMENT,
CRAWLSPACE, FINISHED
WALKOUT BASEMENT

■ The contemporary look of this modern country design is both impressive and unique. Enormous windows brighten and enliven every interior space. The vaulted family room features a fireplace, and a two-sided fireplace warms the formal living and dining rooms. The gourmet island kitchen is open to a nook. Double doors open to a den that accesses a front deck. Upstairs, the master bedroom features a private bath with linen storage and a walk-in closet. Two family bedrooms share a Jack-and-Jill bath. The two-car garage features a storage area on the lower level.

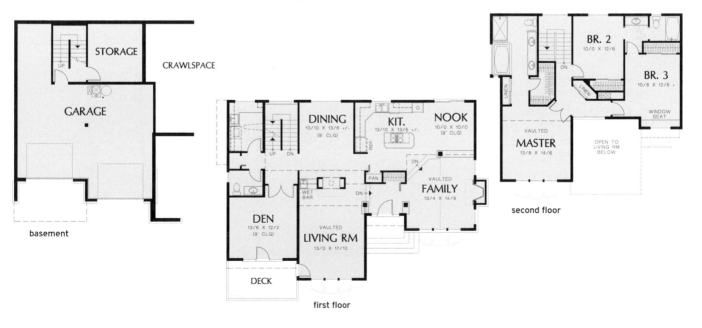

PLAN: HPK1400024

STYLE: NW CONTEMPORARY

FIRST FLOOR: 1,328 SQ. FT.

SECOND FLOOR: 503 SQ. FT.

TOTAL: 1,831 SQ. FT.

BEDROOMS: 4

BATHROOMS: 2

WIDTH: 44' - 0"

DEPTH: 52' - 0"

FOUNDATION: UNFINISHED BASEMENT

■ This lakeside home provides the perfect place to take in the view with its sheltered patio, raised deck, and abundant windows. Inside, the foyer flows into the living room, which offers a built-in fireplace for cool evenings. A sunlit breakfast nook and compact kitchen that opens to a utility room follow. A master bedroom with plenty of closet space, along with one family bedroom, complete the first level. The second level offers two more family bedrooms, a full bath, and a loft area—make it a computer room or a studio. A lower level features the finished basement, a full bath, and a patio area.

side exterior

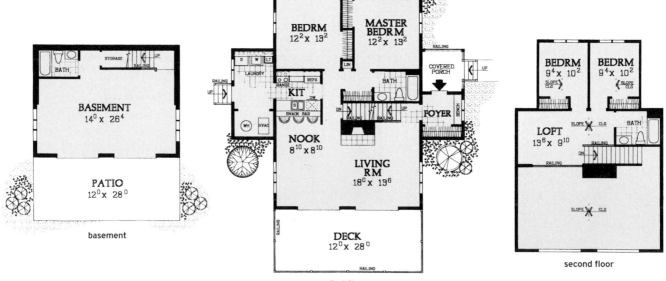

basement

first floor

second floor

PLAN: HPK1400025

STYLE: RESORT LIFESTYLES

MAIN LEVEL: 1,017 SQ. FT.

UPPER LEVEL: 384 SQ. FT.

LOWER LEVEL: 716 SQ. FT.

TOTAL: 2,117 SQ. FT.

BEDROOMS: 3

BATHROOMS: 2

WIDTH: 38' - 0"

DEPTH: 30' - 0"

FOUNDATION: UNFINISHED

WALKOUT BASEMENT

■ With 2,100 square feet of living space on three levels, this charming vacation house offers a lot of efficiency plus room for expansion. An open great room, with its loft above, gives everyone cozy access to the fireplace and plenty of room to gather together for a variety of activities. Three bedrooms with additional areas to put up guests mean this compact home has all the amenities of a larger design without all the maintenance. French doors and a private balcony offer views to the natural wonders outside.

lower level

main level

upper level

PLAN: HPK1400026

STYLE: TRADITIONAL

FIRST FLOOR: 1,032 SQ. FT.

SECOND FLOOR: 923 SQ. FT.

TOTAL: 1,955 SQ. FT.

BONUS SPACE: 317 SQ. FT.

BEDROOMS: 3

BATHROOMS: 2½

WIDTH: 42' - 0"

DEPTH: 50' - 0"

FOUNDATION: UNFINISHED
WALKOUT BASEMENT

■ A beautiful, traditional-style home that features multi-levels of living welcomes you here. Bayed windows and a covered porch with stairway front the exterior. A bonus room is positioned over the garage and is convenient to the laundry room and powder room. A large living and dining room combination creates ideal space utilization for more formal occasions. The family room, breakfast nook, and kitchen round out the main level. Upstairs, the master bedroom and two family bedrooms share a common gallery.

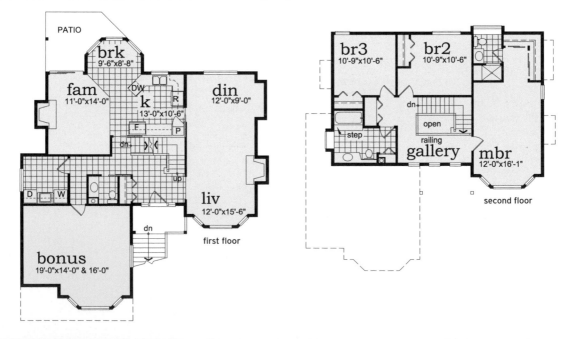

PLAN: HPK1400027

STYLE: BUNGALOW

MAIN LEVEL: 1,920 SQ. FT.

LOWER LEVEL: 1,400 SQ. FT.

TOTAL: 3,320 SQ. FT.

BEDROOMS: 3

BATHROOMS: 2½

WIDTH: 69' - 8"

DEPTH: 56' - 4"

FOUNDATION: FINISHED WALKOUT BASEMENT

■ Elegant hipped and gabled rooflines dress up this country bungalow design. A copper-topped bay window enhances the roomy first-floor study just off the foyer. A full bath with compartmented toilet, separate shower and tub, and a walk-in closet outfit the nearby master suite. Modern convenience places the spacious kitchen, dining bay, hearth room, and great room within a few steps of each other. A beautiful see-through fireplace defines the space between the hearth and great rooms. A lower level opens to the rear property to take advantage of a sloped lot. Two family bedrooms, full bath, large family room, adjoining game room, and plenty of storage complete this level.

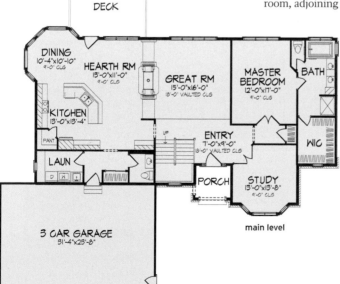

main level

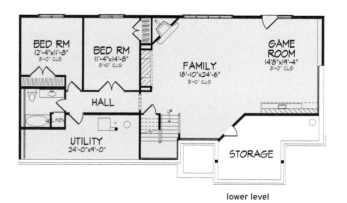

lower level

PLAN: HPK1400028

STYLE: CONTEMPORARY

SQUARE FOOTAGE: 1,067

BEDROOMS: 3

BATHROOMS: 2

WIDTH: 38' - 0"

DEPTH: 30' - 0"

FOUNDATION: UNFINISHED

WALKOUT BASEMENT

■ A handsome front entrance with trim flatters this Contemporary's exterior. Steps take you up to the front door, where the entry is bounded by a staircase on the right, and the main living area ahead and to the left. The dining room affords access and views to the rear deck, and the main living room offers cozy family time or private relaxation in front of the fire. An L-shaped counter along the far kitchen wall provides efficient space in the kitchen, and a snack bar permits informal, intimate meal-times. The master suite is separated into bedroom and very spacious bath, each accessible from the main hallway. A huge entertainment room is found on the second floor, along with two more bedrooms and the second bathroom with an enclosed tub and shower.

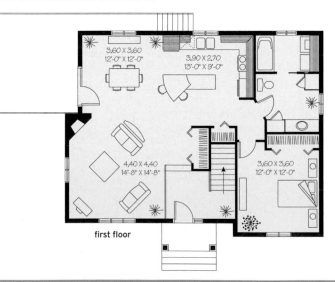

first floor

second floor

PLAN: HPK1400029

STYLE: TRADITIONAL

SQUARE FOOTAGE: 2,499

BONUS SPACE: 733 SQ. FT.

BEDROOMS: 3

BATHROOMS: 2½

WIDTH: 64' - 0"

DEPTH: 72' - 4"

FOUNDATION: UNFINISHED
WALKOUT BASEMENT,
CRAWLSPACE

■ Decorative columns adorn a pedimented porch on this charming brick home. Elegance marks the formal areas with high ceilings and columns. Radius windows enhance the family room, living room, and master bath. The master suite and two additional bedrooms are located on the first floor, while an optional second floor contains space for another bedroom and bath.

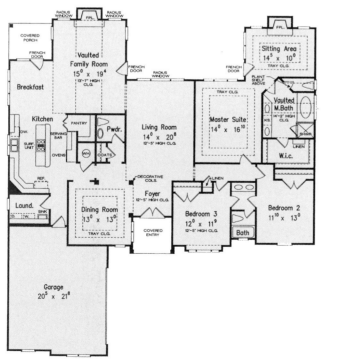

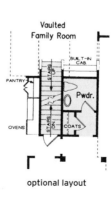

optional layout

PLAN: HPK1400030

STYLE: BUNGALOW

SQUARE FOOTAGE: 1,475

BEDROOMS: 2

BATHROOMS: 2

WIDTH: 46' - 4"

DEPTH: 47' - 4"

FOUNDATION: UNFINISHED

WALKOUT BASEMENT

■ A brick-and-siding facade and a tapered roof lend character and tasteful charm to this bungalow. An angled front porch and foyer introduce you and your guests to the main level. First stop, through double doors to the left, is the kitchen and breakfast area, conveniently arranged around a half-wall and including a pantry. The nook offers a view through perpendicular windows, for a cheery start to one's morning. Through one end of the kitchen access the dining room and adjoining living area. A gas fireplace and views of the deck await. A comfortable master bedroom with private bath is found to the right of the foyer and around the staircase, with angled walk-in closet and tiled flooring in the bathroom. Also here is a space for laundry with handy chute opening from upstairs and a full bath. Heading back toward the front door, don't miss the access point to the double garage or extra bedroom with a vaulted ceiling and window seat just off the foyer. Upstairs is plenty of freedom to develop your own ideas, with double doors and windows facing the rear.

PLAN: HPK1400031

STYLE: RANCH

SQUARE FOOTAGE: 1,354

BONUS SPACE: 246 SQ. FT.

BEDROOMS: 3

BATHROOMS: 2

WIDTH: 51' - 0"

DEPTH: 48' - 4"

FOUNDATION: UNFINISHED
WALKOUT BASEMENT

■ Single-level living is the hottest house trend today—as you look ahead to your future you will probably discover that you want a plan that will accommodate your changing family; this lovely ranch home is ready to do just that. A raised-ceiling foyer welcomes family and friends, leading to a vaulted great room ahead. A cozy fireplace makes this space intimate. Follow the vault to a formal dining room, serviced by an angled kitchen with a serving bar. The left wing holds the sleeping quarters, including an indulgent vaulted master suite with a private spa bath. Two additional bedrooms share a full bath. An optional bonus room is available, great for an extra bedroom, home office or studio.

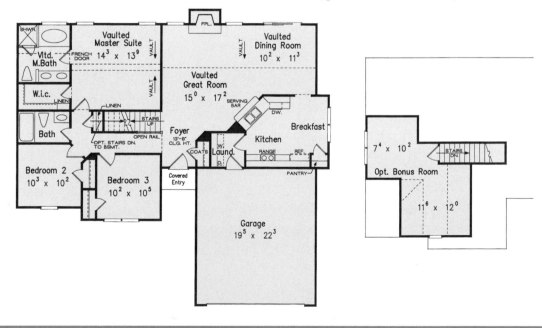

PLAN: HPK1400032

STYLE: COUNTRY COTTAGE

FIRST FLOOR: 1,804 SQ. FT.

SECOND FLOOR: 1,041 SQ. FT.

TOTAL: 2,845 SQ. FT.

BEDROOMS: 4

BATHROOMS: 3½

WIDTH: 57' - 3"

DEPTH: 71' - 0"

FOUNDATION: FINISHED

WALKOUT BASEMENT

■ There's a feeling of old Charleston in this stately home—particularly on the quiet side porch that wraps around the kitchen and breakfast room. The interior of this home revolves around a spacious great room with a welcoming fireplace. The left wing is dedicated to the master suite, which boasts wide views of the rear property. A corner kitchen easily serves planned events in the formal dining room, as well as family meals in the breakfast area. Three family bedrooms, one with a private bath and the others sharing a bath, are tucked upstairs.

rear exterior

first floor

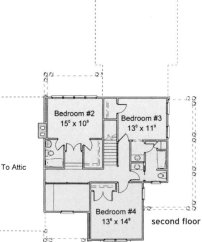

second floor

PLAN: HPK1400033

STYLE: FARMHOUSE

FIRST FLOOR: 797 SQ. FT.

SECOND FLOOR: 886 SQ. FT.

TOTAL: 1,683 SQ. FT.

BEDROOMS: 3

BATHROOMS: 2½

WIDTH: 44' - 0"

DEPTH: 34' - 5"

FOUNDATION: CRAWLSPACE, SLAB, UNFINISHED BASEMENT

■ The front of this home creates an inviting feel with its full front porch and gabled accents. The combination of brick and siding mixed with metal roof accents adds interest. The dramatic, angled staircase in the two-story foyer increases the sense of space. A spacious living area that's open to the breakfast nook and kitchen opens up the entire rear of the house. Create an herb garden in the corner window of the kitchen sink. Upstairs, two secondary bedrooms share a vanity area which opens to a private commode and tub room. The master bath features a garden tub, His and Her vanities, and a commode closet.

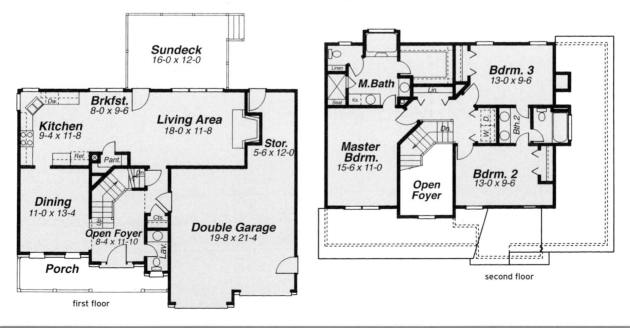

first floor

second floor

PLAN: HPK1400034

STYLE: TRADITIONAL

SQUARE FOOTAGE: 1,681

BASEMENT: 415 SQ. FT.

BEDROOMS: 2

BATHROOMS: 2

WIDTH: 55' - 8"

DEPTH: 46' - 0"

FOUNDATION: UNFINISHED

WALKOUT BASEMENT

■ The grand Palladian window lends plenty of curb appeal to this charming home. The wraparound country porch is perfect for peaceful evenings. The vaulted great room enjoys a large bay window, stone fireplace, pass-through to the kitchen and awesome rear views through the atrium window wall. The master suite features double entry doors, a walk-in closet, and a fabulous bath. The optional lower level includes a family room.

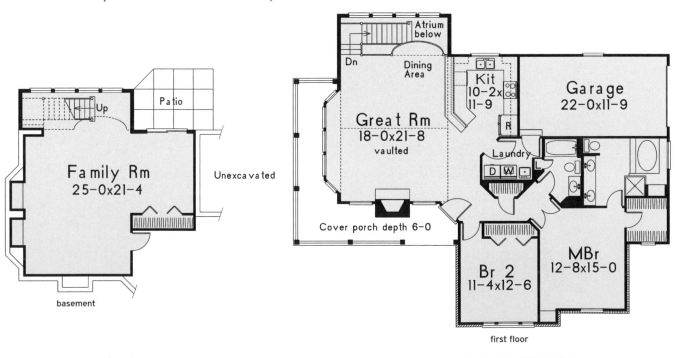

PLAN: HPK1400035

STYLE: FARMHOUSE

FIRST FLOOR: 1,351 SQ. FT.

SECOND FLOOR: 1,257 SQ. FT.

TOTAL: 2,608 SQ. FT.

BONUS SPACE: 115 SQ. FT.

BEDROOMS: 4

BATHROOMS: 2½

WIDTH: 60' - 0"

DEPTH: 46' - 4"

FOUNDATION: CRAWLSPACE, UNFINISHED WALKOUT BASEMENT

■ Attention to detail and a stylish design give this wonderful country home distinct appeal. Inside, the foyer leads to an elegant dining room and a spacious living room with French doors to the covered rear porch. The heart of the home is a two-story family room with a focal-point fireplace and a French door to the rear property. A breakfast room offers a walk-in pantry and shares a snack bar with the kitchen, which in turn leads to the formal dining room through a butler's pantry. The second-floor master suite features an impressive private bath with a vaulted ceiling and an optional sitting room.

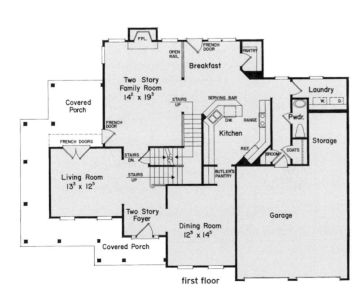

first floor

second floor

PLAN: HPK1400036

STYLE: TRADITIONAL
SQUARE FOOTAGE: 1,826
BEDROOMS: 3
BATHROOMS: 2
WIDTH: 53' - 4"
DEPTH: 61' - 6"
FOUNDATION: UNFINISHED
WALKOUT BASEMENT

■ Quaint country elements give this traditional home a touch of charm that sets it apart from the crowd. Ceilings in the main living areas soar to over 12 feet high, increasing a feeling of spaciousness. An efficient kitchen features a serving bar to the breakfast nook and a pass-through to the hearth-warmed family room. At the rear of the plan, two family bedrooms share a full bath. The master suite is a relaxing getaway with a pampering vaulted bath and enormous walk-in closet.

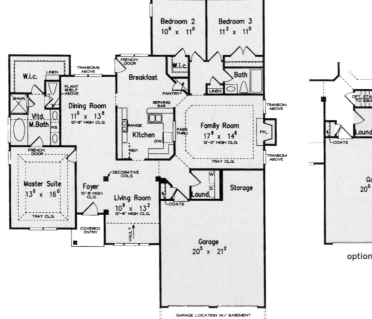

optional layout

PLAN: HPK1400037

STYLE: COUNTRY COTTAGE

FIRST FLOOR: 1,210 SQ. FT.

SECOND FLOOR: 555 SQ. FT.

TOTAL: 1,765 SQ. FT.

BASEMENT: 414 SQ. FT.

BEDROOMS: 3

BATHROOMS: 2½

WIDTH: 43' - 4"

DEPTH: 37' - 0"

FOUNDATION: UNFINISHED BASEMENT

■ This charming country cottage exhibits a drive-under garage design. The Palladian window accented by the stone gable adds a new look to a popular cottage design. Inside, dormers open into a vaulted living area. The master bedroom opens off the foyer. A modified cathedral ceiling makes the front Palladian window a focal point both inside and out. The master-bath also features a cathedral ceiling that extends over the tub and vanity, adding drama. The kitchen opens to a glassed breakfast room with access to a sun deck. The laundry and half-bath are conveniently located near this rear door. U-shaped stairs lead to a balcony overlooking the foyer and two additional bedrooms.

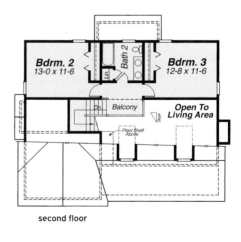

second floor

basement

first floor

PLAN: HPK1400038

STYLE: TRADITIONAL

SQUARE FOOTAGE: 1,348

BEDROOMS: 3

BATHROOMS: 2

WIDTH: 48' - 0"

DEPTH: 53' - 4"

FOUNDATION: UNFINISHED

WALKOUT BASEMENT

■ This compact family home is more than meets the eye. With a thoughtful floor plan and all of today's most asked-for amenities, this design challenges its modest square footage and provides a functional home. An impressive foyer leads to a vaulted great room, highlighted by a focal-point hearth. The galley kitchen easily serves a sunny breakfast nook and elegant formal dining room. Situated for privacy, the master suite enjoys a tray ceiling and spa bath. Two secondary bedrooms—or make one an office—share a full bath. A two-car garage completes the plan.

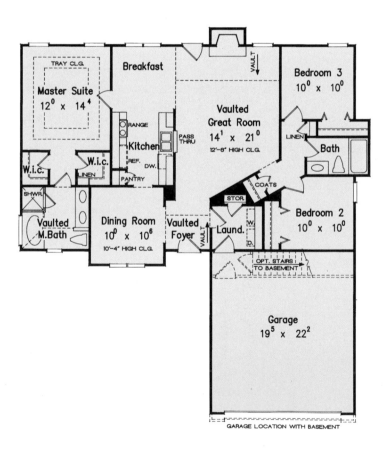

PLAN: HPK1400039

STYLE: COUNTRY COTTAGE

SQUARE FOOTAGE: 1,795

BONUS SPACE: 254 SQ. FT.

BEDROOMS: 3

BATHROOMS: 2

WIDTH: 54' - 0"

DEPTH: 53' - 0"

FOUNDATION: UNFINISHED WALKOUT BASEMENT, CRAWLSPACE

■ This traditional home exudes a sense of welcome. Vaulted ceilings adorn the foyer, dining room, great room, and master bath. The great room enjoys a fireplace flanked by radius windows. The kitchen shares a snack bar with the breakfast area. The living room boasts a bay window. The master suite features a tray ceiling and a private bath with a vaulted ceiling and angled oval tub.

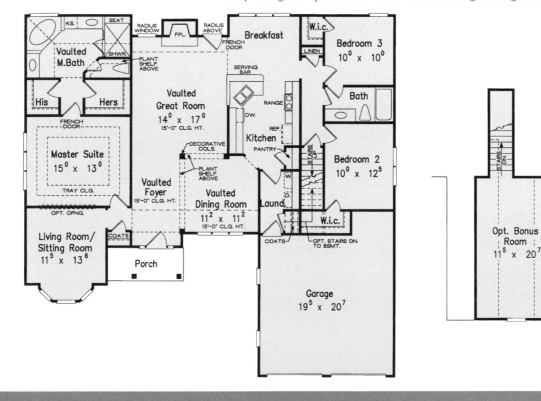

PLAN: HPK1400234

STYLE: PRAIRIE

FIRST FLOOR: 1,440 SQ. FT.

SECOND FLOOR: 1,440 SQ. FT.

TOTAL: 2,880 SQ. FT.

BONUS SPACE: 140 SQ. FT.

BEDROOMS: 4

BATHROOMS: 2½

WIDTH: 30' - 0"

DEPTH: 56' - 0"

FOUNDATION: UNFINISHED BASEMENT

■ The impressive exterior gives way to an interior without boundaries. The lack of unnecessary walls creates a feeling of spaciousness. Access to the sundeck from the family room extends the living space, encouraging entertaining. The second floor houses the master suite and three additional family bedrooms. Bedrooms 2 and 3 enjoy private access to a front-facing covered porch. A second-floor laundry room is an added convenience. The finished basement, boasting a sizable recreation room, completes this plan.

PLAN: HPK1400235

STYLE: CRAFTSMAN

FIRST FLOOR: 1,440 SQ. FT.

SECOND FLOOR: 1,514 SQ. FT.

TOTAL: 2,954 SQ. FT.

BEDROOMS: 4

BATHROOMS: 3½

WIDTH: 30' - 0"

DEPTH: 68' - 0"

FOUNDATION: UNFINISHED WALKOUT BASEMENT

■ A stylish Craftsman at just under 3,000 square feet, this home features an open layout ideal for entertaining. Rooms are distinguished by columns, eliminating the use of unnecessary walls. At the rear of the home, the expansive family room, warmed by a fireplace, faces the adjoining breakfast area and kitchen. Access to the sundeck makes alfresco meals an option. A walk-in pantry is an added bonus. The second floor houses the family bedrooms, including the lavish master suite, two bedrooms separated by a Jack-and-Jill bath, and a fourth bedroom with a private, full bath. The second-floor laundry room is smart and convenient. A centrally located, optional computer station is perfect for a family computer. A sizable recreation room on the basement level completes this plan.

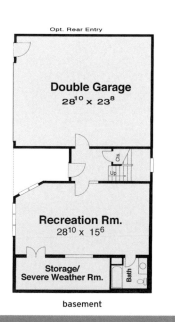

basement

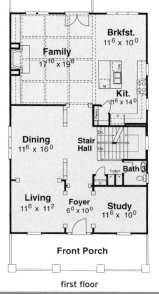

first floor

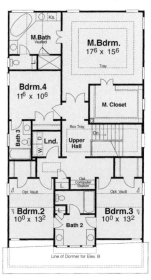

second floor

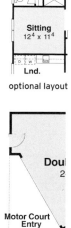

optional layout

optional layout

PLAN: HPK1400040

STYLE: CRAFTSMAN
MAIN LEVEL: 2,170 SQ. FT.
LOWER LEVEL: 1,076 SQ. FT.
TOTAL: 3,246 SQ. FT.
BEDROOMS: 3
BATHROOMS: 2½
WIDTH: 74' - 0"
DEPTH: 54' - 0"
FOUNDATION: SLAB, FINISHED
WALKOUT BASEMENT

■ Perfect for a sloping lot, this Craftsman design boasts two levels of living space. Plenty of special amenities—vaulted ceilings in the living, dining, and family rooms, as well as in the master bedroom; built-ins in the family room and den; a large island cooktop in the kitchen; and an expansive rear deck—make this plan stand out. All three of the bedrooms—a main-level master suite and two lower-level bedrooms—include walk-in closets. Also on the lower level, find a recreation room with built-ins and a fireplace.

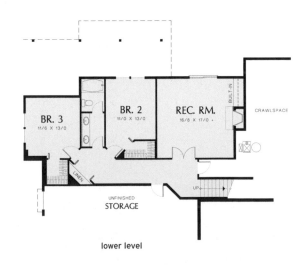

lower level

main level

PLAN: HPK1400041

STYLE: BUNGALOW

SQUARE FOOTAGE: 2,385

BEDROOMS: 3

BATHROOMS: 3

WIDTH: 60' - 0"

DEPTH: 52' - 0"

FOUNDATION: UNFINISHED
WALKOUT BASEMENT

■ This cabin is the ideal vacation home for a retreat to the mountains or the lake. Beyond the covered front porch, the foyer steps lead up to the formal living areas on the main floor. The study is enhanced by a vaulted ceiling and double doors that open onto the front balcony. The vaulted central great room overlooks the rear deck. The island kitchen is open to an adjacent breakfast nook. The master suite is thoughtfully placed on the left side of the plan for privacy and offers two walk-in closets and a pampering master bath with a whirlpool tub.

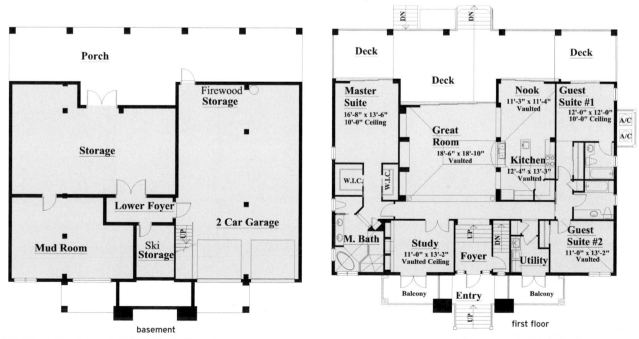

PLAN: HPK1400042

STYLE: CRAFTSMAN

FIRST FLOOR: 897 SQ. FT.

SECOND FLOOR: 740 SQ. FT.

TOTAL: 1,637 SQ. FT.

BEDROOMS: 3

BATHROOMS: 2½

WIDTH: 30' - 0"

DEPTH: 42' - 6"

FOUNDATION: UNFINISHED

WALKOUT BASEMENT

■ With a garage on the ground level, this home takes a much smaller footprint and is perfect for narrow-lot applications. Take a short flight of stairs up to the entry, which opens to a receiving hall and then to the living and dining combination. The living room features a fireplace flanked by bookshelves. The island kitchen and nook are to the rear, near a half-bath. Upstairs are two family bedrooms sharing a full bath and the vaulted master suite, with a private bath and dual walk-in closets.

second floor

basement

first floor

PLAN: HPK1400043

STYLE: CRAFTSMAN

FIRST FLOOR: 1,005 SQ. FT.

SECOND FLOOR: 620 SQ. FT.

TOTAL: 1,625 SQ. FT.

BEDROOMS: 2

BATHROOMS: 2½

WIDTH: 30' - 0"

DEPTH: 44' - 6"

FOUNDATION: FINISHED
WALKOUT BASEMENT

■ A mixture of materials and modern styling creates a lovely home plan for the small family. The main level provides formal living and dining rooms as well as a kitchen area. The quiet study may be converted to an additional bedroom as space is needed. A laundry and powder room are located nearby. The vaulted master bedroom boasts a private bath with a double-bowl vanity and a walk-in closet. Bedroom 2 provides its own bath.

basement

first floor

second floor

PLAN: HPK1400044

STYLE: CRAFTSMAN

MAIN LEVEL: 1,106 SQ. FT.

UPPER LEVEL: 872 SQ. FT.

TOTAL: 1,978 SQ. FT.

BEDROOMS: 3

BATHROOMS: 2½

WIDTH: 38' - 0"

DEPTH: 35' - 0"

FOUNDATION: SLAB,

UNFINISHED BASEMENT

■ Though this home gives the impression of the Northwest, it will be the winner of any neighborhood. From the foyer, the two-story living room is just a couple of steps up and features a through-fireplace. The U-shaped kitchen has a cooktop work island, an adjacent nook, and easy access to the formal dining room. A spacious family room shares the fireplace with the living room, is enhanced by built-ins, and also offers a quiet deck for stargazing. The upstairs consists of two family bedrooms sharing a full bath and a vaulted master suite complete with a walk-in closet and sumptuous bath. A two-car, drive-under garage has plenty of room for storage.

upper level

lower level

main level

PLAN: HPK1400045

STYLE: BUNGALOW

SQUARE FOOTAGE: 3,074

BEDROOMS: 3

BATHROOMS: 3½

WIDTH: 77' - 0"

DEPTH: 66' - 8"

FOUNDATION: UNFINISHED
WALKOUT BASEMENT

■ With a rugged stone-and-siding facade, this neighborhood-friendly home sets the pace in ultra-chic places with timeless character. A stately portico presents a warm welcome, while a mid-level foyer eases the transition to the elevated grand salon. Interior vistas extend throughout the living area, made even more inviting by rows of graceful arches and stunningly wide views. A wet bar and pantry serve planned events, and the formal dining room is spacious enough for the most elegant occasions. In the gourmet kitchen, wide counters and a walk-in pantry surround a food-preparation island that sports a vegetable sink. A rambling master suite includes a spacious bath with a whirlpool tub and oversized shower. A private hall leads through a pocket door to a quiet study with built-in cabinetry.

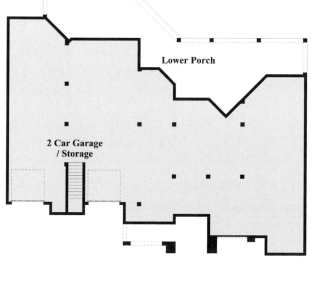

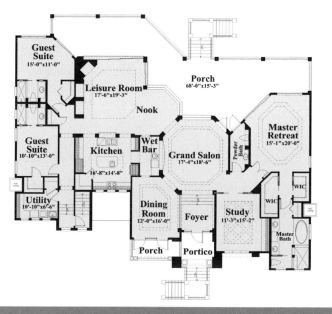

PLAN: HPK1400046

STYLE: CRAFTSMAN

FIRST FLOOR: 993 SQ. FT.

SECOND FLOOR: 642 SQ. FT.

TOTAL: 1,635 SQ. FT.

BEDROOMS: 2

BATHROOMS: 2½

WIDTH: 28' - 0"

DEPTH: 44' - 0"

FOUNDATION: FINISHED

WALKOUT BASEMENT

■ This modern three-level home is just right for a young family. The main level features a study, kitchen, dining room, laundry, and two-story living room with a corner fireplace. A rear patio makes summertime grilling fun. The master bedroom is vaulted and features a double-bowl vanity bath and walk-in closet. Bedroom 2 offers its own full bath as well. The basement level boasts a spacious garage and storage area.

second floor

CRAWLSPACE

GARAGE
19/0 X 21/0

UP

basement

UP

PATIO

DINING
12/0 X 11/0
(9' CLG.)

(VAULTED)
LIVING
14/6 X 13/0

MEDIA

REF

PAN.

UP

DN.   UP

BUILT-IN

D. W.

STUDY
12/0X 11/6
(9' CLG.)

DN.

first floor

PLAN: HPK1400047

STYLE: BUNGALOW

SQUARE FOOTAGE: 2,137

BEDROOMS: 3

BATHROOMS: 2

WIDTH: 44' - 0"

DEPTH: 63' - 0"

FOUNDATION: UNFINISHED
WALKOUT BASEMENT

■ The horizontal lines and straightforward details of this rustic plan borrow freely from the Arts and Crafts style, with a dash of traditional warmth. At the heart of the home, the kitchen and nook bring people together for easy meals and conversation. Clustered sleeping quarters ramble across the right wing and achieve privacy and convenience for the homeowners. The master suite is all decked out with a wall of glass, two walk-in closets, and generous dressing space. On the lower level, a mud area leads in from a covered porch, and the two-car garage leaves plenty of room for bicycles.

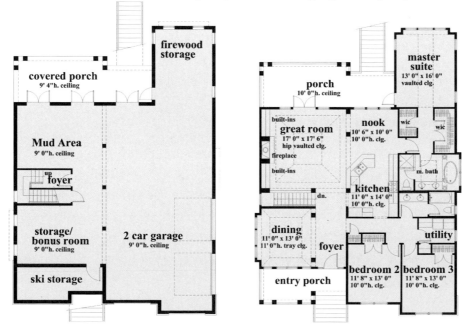

PLAN: HPK1400048

STYLE: CRAFTSMAN

FIRST FLOOR: 630 SQ. FT.

SECOND FLOOR: 1,039 SQ. FT.

TOTAL: 1,669 SQ. FT.

BEDROOMS: 3

BATHROOMS: 2

WIDTH: 44' - 6"

DEPTH: 32' - 0"

FOUNDATION: SLAB

■ This design looks cozy, yet the interior provides all the amenities a home-owner could want. A covered porch leads to the vaulted dining area, directly next to the island kitchen, complete with plenty of counter space and a pantry. The vaulted living room is graced with a fireplace, perfect for chilly evenings. Upstairs, a vaulted master suite enjoys a linen closet, a large walk-in closet, and a separate tub and shower. Two additional bedrooms sharing a hall bath reside downstairs. Bedroom 2 boasts a desk/seat area for studying.

second floor

first floor

PLAN: HPK1400049

STYLE: CRAFTSMAN

MAIN LEVEL: 1,984 SQ. FT.

LOWER LEVEL: 1,451 SQ. FT.

TOTAL: 3,435 SQ. FT.

BEDROOMS: 4

BATHROOMS: 3½

WIDTH: 56' - 0"

DEPTH: 65' - 0"

FOUNDATION: FINISHED
WALKOUT BASEMENT

■ This charming vacation retreat will feel like home in the mountains as well as by a wooded lakefront. With a covered deck, screened porch, and spacious patio, this home is designed for lovers of the outdoors. Inside, a comfy, rustic aura dominates. On the main level, a lodge-like living area with an extended-hearth fireplace and snack bar dominates. A library, easy-to-use kitchen, and enchanting master suite are also located on this floor. Downstairs, there are two more bedrooms, a huge recreation room, a hobby room (or make it into another bedroom), and lots of storage space.

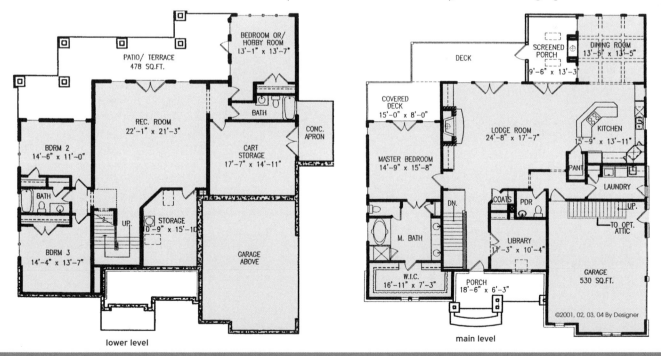

lower level

main level

Set Your Sites
To *make the most of your location, take care when siting your home on your land*

There are seemingly endless decisions to make when looking for a house plan: the style, number of stories, and how many bedrooms and baths, just to begin. But because available, affordable land today often means a less-than-perfect building site, it is also important to find the right plan to fit your lot. Choosing the right plan and siting it properly can mitigate problems and save on energy costs.

Sloping lots, wetlands acreage, and narrow-width sites are all buildable, with the right home plan.

Sloping lots—which generally offer great views and cool breezes—are tamed when paired with a hillside plan designed to fit a slope to the front, back, or side, as needed for the lot. Consider a plan that places your garage on the high side of a slope, thereby minimizing foundation costs and eliminating stairs to the garage. Alternately, pick a plan with a drive-under garage that makes perfect use of a sloping lot.

Wetlands or other areas prone to swampy ground or high water, at least part of the year, tend not to be a problem on sloped lots. But a home with a pier or raised foundation can meet the challenges presented by either a hillside or a water-prone site. These foundations raise the main body of the home up and away from soggy sites and often are in accordance with local laws protecting wetlands areas. In dry seasons, the area under the piers provides storage for a boat or other waterfront perks.

Regardless of the size, shape, and location of your lot, you want to be sure to take advantage of proper "siting." That means situating your home on the lot with consideration to sun exposure, prevailing winds, views, and access.

Both lot siting and home siting are important. Lot siting involves the specifics of your building site and its neighborhood. Does it have a view? Does it allow for privacy? How is it shaped or sized? These fac-

This lot slopes to the side and the back, creating a perfect setting for a walkout basement that includes a rec room and guest suite (page 106).

Left: Blending perfectly into the landscape, this home—found on page 101—features a covered porch and deck on the main level, with a patio off of the walkout basement. Below: A rugged design like this one fits perfectly on a mountainside lot. See page 75 for details.

tors will determine some of the details you'll want to feature in your home, which may include: large windows to capture a view, a privacy court to block out street noise, a garage that opens to the side or rear, or a particular footprint to allow for easements and setbacks from the property line.

Home siting involves the specific relationship of the home to its lot, taking into account grade changes, available views, orientation to the sun, prevailing winds, and existing vegetation. Your designer or builder should be able to help you develop a site plan, which places your home optimally on your lot. Some local building departments require a site plan before they will approve plans and issue permits. If your house plan doesn't completely meet site requirements, you should be able to make appropriate modifications.

Also consider the specific climatic conditions in your area. Correctly orientating your home will help keep you comfortable, while saving on heating and cooling bills. In hot climates, for example, locate the living areas in your home on the north or east side of the plan, reserving the south and west sides of the home for non-living spaces such as the garage or storage areas.

Homes built in temperate climates should emphasize sun exposure in the cool months and shade in the summer, while reducing the impact of winter wind and increasing the flow of summer breezes. Protect yourself from winter winds by choosing a plan with a steeply pitched roof that can be placed on the windward side of the lot. If possible, minimize windows on the north side of the home as well.

Finding a great home plan is a big step in realizing your dreams. But in the end, you'll be happiest if your home and your site are working together to make your dreams come true. ∎

OUTER SPACE

To enjoy your beautiful setting to the fullest, plan your outdoor spaces early in the building process. Consider patios, porches, and decks, and place them where they will receive afternoon sun exposure. The best outdoor living spaces will be well organized, easily accessible from multiple indoor rooms, and inviting thanks to a mix of hardscape and natural planting. Add a focal point to your outdoor living space—like a dining area, outdoor fireplace, or gazebo in the garden—for an even bigger impact.

Fit for a King

The distinctive turret at the front of this home hints at the luxury within

Blessed with plenty of curb appeal thanks to an elegant yet rustic stone exterior, this home continues to impress once you step inside. The layout includes a number of in-demand features, from a sun room to a home theater, while the attention to detail shown throughout—such as in the exposed wood beams on the main level—is sure to please.

A see-through fireplace stands in the middle of the main level, providing a division between the great room and the hearth room, but still allowing light and traffic to move freely between the two spaces. The kitchen and dining area share in the open

**Above: Built-ins add storage and character in the great room.
Right: The home's front entrance strikes a stately pose.**

design, all with terrific views of the backyard. The best views of all are saved for the sunroom, which features an octagonal design with built-ins and doorways to the kitchen and dining room.

A pair of stairways—one at each end of the sprawling, 6,300-square-foot home—facilitate access to and from the lower level, which matches the main level for space and amenities. Three bedrooms occupy the left side of the lower level, and one has a private bath—making it a perfect guest suite. A family room, rec room, craft room, and home theater fill the rest of the space, with a wet bar built in to the center of the room to serve everyone. ■

Above Left: The octagonal sun room features a fireplace. Above: The lower-level family room has large windows overlooking the backyard.

PLAN: HPK1400050

STYLE: EUROPEAN COTTAGE

MAIN LEVEL: 3,394 SQ. FT.

LOWER LEVEL: 2,966 SQ. FT.

TOTAL: 6,360 SQ. FT.

BEDROOMS: 4

BATHROOMS: 3½ + ½

WIDTH: 94' - 0"

DEPTH: 82' - 0"

FOUNDATION: FINISHED WALKOUT BASEMENT

main level

lower level

Double the Fun

The main level of this home is fantastic; the walkout basement makes it irresistible

This luxurious design is unassuming from the exterior—but step inside and you'll be blown away. An open floor plan greets visitors through the front door, with a massive great room and kitchen joining to command center stage. A

**Above: The home's unassuming facade hides a spacious interior.
Right: A work island highlights the kitchen.**

deck and porch combination stretches across the back of the house, and the breakfast area shares its tremendous views.

The home's stunning master suite can nearly overshadow the rest of its splendor. Not only does it have a gigantic walk-in closet, twin vanities, shower, and oversize garden tub, it enjoys an exercise room, easy access to a library, and a private entry to the rear deck.

A guest suite is also found on the main floor, and two more bedrooms share the

SMART DESIGN *The open design of the bar, billiards room, rec room, and media room will allow light to flow through the basement and make an already large space seem even bigger.*

lower level with a spacious recreation room and entertainment center. A full bar is ready to serve guests in the rec room and throughout the lower level—saving trips upstairs. In addition, a hobby room offers extra space and privacy. ∎

PLAN: HPK1400051

STYLE:	CONTEMPORARY
SQUARE FOOTAGE:	3,990
BASEMENT:	2,669 SQ. FT.
BEDROOMS:	2
BATHROOMS:	2½
WIDTH:	99' - 6"
DEPTH:	84' - 2"
FOUNDATION:	FINISHED WALKOUT BASEMENT

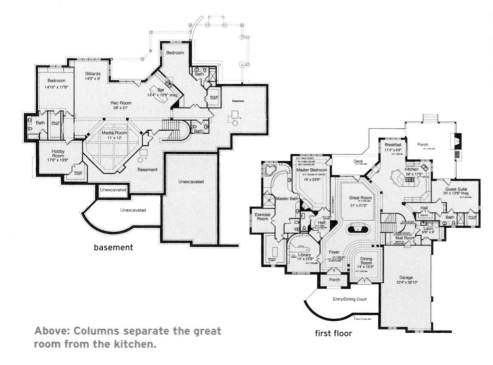

THIS HOME, AS SHOWN IN THE PHOTOGRAPH, MAY DIFFER FROM THE ACTUAL BLUEPRINTS. FOR MORE DETAILED INFORMATION, PLEASE CHECK THE FLOOR PLANS CAREFULLY.

basement

first floor

Above: Columns separate the great room from the kitchen.

PLAN: HPK1400052

STYLE: CRAFTSMAN

FIRST FLOOR: 3,203 SQ. FT.

SECOND FLOOR: 1,689 SQ. FT.

TOTAL: 4,892 SQ. FT.

BASEMENT: 2,135 SQ. FT.

BEDROOMS: 5

BATHROOMS: 5½ + ½

WIDTH: 96' - 9"

DEPTH: 91' - 10"

FOUNDATION: FINISHED WALKOUT BASEMENT

■ This magnificent five-bedroom home offers a rustic shingled exterior that is reminiscent of Old World Europe. The elegant foyer opens to the gallery and formal dining room. The living room, to the rear, enjoys a majestic fireplace accented by built-in book shelves. The spacious kitchen to the left adjoins the breakfast nook that boasts a curved window wall. The cozy and informal gathering room sits on the far left. The lavish master suite occupies the right side of the plan with a fireplace and private bath. Three additional bedrooms reside on the second floor; each has a private bath.

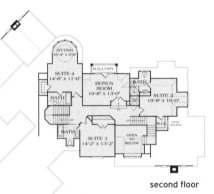

second floor

basement

first floor

PLAN: HPK1400053

STYLE: CRAFTSMAN

MAIN LEVEL: 2,922 SQ. FT.

LOWER LEVEL: 3,027 SQ. FT.

TOTAL: 5,949 SQ. FT.

BEDROOMS: 4

BATHROOMS: 4½ + ½

WIDTH: 98' - 0"

DEPTH: 76' - 0"

FOUNDATION: FINISHED WALKOUT BASEMENT

■ Looks can be deceiving! Although the exterior of this home appears as rustic as a mountain cabin, the interior is nothing but lavish. From a grand foyer, the great room has a warming fireplace and built-in media center. Covered-deck access is perfect year-round, with built-in deck furniture storage for those colder months. The kitchen is marvelous, with a six-burner cooktop island and a butler's pantry to the dining room, surrounded by glass. The inspiring master suite relishes a luxurious spa bath and tons of natural light. Downstairs, a games room, wine cellar, and theater are special touches. Two generous bedrooms share a full bath and a computer center to the right; to the left, Bedroom 4 enjoys a private spa bath.

lower level

main level

PLAN: HPK1400054

STYLE: CRAFTSMAN
SQUARE FOOTAGE: 1,899
BASEMENT: 1,899 SQ. FT.
BEDROOMS: 2
BATHROOMS: 2½
WIDTH: 62' - 0"
DEPTH: 68' - 8"

■ A hipped dormer on the exterior and a tray ceiling inside highlight the dining room of this traditional craftsman. Escape to the privacy of your master suite and its own whirlpool tub (four extra bathrooms throughout the house means no sharing!). The kitchen is tucked away from traffic, but within view of the amply-spaced eating area. The main floor of this house has an additional covered porch in the rear corner leading off of the garage. Both the den and family bedroom feature built-in desks. These conveniences are mirrored upstairs with a ready-to-use bookcase, hutch, wine storage, and bar. Entertain upstairs in style, and still have plenty of space available for all of your storage needs.

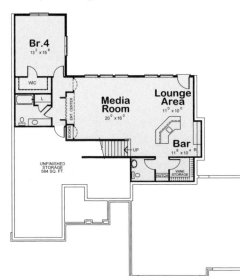

PLAN: HPK1400236

STYLE: COUNTRY COTTAGE

FIRST FLOOR: 1,285 SQ. FT.

SECOND FLOOR: 1,726 SQ. FT.

TOTAL: 3,011 SQ. FT.

BEDROOMS: 4

BATHROOMS: 3½

WIDTH: 44' - 0"

DEPTH: 50' - 0"

FOUNDATION: UNFINISHED
WALKOUT BASEMENT

rear exterior

■ A picture-perfect addition to any neighborhood, this Craftsman home is brimming with curb appeal. Inside, the imaginative design is abound with amenities. Highlights include intricate ceiling treatments, built-in bookcases and desks, and plant shelves. The island kitchen is open to the family room enabling constant interaction. Access to a rear patio invites the option of alfresco meals. The second floor houses four bedrooms, including the master suite. The fourth bedroom can be used as an office or a guest suite. Extra storage space in the two-car garage is an added bonus.

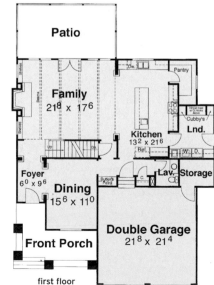

first floor

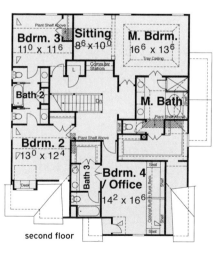

second floor

©1999 Donald A. Gardner, Inc.

PLAN: HPK1400055

STYLE: BUNGALOW

MAIN LEVEL: 1,734 SQ. FT.

UPPER LEVEL: 546 SQ. FT.

LOWER LEVEL: 788 SQ. FT.

TOTAL: 3,068 SQ. FT.

BONUS SPACE: 381 SQ. FT.

BEDROOMS: 4

BATHROOMS: 3½

WIDTH: 60' - 8"

DEPTH: 68' - 0"

■ Multiple gables, cedar shakes, stucco, and stone provide plenty of enchantment for the exterior of this hillside home. Craftsman character abounds inside as well as out, evidenced by the home's functional floor plan. Built-ins flank the great room's fireplace for convenience, and a rear deck extends living space outdoors. The exceptionally well-designed kitchen features an island cooktop and an adjacent breakfast bay. The master suite, also with a bay window, enjoys two walk-in closets and a delightful bath with dual vanities. Two upstairs bedrooms are divided by an impressive balcony that overlooks the foyer and great room.

rear exterior

lower level

main level

upper level

©1999 Donald A. Gardner, Inc.

PLAN: HPK1400056

STYLE: CRAFTSMAN

SQUARE FOOTAGE: 1,544

BASEMENT: 1,018 SQ. FT.

BEDROOMS: 2

BATHROOMS: 2

WIDTH: 40' - 0"

DEPTH: 60' - 0"

FOUNDATION: FINISHED WALKOUT BASEMENT

■ This Cape Cod design is enhanced with shingles, stone detailing, and muntin windows. The entry is flanked on the left by a bedroom/den, perfect for overnight guests or a cozy place to relax. The hearth-warmed great room enjoys expansive views of the rear deck area. The dining room is nestled next to the island kitchen, which boasts plenty of counter space. The master bedroom is positioned at the rear of the home for privacy and accesses a private bath. Two family bedrooms and a spacious games room complete the finished basement.

basement

first floor

PLAN: HPK1400057

STYLE: BUNGALOW
FIRST FLOOR: 2,391 SQ. FT.
SECOND FLOOR: 1,539 SQ. FT.
TOTAL: 3,930 SQ. FT.
BONUS SPACE: 429 SQ. FT.
BEDROOMS: 3
BATHROOMS: 4½
WIDTH: 71' - 0"
DEPTH: 69' - 0"
FOUNDATION: ISLAND
BASEMENT

■ Climate is a key component of any mountain retreat, and outdoor living is an integral part of its design. This superior cabin features open and covered porches. A mix of matchstick details and rugged stone sets off this lodge-house facade, concealing a well-defined interior. Windows line the breakfast bay and brighten the kitchen, which features a center cooktop island. A door leads out to a covered porch with a summer kitchen. The upper level features a secluded master suite with a spacious bath beginning with a double walk-in closet and ending with a garden view of the porch. A two-sided fireplace extends warmth to the whirlpool spa-style tub.

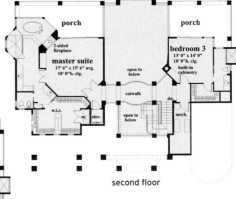

second floor

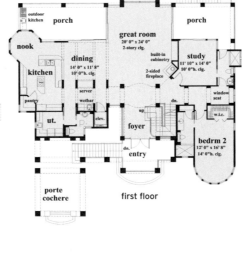

first floor

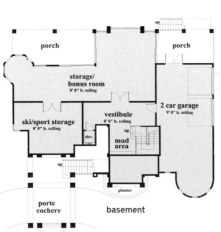

basement

PLAN: HPK1400058

STYLE: BUNGALOW

MAIN LEVEL: 1,810 SQ. FT.

LOWER LEVEL: 1,146 SQ. FT.

TOTAL: 2,956 SQ. FT.

BEDROOMS: 4

BATHROOMS: 3

WIDTH: 68' - 4"

DEPTH: 60' - 10"

rear exterior

■ This hillside home combines stucco, stone, and cedar shakes for exceptional Craftsman character. A dramatic cathedral ceiling heightens the open living room with a central fireplace and built-ins. Porches flank the living room to allow its rear wall of windows uninterrupted views of the outdoors. Exit to the two rear porches from the dining room and master bedroom. The breakfast and dining rooms enjoy screened-porch access. A tray ceiling tops the master bedroom, which features a lovely private bath and walk-in closet. A versatile bedroom/study and full bath are nearby. Downstairs are two more bedrooms, each with an adjacent covered patio, another full bath, and a generous family room with a fireplace.

lower level

main level

PLAN: HPK1400004

STYLE: COUNTRY COTTAGE

FIRST FLOOR: 1,561 SQ. FT.

SECOND FLOOR: 578 SQ. FT.

TOTAL: 2,139 SQ. FT.

BONUS SPACE: 284 SQ. FT.

BEDROOMS: 3

BATHROOMS: 2½

WIDTH: 50' - 0"

DEPTH: 57' - 0"

FOUNDATION: CRAWLSPACE, FINISHED WALKOUT BASEMENT

rear exterior

■ Nostalgic and earthy, this Craftsman design has an attractive floor plan and thoughtful amenities. A column-lined covered porch is the perfect welcome to guests. A large vaulted family room, enhanced by a fireplace, opens to the spacious island kitchen and roomy breakfast area. The private master suite is embellished with a vaulted ceiling, walk-in closet, and vaulted super bath with French-door entry. With family in mind, two secondary bedrooms—each with a walk-in closet—share a computer workstation or loft area. A bonus room can be used as bedroom or home office.

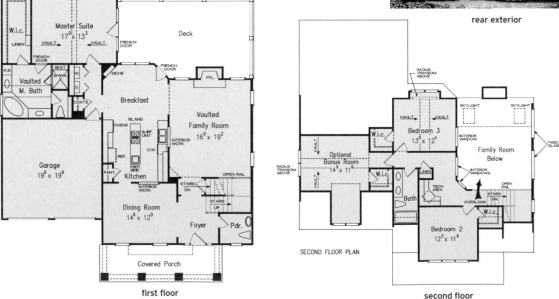

first floor

second floor

PLAN: HPK1400059

STYLE: CRAFTSMAN

MAIN LEVEL: 3,171 SQ. FT.

LOWER LEVEL: 1,897 SQ. FT.

TOTAL: 5,068 SQ. FT.

BEDROOMS: 5

BATHROOMS: 3½

WIDTH: 86' - 2"

DEPTH: 63' - 8"

FOUNDATION: FINISHED WALKOUT BASEMENT

rear exterior

■ A brick, stone, and shake-shingle facade makes this beautiful home a perfect choice for any neighborhood. A large great room, breakfast area, and kitchen create a comfortable and inviting atmosphere. Columns introduce the great room from the foyer, and 12-foot high ceilings top the great room, breakfast area, kitchen, dining room, and master bedroom. Formal dining is available for special occasions. A covered deck with fireplace and built-in grill offers stylish outdoor living. Angled stairs lead to a lower level where a large party room offers a bar, billiards area, recreation room, and media room. Additional bedrooms are available for the occasional overnight guest.

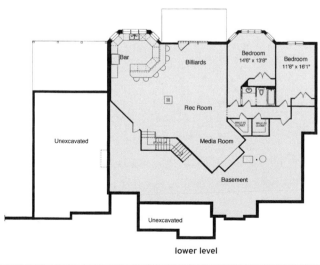

lower level

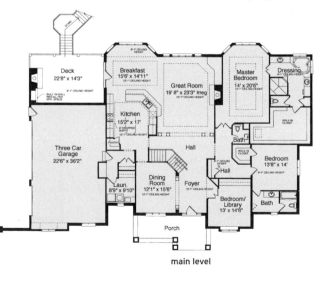

main level

PLAN: HPK1400060

STYLE: CRAFTSMAN

SQUARE FOOTAGE: 1,860

BEDROOMS: 3

BATHROOMS: 2

WIDTH: 64' - 2"

DEPTH: 44' - 2"

FOUNDATION: FINISHED WALKOUT BASEMENT

■ A brick, stone, and cedar-shake facade provide color and texture to the exterior of this delightful one-level home. A spacious great room is decorated with a wood-burning fireplace, high ceiling, and French doors. Grand openings to both the breakfast room and dining room offer expanded space for formal or informal occasions. A breakfast bar offers additional seating and a comfortable gathering place. A covered porch provides a pleasant retreat and is located for convenient access from the kitchen and breakfast area. Alcoves in the great room and master bedroom are created for furniture placement. An angled entry in the master suite introduces a spectacular bath with a whirlpool tub and double-bowl vanity.

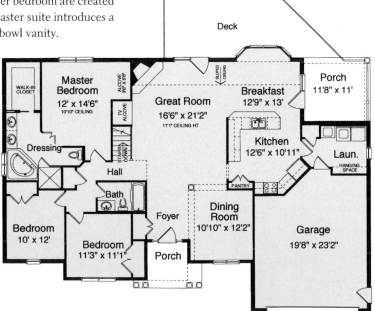

PLAN: HPK1400061

STYLE: BUNGALOW

MAIN LEVEL: 1,864 SQ. FT.

LOWER LEVEL: 999 SQ. FT.

TOTAL: 2,863 SQ. FT.

BONUS SPACE: 417 SQ. FT.

BEDROOMS: 4

BATHROOMS: 3

WIDTH: 60' - 0"

DEPTH: 67' - 2"

© 1999 Donald A. Gardner Inc.

rear exterior

■ Cedar shakes, siding, and stone blend artfully together on the exterior of this attractive Craftsman-style home. Inside, a remarkably open floor plan separates the master suite from two family bedrooms for homeowner privacy. Optimizing family togetherness, the common areas of the home are surprisingly open with few interior walls to divide the rooms from one another. A tray ceiling adds definition to the dining room, while the great room is amplified by a cathedral ceiling. A tray ceiling also tops the master bedroom, which enjoys a lovely private bath with a walk-in closet. Two family bedrooms share a hall bath on the opposite side of the home; another bedroom is located downstairs, along with a large recreation room and an unfinished storage area.

lower level

main level

BONUS RM.
14-8 x 23-4

© 1997 Donald A. Gardner Architects, Inc.

PLAN: HPK1400062

STYLE: CONTEMPORARY

SQUARE FOOTAGE: 1,680

BASEMENT: 1,653 SQ. FT.

BEDROOMS: 3

BATHROOMS: 2

WIDTH: 62' - 8"

DEPTH: 59' - 10"

■ This rustic retreat is updated with contemporary angles and packs a lot of living into a small space. The covered front porch leads to a welcoming foyer. The beamed-ceiling great room opens directly ahead and features a fireplace, a wall of windows, and access to the screened porch (with its own fireplace!) and is adjacent to the angled dining area. A highly efficient island kitchen is sure to please with tons of counter and cabinet space. Two family bedrooms, sharing a full bath, are located on one end of the plan; the master suite is secluded for complete privacy at the other end.

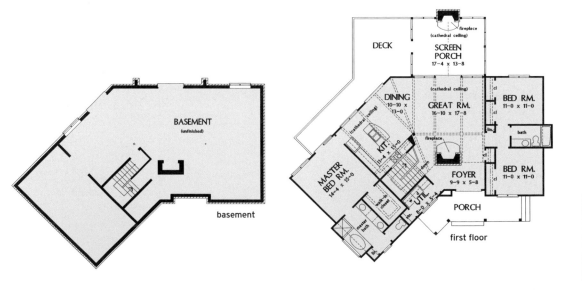

basement

first floor

GARAGE
22-0 x 22-0

PLAN: HPK1400063

STYLE: CRAFTSMAN

MAIN LEVEL: 3,040 SQ. FT.

LOWER LEVEL: 1,736 SQ. FT.

TOTAL: 4,776 SQ. FT.

BEDROOMS: 5

BATHROOMS: 4½ + ½

WIDTH: 106' - 5"

DEPTH: 104' - 2"

rear exterior

■ Looking a bit like a mountain resort, this fine rustic-style home is sure to be the envy of your neighborhood. Entering through the elegant front door, one finds an open staircase to the right and a spacious great room directly ahead. Here, a fireplace and a wall of windows give a cozy welcome. A lavish master suite begins with a sitting room complete with a fireplace and continues to a private porch, large walk-in closet, and sumptuous bedroom area. The gourmet kitchen adjoins a sunny dining room that offers access to a screened porch.

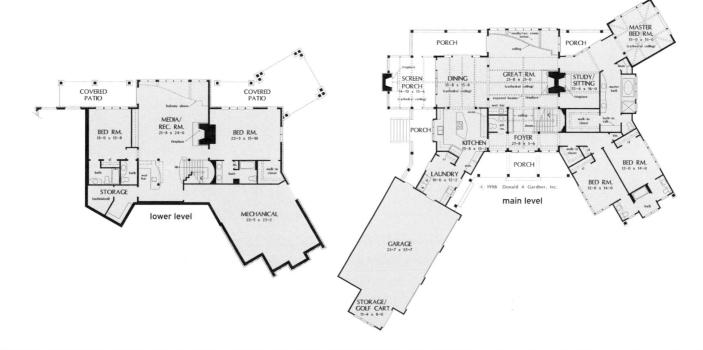

PLAN: HPK1400002

STYLE: CAPE COD

FIRST FLOOR: 1,024 SQ. FT.

SECOND FLOOR: 456 SQ. FT.

TOTAL: 1,480 SQ. FT.

BEDROOMS: 2

BATHROOMS: 2

WIDTH: 32' - 0"

DEPTH: 40' - 0"

FOUNDATION: FINISHED
WALKOUT BASEMENT

■ Pillars, a large front porch, and plenty of window views lend a classic feel to this lovely country cottage. Inside, the entry room has a coat closet and an interior entry door to eliminate drafts. The light-filled L-shaped kitchen lies conveniently near the entrance. A large room adjacent to the kitchen serves as a dining and living area where a fireplace adds warmth. A master suite boasts a walk-in closet and full bath. The second floor holds a loft, a second bedroom, and a full bath.

first floor

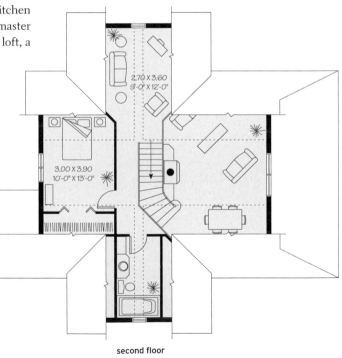

second floor

PLAN: HPK1400064

STYLE: FRENCH

FIRST FLOOR: 2,346 SQ. FT.

SECOND FLOOR: 1,260 SQ. FT.

TOTAL: 3,606 SQ. FT.

BEDROOMS: 4

BATHROOMS: 3½

WIDTH: 68' - 11"

DEPTH: 58' - 9"

FOUNDATION: FINISHED

WALKOUT BASEMENT

■ The European character of this home is enhanced through the use of stucco and stone on the exterior, giving this French Country estate home its charm and beauty. The foyer leads to the dining room and study/living room. The two-story family room is positioned for convenient access to the back staircase, kitchen, wet bar, and deck area. The master bedroom is privately located on the right side of the home with an optional entry to the study and a large garden bath. Upstairs are three additional large bedrooms; two have a shared bath and private vanities and one has a full private bath. All bedrooms conveniently access the back staircase and have open-rail views to the family room below.

first floor

second floor

PLAN: HPK1400065

STYLE: VACATION

MAIN LEVEL: 787 SQ. FT.

LOWER LEVEL: 787 SQ. FT.

TOTAL: 1,574 SQ. FT.

BEDROOMS: 3

BATHROOMS: 2

WIDTH: 32' - 4"

DEPTH: 24' - 4"

FOUNDATION: UNFINISHED BASEMENT

■ This chalet-style design offers wonderful views for vacations and plenty of comfort for year-round living. The main level includes complete living quarters, with one bedroom, a full bath, and an open living and dining area that accesses the front. Sliding glass doors lead from the eat-in kitchen to the wraparound deck, and a V-shaped fireplace warms the entire area. The lower level provides two additional bedrooms, a full bath with laundry facilities, and a family room with outdoor access.

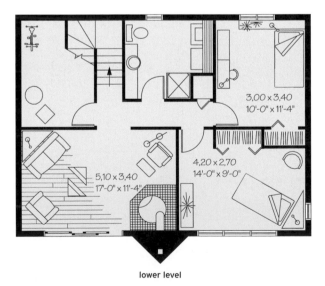

lower level

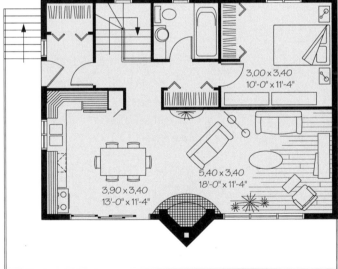

main level

PLAN: HPK1400066

STYLE: EUROPEAN COTTAGE
MAIN LEVEL: 787 SQ. FT.
LOWER LEVEL: 787 SQ. FT.
TOTAL: 1,574 SQ. FT.
BEDROOMS: 3
BATHROOMS: 2
WIDTH: 32' - 4"
DEPTH: 24' - 4"
FOUNDATION: UNFINISHED
WALKOUT BASEMENT

■ This mountain-top chalet takes advantage of views with tall floor-to-ceiling windows. A central fireplace runs straight up from the lower-level family room to the living/dining room as a visual statement of warmth. A large efficient kitchen, living room, dining area, bedroom, and full bath complete the main level. Downstairs, two bedrooms share a full bath and a laundry room. A family room accesses the patio through sliding glass doors.

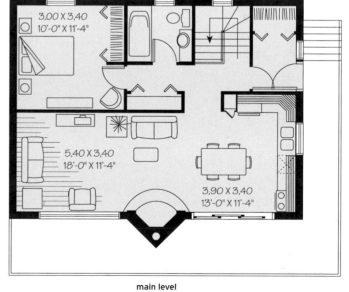

main level

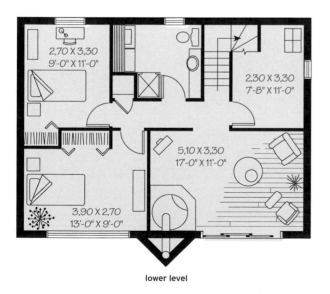

lower level

PLAN: HPK1400067

STYLE: COUNTRY COTTAGE

FIRST FLOOR: 792 SQ. FT.

SECOND FLOOR: 573 SQ. FT.

TOTAL: 1,365 SQ. FT.

BEDROOMS: 3

BATHROOMS: 2

WIDTH: 42' - 0"

DEPTH: 32' - 0"

FOUNDATION: CRAWLSPACE, UNFINISHED BASEMENT

■ This distinctive vacation home is designed ideally for a gently sloping lot, which allows for a daylight basement. It can, however, accommodate a flat lot nicely. An expansive veranda sweeps around two sides of the exterior and is complemented by full-height windows. Decorative woodwork and traditional multipane windows belie the contemporary interior. An open living/dining room, with a woodstove and two bay windows, is complemented by a galley-style kitchen. A bedroom, or den, on the first floor has the use of a full bath. The second floor includes a master bedroom with a balcony, and one family bedroom. Both second-floor bedrooms have dormer windows and share a full bath that has a vaulted ceiling.

rear exterior

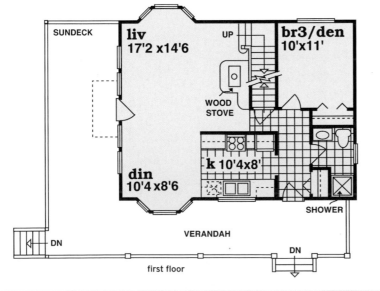

first floor

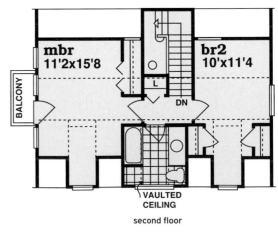

second floor

PLAN: HPK1400068

STYLE: COUNTRY COTTAGE

MAIN LEVEL: 1,230 SQ. FT.

LOWER LEVEL: 769 SQ. FT.

TOTAL: 1,999 SQ. FT.

BEDROOMS: 3

BATHROOMS: 2½

WIDTH: 40' - 0"

DEPTH: 52' - 6"

FOUNDATION: FINISHED
WALKOUT BASEMENT

■ This petite country cottage design is enhanced with all the modern amenities. Inside, through a pair of double doors, the family den is illuminated by a large window. The kitchen, which features efficient pantry space, opens to the living/dining area. This spacious room is highlighted by a scissor vaulted ceiling, and features a warming fireplace and nook space. The living/dining room also overlooks a large rear deck, which is accessed through a back door. Secluded on the ground level for extra privacy, the vaulted master bedroom includes a private full bath and a walk-in closet. A laundry room, two-car garage, and powder room all complete this floor. Downstairs, two additional family bedrooms share a hall bath. The recreation room is an added bonus. Extra storage space is also available on this floor.

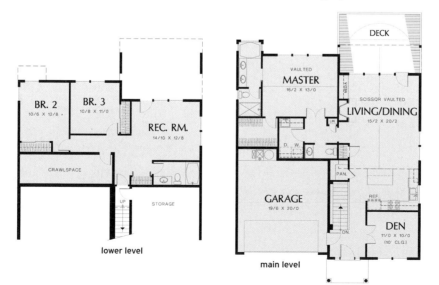

lower level

main level

PLAN: HPK1400069

STYLE: COUNTRY COTTAGE

MAIN LEVEL: 2,920 SQ. FT.

UPPER LEVEL: 1,362 SQ. FT.

LOWER LEVEL: 1,860 SQ. FT.

TOTAL: 6,142 SQ. FT.

BEDROOMS: 5

BATHROOMS: 2½

WIDTH: 76' - 2"

DEPTH: 74' - 0"

FOUNDATION: FINISHED BASEMENT

■ This comfortable country cottage is designed with a lovely siding facade and a pleasing floor plan for a home with lots of personality. From the foyer, the living room (or make it a guest suite) has pocket doors and built-ins and access to a full bath. The dining room is nearby, with a butler's pantry that makes entertaining a breeze. The kitchen is made for conversation, opening to the family room, breakfast bay, and sun room. The master suite is located on the right, resplendent with vaults in the bedroom and sitting bay, dual walk-in closets, and a garden tub. Upstairs, three generous bedrooms each have a walk-in closet. Future space allows for growth. The lower level provides a bedroom and full bath, recreation room, study, workshop, ancillary kitchen and dining area, and a craft room.

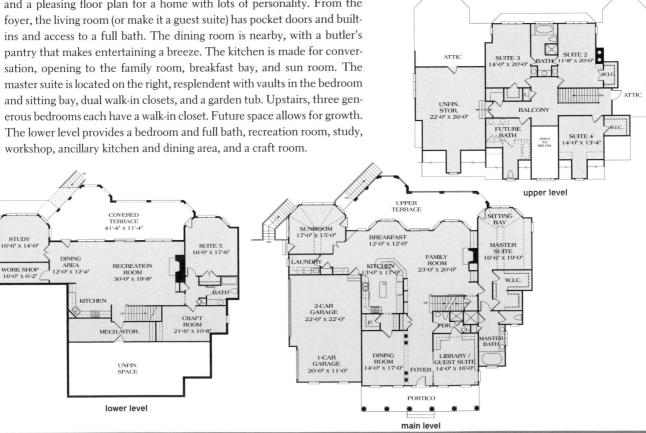

upper level

lower level

main level

PLAN: HPK1400070

STYLE: TRADITIONAL

FIRST FLOOR: 2,565 SQ. FT.

SECOND FLOOR: 1,375 SQ. FT.

TOTAL: 3,940 SQ. FT.

BEDROOMS: 4

BATHROOMS: 3½

WIDTH: 88' - 6"

DEPTH: 58' - 6"

FOUNDATION: FINISHED WALKOUT BASEMENT

rear exterior

■ A symmetrical facade with twin chimneys makes a grand statement. A covered porch welcomes visitors and provides a pleasant place to spend a mild evening. The entry foyer is flanked by formal living areas—a dining room and a living room—each with a fireplace. A third fireplace is the highlight of the expansive great room to the rear. An L-shaped kitchen offers a work island and a walk-in pantry and easily serves the nearby breakfast and sunrooms. The master suite provides lavish luxuries.

first floor

second floor

PLAN: HPK1400071

STYLE: FARMHOUSE

MAIN LEVEL: 1,709 SQ. FT.

LOWER LEVEL: 1,051 SQ. FT.

TOTAL: 2,760 SQ. FT.

BEDROOMS: 3

BATHROOMS: 3½

WIDTH: 60' - 10"

DEPTH: 69' - 3"

FOUNDATION: SLAB,

UNFINISHED BASEMENT

■ A lovely traditional facade complements this up-to-date ranch-style plan. Inside, an elegant arch connects the kitchen and breakfast room to the main living area beyond. The great room features a cozy fireplace and the dining room is easily served from the kitchen. The first-floor master suite features a roomy walk-in closet, double vanities, and a separate shower and whirlpool tub. Downstairs, Bedrooms 2 and 3 share a bath and are located on either side of a casual den.

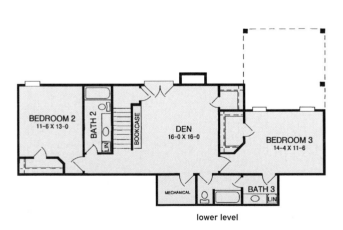

lower level

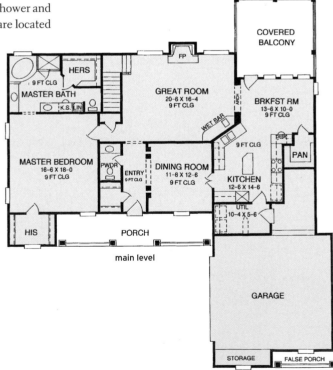

main level

PLAN: HPK1400072

STYLE: TRADITIONAL

SQUARE FOOTAGE: 2,500

BEDROOMS: 3

BATHROOMS: 3

WIDTH: 64' - 0"

DEPTH: 52' - 0"

FOUNDATION: UNFINISHED
BASEMENT

■ This Florida "Cracker"-style home is warm and inviting. Unpretentious use of space is the hallmark of the Florida Cracker. This design shows the style at its best. Private baths for each of the bedrooms are a fine example of this. The huge great room, which sports a volume ceiling, opens to the expansive rear porch for extended entertaining. Traditional Cracker homes had sparse master suites. Not this one! It has a lavish bedchamber and a luxurious bath with His and Hers closets and a corner soaking tub. Perfect for a sloping lot, this home can be expanded with a lower garage and bonus space in the basement.

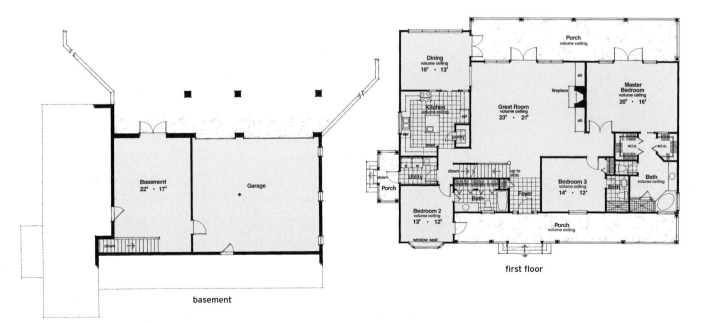

basement

first floor

PLAN: HPK1400073

STYLE: COUNTRY COTTAGE

FIRST FLOOR: 2,076 SQ. FT.

SECOND FLOOR: 843 SQ. FT.

TOTAL: 2,919 SQ. FT.

BEDROOMS: 4

BATHROOMS: 3½

WIDTH: 57' - 6"

DEPTH: 51' - 6"

FOUNDATION: FINISHED WALKOUT BASEMENT

■ This lovely home's foyer opens to the formal dining room, defined by decorative columns, and leads to the two-story great room. The kitchen and breakfast room join the great room to create a casual family area. The master suite is finished with a coffered ceiling and a sumptuous bath. A guest suite with a private bath is located just off the kitchen. Upstairs, two family bedrooms share a compartmented bath and a raised loft.

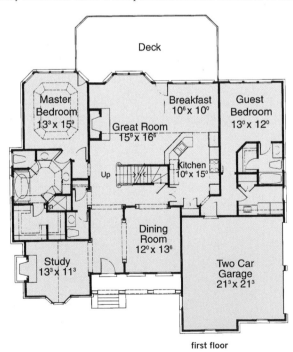

first floor

second floor

PLAN: HPK1400074

STYLE: BUNGALOW

MAIN LEVEL: 2,065 SQ. FT.

LOWER LEVEL: 1,216 SQ. FT.

TOTAL: 3,281 SQ. FT.

BEDROOMS: 4

BATHROOMS: 3½

WIDTH: 82' - 2"

DEPTH: 43' - 6"

rear exterior

©1998 Donald A. Gardner, Inc.

■ Stone, siding, and multiple gables combine beautifully on the exterior of this hillside home. Taking advantage of rear views, the home's most oft-used rooms are oriented at the back with plenty of windows. Augmented by a cathedral ceiling, the great room features a fireplace, built-in shelves, and access to the rear deck. Twin walk-in closets and a private bath infuse the master suite with luxury. The nearby powder room offers an optional full-bath arrangement, allowing the study to double as a bedroom. Downstairs, a large media/recreation room with a wet bar and fireplace separates two more bedrooms, each with a full bath and walk-in closet.

PLAN: HPK1400075

STYLE: TRADITIONAL

MAIN LEVEL: 2,464 SQ. FT.

LOWER LEVEL: 1,887 SQ. FT.

TOTAL: 4,351 SQ. FT.

BEDROOMS: 4

BATHROOMS: 3½

WIDTH: 59' - 0"

DEPTH: 81' - 0"

FOUNDATION: FINISHED

WALKOUT BASEMENT, SLAB

■ Here is a gorgeous hillside design that offers an unassuming front perspective, but behold the side view with its elegant deck flanked by the great room and master bedroom, each with an enormous arch-top window. Inside, the dining room, island kitchen, nook, and great room enjoy an open plan with decorative columns and tray ceilings defining the dining and great rooms. The master suite finds privacy to the right with a luxurious bath. The staircase near the kitchen leads to the lower level where three additional bedrooms are found. The game room offers a built-in media center with a wet-bar and wine cellar close at hand.

rear exterior

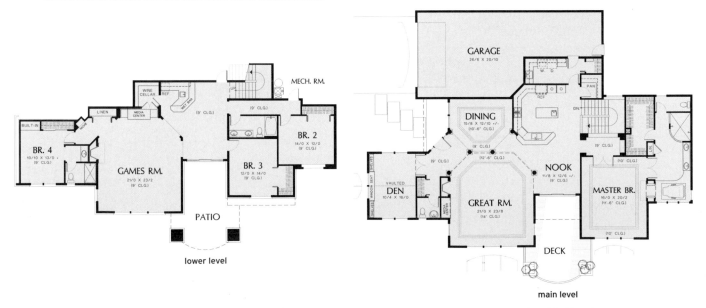

lower level

main level

PLAN: HPK1400003

STYLE: COUNTRY COTTAGE

SQUARE FOOTAGE: 2,170

BEDROOMS: 4

BATHROOMS: 3

WIDTH: 62' - 0"

DEPTH: 61' - 6"

FOUNDATION: FINISHED
WALKOUT BASEMENT

■ This classic cottage boasts a stone-and-wood exterior with a welcoming arch-top entry that leads to a columned foyer. An extended-hearth fireplace is the focal point of the family room, and a nearby sunroom with covered porch access opens up the living area to the outdoors. The gourmet island kitchen opens through double doors from the living area; the breakfast area looks out to a porch. Sleeping quarters include a master wing with a spacious, angled bath, and a sitting room or den that has its own full bath—perfect for a guest suite. On the opposite side of the plan, two family bedrooms share a full bath.

QUOTE ONE®

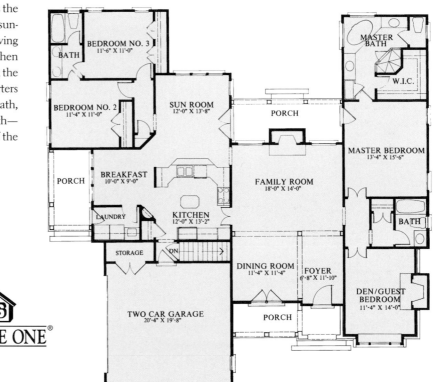

PLAN: HPK1400076

STYLE: COUNTRY COTTAGE

SQUARE FOOTAGE: 2,090

BEDROOMS: 4

BATHROOMS: 3

WIDTH: 61' - 0"

DEPTH: 70' - 6"

FOUNDATION: FINISHED
WALKOUT BASEMENT

■ This traditional home features board-and-batten and cedar shingles in a well-proportioned, country-flavored exterior. The foyer opens to the dining room and leads to the great room, which offers French doors to the rear columned porch. An additional bedroom or study shares a full bath with Bedroom 2. The lavish master suite enjoys a luxurious private bath and two walk-in closets. A fourth bedroom—or make it a home office—resides just off the kitchen.

QUOTE ONE®

PLAN: HPK1400077

STYLE: TRADITIONAL

FIRST FLOOR: 1,619 SQ. FT.

SECOND FLOOR: 372 SQ. FT.

TOTAL: 1,991 SQ. FT.

BONUS SPACE: 82 SQ. FT.

BEDROOMS: 3

BATHROOMS: 3

WIDTH: 46' - 8"

DEPTH: 70' - 8"

■ Euro-French, country traditional sums up this exquisite hideaway. A complex roof line sits astride rustic exteriors and a chimney sure to charm! Cathedral-style ceilings adorn the main level. Enter your home and be greeted by a fireplace in the foyer on your immediate right, and a den on the left. Continue straight ahead to the great room, where you can view your enclosed deck and access your kitchen with accompanying eating area. A master suite with walk-in closet is to the right of the kitchen. A second bathroom and garage are accessed through the kitchen as well. Upstairs you will find plenty to do, including an office with built-in desk, and an extra kitchen!

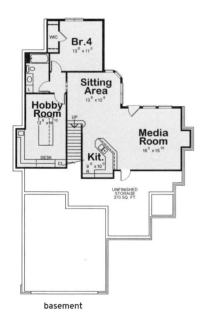

basement

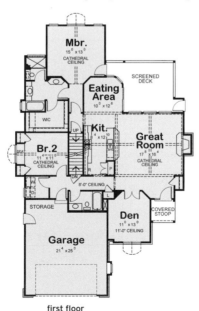

first floor

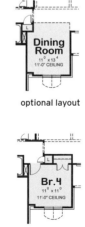

second floor

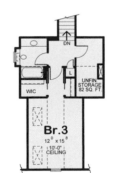

optional layout

optional layout

PLAN: HPK1400078

STYLE: TRADITIONAL

SQUARE FOOTAGE: 2,176

BASEMENT: 957 SQ. FT.

BEDROOMS: 2

BATHROOMS: 2

WIDTH: 70' - 8"

DEPTH: 68' - 8"

■ Brick with window shutters on the outside lend old-fashioned appeal to this plan. Inside, the great room serves as the focal point, located directly off the foyer. Windows looking out to the rear frame a fireplace, and an arch separates the dining room. The kitchen area is easily accessible from the great room, and is built for all of your food storage, serving and preparation needs. The dining room offers access onto the deck (covered!) and to the second bedroom and to the study. The kitchen offers access to the garage with shop. The master bedroom is accessed via double doors from the great room, and comes with luxurious bath and incredible walk-in closet. Upstairs is the third bedroom with private bath and separate dressing area, family room, rec room and storage.

PLAN: HPK1400079

STYLE: EUROPEAN COTTAGE

MAIN LEVEL: 2,297 SQ. FT.

LOWER LEVEL: 1,212 SQ. FT.

TOTAL: 3,509 SQ. FT.

BEDROOMS: 5

BATHROOMS: 5½

WIDTH: 70' - 10"

DEPTH: 69' - 0"

©1998 Donald A. Gardner, Inc.

rear exterior

■ A variety of exterior materials and interesting windows combine with an unusual floor plan to make this an exceptional home. It is designed for a sloping lot, with full living quarters on the main level, but with two extra bedrooms and a family room added to the lower level. A covered porch showcases a wonderful dining room window and an attractive front door. The living room, enhanced by a fireplace, adjoins the dining room for easy entertaining. The island kitchen and a bayed breakfast room are to the left. Three bedrooms on this level include one that could serve as a study and one as a master suite with dual vanities, a garden tub, and a walk-in closet. A deck on this floor covers the patio off the lower-level family room, which has its own fireplace.

lower level

main level

PLAN: HPK1400080

STYLE: TRADITIONAL

FIRST FLOOR: 1,580 SQ. FT.

SECOND FLOOR: 595 SQ. FT.

TOTAL: 2,175 SQ. FT.

BONUS STORAGE: 290 SQ. FT.

BEDROOMS: 3

BATHROOMS: 2½

WIDTH: 50' - 2"

DEPTH: 70' - 11"

FOUNDATION: FINISHED WALKOUT BASEMENT

■ This home is a true Southern original. Inside, the spacious foyer leads directly to a large vaulted great room with its handsome fireplace. The dining room, just off the foyer, features a dramatic vaulted ceiling. The spacious kitchen offers both storage and large work areas opening up to the breakfast room. At the rear of the home you will find the master suite with its garden bath, His and Hers vanities, and an oversize closet. The second floor provides two additional bedrooms with a shared bath and a balcony overlook to the foyer below.

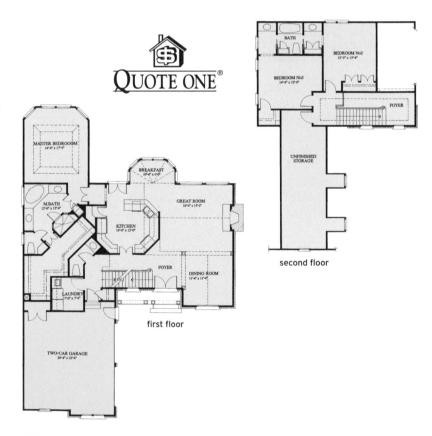

first floor

second floor

PLAN: HPK1400081

STYLE: COUNTRY COTTAGE

FIRST FLOOR: 1,475 SQ. FT.

SECOND FLOOR: 1,460 SQ. FT.

TOTAL: 2,935 SQ. FT.

BEDROOMS: 4

BATHROOMS: 3½

WIDTH: 57' - 6"

DEPTH: 46' - 6"

FOUNDATION: FINISHED
WALKOUT BASEMENT

■ Quaint keystones and shutters offer charming accents to the stucco-and-stone exterior of this stately English Country home. The two-story foyer opens through decorative columns to the formal living room, which offers a wet bar. The nearby media room shares a through-fireplace with the two-story great room, which has double doors that lead to the rear deck. A bumped-out bay holds a breakfast area that shares its light with an expansive cooktop-island kitchen. This area opens to the formal dining room through a convenient butler's pantry. One wing of the second floor is dedicated to the rambling master suite, which boasts unusual amenities with angled walls, a tray ceiling, and a bumped-out bay with a sitting area in the bedroom.

QUOTE ONE®

first floor

second floor

PLAN: HPK1400082

STYLE: TRADITIONAL

SQUARE FOOTAGE: 2,377

BEDROOMS: 3

BATHROOMS: 2

WIDTH: 69' - 0"

DEPTH: 49' - 6"

FOUNDATION: FINISHED WALKOUT BASEMENT

■ One-story living takes a lovely traditional turn in this brick home. The entry foyer opens to the formal dining room and the great room through graceful columned archways. The open gourmet kitchen, bayed breakfast nook, and keeping room with a fireplace will be a magnet for family activity. Sleeping quarters offer two family bedrooms, a hall bath, and a rambling master suite with a bayed sitting area and a sensuous bath.

QUOTE ONE®

PLAN: HPK1400083

STYLE: TRADITIONAL

FIRST FLOOR: 1,621 SQ. FT.

SECOND FLOOR: 1,766 SQ. FT.

TOTAL: 3,387 SQ. FT.

BEDROOMS: 4

BATHROOMS: 3½

WIDTH: 52' - 0"

DEPTH: 50' - 6"

FOUNDATION: FINISHED

WALKOUT BASEMENT

■ An all-American charm springs from the true Colonial style of this distinguished home. Double French doors partition the casual region of the home, which features the comfortable family room and its lovely fireplace. A guest room is located behind the kitchen area, making it a perfect maid's or nurse's room. The master suite has a private study, a fireplace, and an amenity-laden bath with an extended walk-in closet. Two additional bedrooms share a private, compartmented bath.

first floor

second floor

PLAN: HPK1400084

STYLE: MEDITERRANEAN
FIRST FLOOR: 2,502 SQ. FT.
SECOND FLOOR: 677 SQ. FT.
TOTAL: 3,179 SQ. FT.
BONUS SPACE: 171 SQ. FT.
BEDROOMS: 4
BATHROOMS: 3½
WIDTH: 71' - 2"
DEPTH: 56' - 10"
FOUNDATION: FINISHED
WALKOUT BASEMENT

■ Stone and stucco bring a chateau welcome to this Mediterranean-style home. A sensational sunroom lights up the rear of the plan and flows to the bayed breakfast nook. The living area opens to the formal dining room. A master suite with rear-deck access leads to a family or guest bedroom with a private bath. Upstairs, two secondary bedrooms and a full bath enjoy easy kitchen access down a side stairway.

first floor

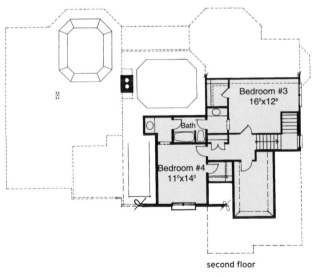

second floor

PLAN: HPK1400085

STYLE: FRENCH

SQUARE FOOTAGE: 1,684

BEDROOMS: 3

BATHROOMS: 2½

WIDTH: 55' - 6"

DEPTH: 57' - 6"

FOUNDATION: FINISHED
WALKOUT BASEMENT

■ Charming and compact, this home is as beautiful as it is practical. The impressive arch over the double front door is repeated with an arched window in the formal dining room. This room opens to a spacious great room with a fireplace and is near the kitchen and bayed breakfast area. Split sleeping arrangements put the master suite at the right of the plan and two family bedrooms at the left.

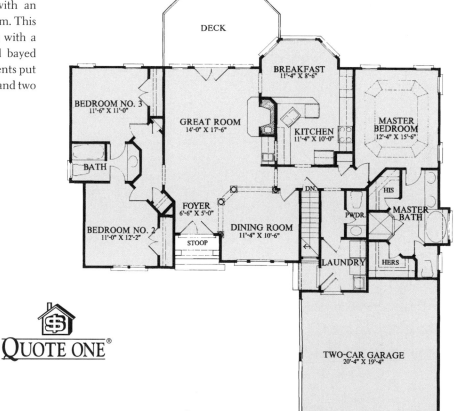

Quote One®

PLAN: HPK1400086

STYLE: TRADITIONAL

FIRST FLOOR: 2,070 SQ. FT.

SECOND FLOOR: 790 SQ. FT.

TOTAL: 2,860 SQ. FT.

BEDROOMS: 4

BATHROOMS: 3½

WIDTH: 58' - 4"

DEPTH: 54' - 10"

FOUNDATION: FINISHED
WALKOUT BASEMENT

■ The striking combination of wood framing, shingles, and glass creates the exterior of this classic cottage. The foyer opens to the main-level layout. To the left of the foyer is a study with a warming hearth and vaulted ceiling; to the right is a formal dining room. A great room with an attached breakfast area sits to the rear near the kitchen. A guest room is nestled in the rear of the plan for privacy. The master suite provides an expansive tray ceiling, a glass sitting area, and easy passage to the outside deck. Upstairs, two bedrooms are accompanied by a loft for a quiet getaway.

QUOTE ONE®

first floor

second floor

PLAN: HPK1400087

STYLE: EUROPEAN COTTAGE

MAIN LEVEL: 2,961 SQ. FT.

LOWER LEVEL: 2,416 SQ. FT.

TOTAL: 5,377 SQ. FT.

BEDROOMS: 3

BATHROOMS: 2½ + ½

WIDTH: 89' - 0"

DEPTH: 59' - 2"

FOUNDATION: FINISHED
WALKOUT BASEMENT

■ Stone accents and a charming turret enhance the exterior of this spacious plan. A beamed ceiling highlights the great room, which shares a two-sided fireplace with the foyer; another fireplace can be found in the hearth room, which overlooks a covered rear porch and deck area. A resplendent master suite, with easy access to the laundry area, sits to the right of the plan and boasts a private sitting bay, a dual-vanity dressing area, and a large walk-in closet. The lower level includes media, billiards, and exercise rooms, two bedrooms, and a gathering area that opens to a patio.

rear exterior

lower level

main level

PHOTO COURTESY OF STUDER RESIDENTIAL DESIGNS, INC. BUILDER: ASHLEY DEVELOPMENT. THIS HOME, AS SHOWN IN THE PHOTOGRAPH, MAY DIFFER FROM THE ACTUAL BLUEPRINTS. FOR MORE DETAILED INFORMATION, PLEASE CHECK THE FLOOR PLANS CAREFULLY.

PLAN: HPK1400088

STYLE: TRANSITIONAL

FIRST FLOOR: 1,362 SQ. FT.

SECOND FLOOR: 1,737 SQ. FT.

TOTAL: 3,099 SQ. FT.

BEDROOMS: 3

BATHROOMS: 2½

WIDTH: 37' - 10"

DEPTH: 52' - 4"

FOUNDATION: FINISHED
WALKOUT BASEMENT

■ An exquisitely designed entry and Palladian window decorate the exterior of this narrow-lot home. A high ceiling in the foyer and adjacent staircase with wood trim creates an elegant entry. A spacious gallery introduces the formal dining room and great room. The wall of windows and doors across the rear wall showcase the exterior view. The gourmet kitchen enjoys a chef's island, walk-in pantry and snack bar with seating. The second-floor loft and hall provide a dramatic view to the foyer, and lead to three bedrooms and a laundry room. The master bedroom suite enjoys a soothing bath and raised ceiling—windows offer a spectacular view from the whirlpool tub and shower. With an array of high-end amenities, this house makes a wonderful narrow-lot choice.

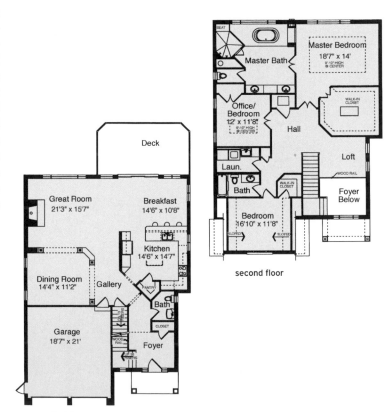

second floor

first floor

PLAN: HPK1400089

STYLE: CRAFTSMAN

FIRST FLOOR: 1,160 SQ. FT.

SECOND FLOOR: 1,531 SQ. FT.

TOTAL: 2,691 SQ. FT.

BASEMENT: 803 SQ. FT.

BEDROOMS: 3

BATHROOMS: 3½

WIDTH: 37' - 8"

DEPTH: 53' - 0"

FOUNDATION: FINISHED
WALKOUT BASEMENT

■ Stone and siding add color and texture to the exterior of this lovely period home. A covered porch introduces a front entry that leads directly into the living room, and through to the rear of the home. The open floor plan includes a great room with fireplace, dining area, and large kitchen with island and seating. A wall of windows across the rear of the home offers a view to the outdoors, and conveys natural light to the interior. Sliding doors from the great room lead to a deck that spans the width of the home. Split stairs lead to a second floor, where the master bedroom enjoys angled walls, a large walk-in closet, a garden bath with whirlpool tub, a double bowl vanity, a shower enclosure, and a view of the rear property. The simple lines remain true to the Arts and Crafts style.

basement

first floor

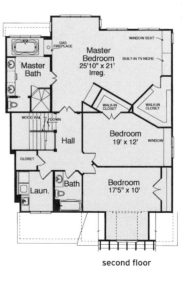

second floor

PLAN: HPK1400090

STYLE: EUROPEAN COTTAGE

SQUARE FOOTAGE: 2,546

BEDROOMS: 2

BATHROOMS: 2½

WIDTH: 66' - 4"

DEPTH: 80' - 8"

FOUNDATION: FINISHED BASEMENT, UNFINISHED BASEMENT

■ The facade of this home is a charming mixture of brick and shingles, with a cupola to complete the the country feel. The vaulted great room—which looks to the rear terrace—is the center of this home, with the dining room flanking it to the right and the master bedroom to the left. The island kitchen has access to a screened porch and a laundry area. The first-floor master suite boasts a walk-in closet, garden tub, separate shower, and a tray ceiling. An additional bedroom resides on this level as well. The second level is resplendent with luxuries: a home theater, storage/workshop area, an exercise room, a recreation room, a family suite, full bath, a private bar, and a covered terrace.

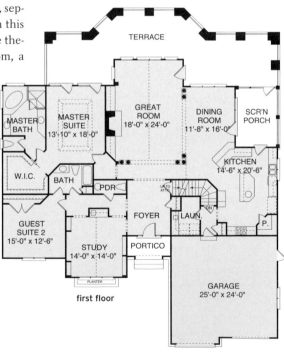

first floor

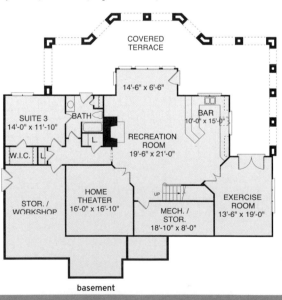

basement

PLAN: **HPK1400091**

STYLE: TRADITIONAL

FIRST FLOOR: 2,274 SQ. FT.

SECOND FLOOR: 972 SQ. FT.

TOTAL: 3,246 SQ. FT.

BASEMENT: 1,187 SQ. FT.

BEDROOMS: 4

BATHROOMS: 3½

WIDTH: 66' - 0"

DEPTH: 89' - 10"

FOUNDATION: FINISHED WALKOUT BASEMENT

■ Looking for a fairy-tale home to raise your family and astound your friends? Look no further than this little slice of heaven. The three-car garage and array of rooflines create a look that everyone will enjoy. Inside, four bedrooms, three full baths, and a powder room provide the perfect setting for a loving family. To the far left is a convenient laundry room which gives way to an island kitchen with serving-bar access to an eating nook. The more formal dining room is also conveniently placed adjacent to the kitchen for seemless dinner parties and holiday meals. The vast two-story great room includes a glowing fireplace and room for everyone to gather. A den with built-in bookshelves sits nestled in front of the master suite—and one look at the master bath with convince you that fairy tales do come true!

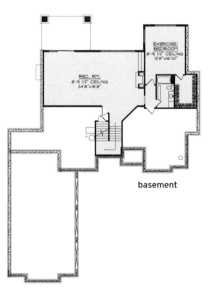

basement

first floor

second floor

PLAN: HPK1400092

STYLE: EUROPEAN COTTAGE

FIRST FLOOR: 2,138 SQ. FT.

SECOND FLOOR: 1,252 SQ. FT.

TOTAL: 3,390 SQ. FT.

BONUS SPACE: 1,332 SQ. FT.

BEDROOMS: 5

BATHROOMS: 4½

WIDTH: 72' - 10"

DEPTH: 49' - 1"

FOUNDATION: FINISHED BASEMENT

■ European grandeur presents a chateau-style manor with all the exterior details you would expect from French Country and from the interior touches that define a family home. From the portico, the two-story foyer leads through a columned arch to the family room, warmed by a fireplace and flooded with natural light. A country kitchen is open and welcoming with an island cooktop. To the right, a morning room is beautiful as a breakfast area or a sun room. The master suite envelopes the left wing, decadent with bay-window light and an opulent bath. Upstairs, three suites share two baths, one with dual compartmented toilets. The lower level includes a fifth suite and full bath, a recreation room with a corner fireplace, and a living room with screened porch access.

second floor

basement

first floor

PLAN: HPK1400093

STYLE: TRADITIONAL

MAIN LEVEL: 1,472 SQ. FT.

LOWER LEVEL: 1,211 SQ. FT.

TOTAL: 2,683 SQ. FT.

BEDROOMS: 3

BATHROOMS: 2½

WIDTH: 54' - 0"

DEPTH: 40' - 8"

©1998 Donald A. Gardner, Inc.

rear exterior

■ A stone-and-stucco exterior and exquisite window detailing give this home its Mediterranean appeal. A covered porch connects the garage to the main house via the breakfast room. The master suite includes two walk-in closets and a bath with separate vanities. Two family bedrooms in the lower level feature walk-in closets and share a compartmented bath and a media/recreation room. Both bedrooms offer private access to the patio. A utility room and storage room complete this level.

PLAN: HPK1400094

STYLE: COUNTRY COTTAGE

FIRST FLOOR: 2,340 SQ. FT.

SECOND FLOOR: 1,806 SQ. FT.

TOTAL: 4,146 SQ. FT.

BASEMENT: 1,608 SQ. FT.

BEDROOMS: 4

BATHROOMS: 4½

WIDTH: 117' - 6"

DEPTH: 74' - 5"

FOUNDATION: FINISHED
WALKOUT BASEMENT, SLAB

■ Full of amenities, this country estate includes a media room and a study. The two-story great room is perfect for formal entertaining. Family and friends will enjoy gathering in the large kitchen, the hearth room, and the breakfast room. The luxurious master suite is located upstairs. Bedrooms 2 and 3 share a bath that includes dressing areas for both bedrooms. Bedroom 4 features a private bath. The rear stair is complete with a dumb-waiter, which goes down to a walkout basement where you'll find an enormous workshop, a game room, and a hobby room.

basement

second floor

first floor

PLAN: HPK1400005

STYLE: FRENCH COUNTRY

MAIN LEVEL: 2,981 SQ. FT.

UPPER LEVEL: 1,017 SQ. FT.

LOWER LEVEL: 1,471 SQ. FT.

TOTAL: 5,469 SQ. FT.

BEDROOMS: 4

BATHROOMS: 4½ + ½

WIDTH: 79' - 4"

DEPTH: 91' - 0"

FOUNDATION: FINISHED
WALKOUT BASEMENT

rear exterior

■ Majestic through and through, this stately home enjoys a stone exterior inspired by classical French architecture. In the center of the main floor, the conservatory and elegant formal dining room reign. The massive country kitchen flows easily into the family room and the casual eating area. It also enjoys a butler's pantry leading to the dining room and a walk-in pantry. An exercise room and resplendent bath are found in the master suite, also on this level. Two more suites with private baths share a sitting room upstairs. The finished basement includes another bedroom suite, a recreation room, office, storage, and a book niche. Additional room is available for setting up a workshop.

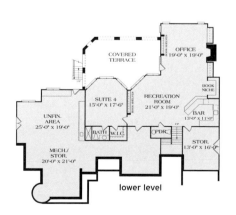

lower level

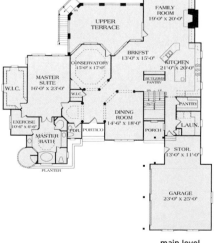

main level

upper level

PLAN: HPK1400095

STYLE: FARMHOUSE

FIRST FLOOR: 3,566 SQ. FT.

SECOND FLOOR: 864 SQ. FT.

TOTAL: 4,430 SQ. FT.

STUDIO/BASEMENT:
556/1,619 SQ. FT.

BEDROOMS: 4

BATHROOMS: 4½

WIDTH: 127' - 9"

DEPTH: 75' - 8"

FOUNDATION: FINISHED
BASEMENT

■ Arch-topped windows, graceful details, and a stunning stucco facade give this manor plenty of appeal. Inside, the foyer is flanked by a cozy drawing room and the formal dining room. Entertaining will be a breeze with the huge keeping room near the efficient kitchen, and the grand room; both rooms have fireplaces and access to the covered rear terrace. A guest suite provides privacy for visitors. The lavish master suite features a walk-in closet, deluxe bath, covered balcony, and fireplace. Upstairs, two amenity-filled suites are separated by a balcony. The basement level of the home expands its livability greatly, with a spacious exercise room (complete with a full bath), a summer kitchen, a gathering room (includes a fireplace and bar), and a suite for future needs. Note the studio apartment over the main garage.

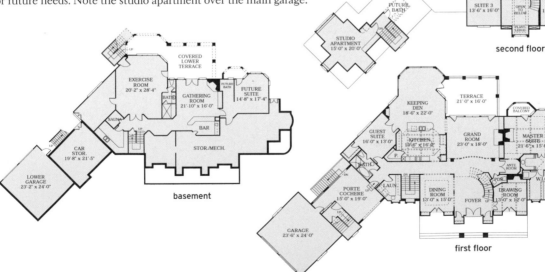

second floor

basement

first floor

PLAN: HPK1400096

STYLE: FRENCH COUNTRY

FIRST FLOOR: 2,844 SQ. FT.

SECOND FLOOR: 1,443 SQ. FT.

TOTAL: 4,287 SQ. FT.

BONUS SPACE: 360 SQ. FT.

BEDROOMS: 4

BATHROOMS: 4½

WIDTH: 72' - 0"

DEPTH: 78' - 6"

FOUNDATION: UNFINISHED

WALKOUT BASEMENT

■ This magnificent home captures the charm of French Country design with its high hipped roof and brick detailing. Inside, the two-story foyer leads directly to the spacious great room with a fireplace and three sets of double doors to the rear porch. The formal dining room sits to the left of the foyer and is near the L-shaped kitchen, which serves a bright breakfast room. The main-floor master suite takes the entire right wing of the house and includes a large sitting area with porch access and an opulent bath. Upstairs, a gallery hall leads to a media room, three more bedrooms (each with a private bath), and a bonus room over the garage.

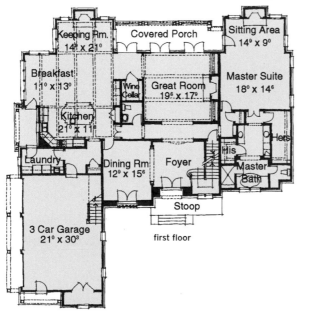

first floor

second floor

PLAN: HPK1400097

STYLE: TRADITIONAL

FIRST FLOOR: 2,262 SQ. FT.

SECOND FLOOR: 1,125 SQ. FT.

TOTAL: 3,387 SQ. FT.

BASEMENT: 1,046 SQ. FT.

BEDROOMS: 4

BATHROOMS: 4½ + ½

WIDTH: 87' - 0"

DEPTH: 85' - 0"

FOUNDATION: FINISHED BASEMENT

■ The grand entrance that leads to the foyer welcomes guests into a gallery where the possibilities are endless. To the right is the formal dining room and to the left is a study. Straight ahead sits a gathering room with a fireplace and access to a covered terrace. The master suite awaits at the end of the gallery. Once inside, it offers a tray ceiling in the bedroom and a garden tub, separate shower, dual vanities, and large walk-in closet in the bathroom. There are two additonal suites upstairs and one in the basement. The recreation area and convenient wet bar afford unlimited casual entertainment. A three-car garage completes the plan.

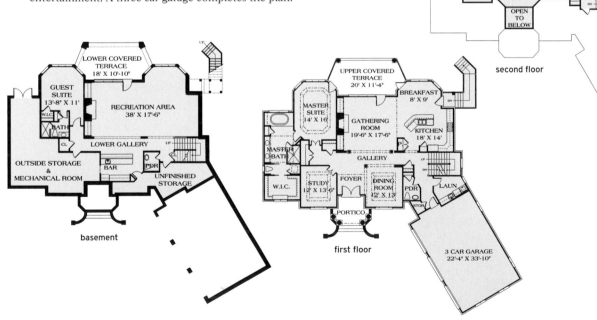

basement

first floor

second floor

PLAN: HPK1400098

STYLE: SW CONTEMPORARY

MAIN LEVEL: 2,662 SQ. FT.

LOWER LEVEL: 1,548 SQ. FT.

TOTAL: 4,210 SQ. FT.

BEDROOMS: 3

BATHROOMS: 2½ + ½

WIDTH: 98' - 0"

DEPTH: 64' - 8"

FOUNDATION: FINISHED BASEMENT

L D

rear exterior

■ Here's a hillside haven for family living with plenty of room to entertain in style. Perfect for the California coast, this dazzling home has it all! Enter the main level from a dramatic columned portico that leads to a large entry hall. The gathering room, graced by a fireplace and sliding glass doors to the rear deck, is straight back and adjoins a formal dining area. A true gourmet kitchen with plenty of room for casual eating and conversation is nearby. The abundantly appointed master suite on this level is complemented by a luxurious bath complete with His and Hers walk-in closets, a whirlpool tub in a bumped-out bay, and a separate shower. On the lower level are two more bedrooms—each with access to the rear terrace, a full bath, a large activity area with a fireplace, and a convenient summer kitchen.

lower level

QUOTE ONE®

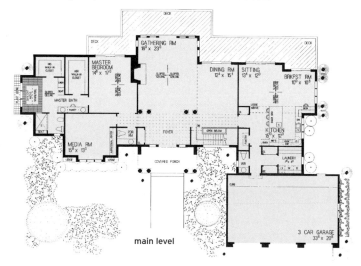

main level

PLAN: HPK1400099

STYLE: SPANISH COLONIAL
FIRST FLOOR: 929 SQ. FT.
SECOND FLOOR: 2,092 SQ. FT.
THIRD FLOOR: 2,437 SQ. FT.
TOTAL: 5,458 SQ. FT.
BEDROOMS: 7
BATHROOMS: 7½
WIDTH: 74' - 10"
DEPTH: 75' - 2"
FOUNDATION: SLAB

■ This captivating Spanish Colonial villa includes three levels of living space to accommodate seven bedrooms and seven full baths—an elevator accesses every level. Enter on the ground floor to find a game room, guest suite, and pool area. Upstairs, the main level supports a comfortable living room, with a cozy fireplace and French doors to the balcony. The kitchen opens to a nook, bathed in light. Three family bedrooms and a guest suite—each with private baths—complete the level. One more flight of stairs leads to the upper living areas, comprising an inviting family room, formal dining room and ancillary kitchen, private study, and two bedrooms. The master suite is a decadent retreat, with two private balconies, a fireplace-warmed bath, a recessed whirlpool tub, and a compartmented toilet and bidet.

second floor

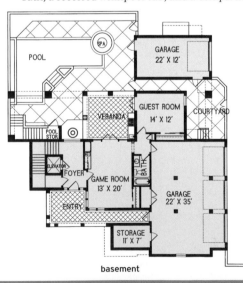

basement

first floor

PLAN: HPK1400100

STYLE: SANTA FE

MAIN LEVEL: 1,946 SQ. FT.

LOWER LEVEL: 956 SQ. FT.

TOTAL: 2,902 SQ. FT.

BEDROOMS: 4

BATHROOMS: 3

WIDTH: 51' - 6"

DEPTH: 70' - 2"

FOUNDATION: FINISHED
WALKOUT BASEMENT

L

rear exterior

■ The simple, Pueblo-style lines borrowed from the early Native American dwellings combine with contemporary planning for the best possible design. From the front, this home appears to be a one-story. However, a lower level provides a two-story rear elevation, making it ideal for sloping lots. The unique floor plan places a circular staircase to the left of the angled foyer. To the right is an L-shaped kitchen with a walk-in pantry, a sun-filled breakfast room, and a formal dining room. Half-walls border the entrance to the formal living room that is warmed by a beehive fireplace. The adjacent covered deck provides shade to the patio below. A roomy master suite, secondary bedroom, full bath, and laundry room complete the first floor. The lower level contains a great room, another full bath, and two family bedrooms.

lower level

main level

PLAN: HPK1400101

STYLE: MEDITERRANEAN
MAIN LEVEL: 2,959 SQ. FT.
UPPER LEVEL: 1,055 SQ. FT.
LOWER LEVEL: 1,270 SQ. FT.
TOTAL: 5,284 SQ. FT.
BEDROOMS: 4
BATHROOMS: 5½
WIDTH: 110' - 4"
DEPTH: 72' - 5"
FOUNDATION: SLAB, FINISHED
WALKOUT BASEMENT

■ Designed for a sloping lot, this fantastic Mediterranean home features all the views to the rear, making it the perfect home for an ocean, lake, or golf-course view. Inside, the great room features a rear wall of windows. The breakfast room, kitchen, dining room, and master suite also feature rear views. A three-level series of porches is located on the back for outdoor relaxing. Two bedroom suites are found upstairs, each with a private bath and a porch. The basement of this home features another bedroom suite and a large game room. An expandable area can be used as an office or Bedroom 5.

PLAN: HPK1400102

STYLE: NW CONTEMPORARY
MAIN LEVEL: 2,300 SQ. FT.
LOWER LEVEL: 1,114 SQ. FT.
TOTAL: 3,414 SQ. FT.
BEDROOMS: 5
BATHROOMS: 3
WIDTH: 56' - 0"
DEPTH: 61' - 6"
FOUNDATION: FINISHED
WALKOUT BASEMENT

■ Looking for all the world like a one-story plan, this elegant hillside design has a surprise on the lower level. The main level is reached through an arched, recessed entry that opens to a 12-foot ceiling. The formal dining room is on the right, next to a cozy den or Bedroom 3. Columns decorate the hall and separate it from the dining room and great room, which contains a tray ceiling and a fireplace flanked by built-ins. The breakfast nook and kitchen are just steps away, on the left. Lower-level space includes another great room with built-ins and two family bedrooms sharing a full bath.

lower level

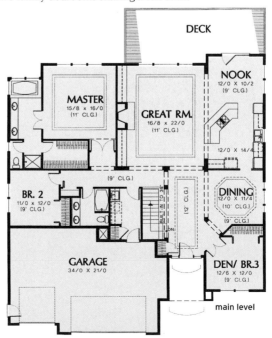

main level

PLAN: HPK1400103

STYLE: MEDITERRANEAN
MAIN LEVEL: 3,300 SQ. FT.
UPPER LEVEL: 1,974 SQ. FT.
LOWER LEVEL: 1,896 SQ. FT.
TOTAL: 7,170 SQ. FT.
BEDROOMS: 5
BATHROOMS: 4½ + ½
WIDTH: 108' - 2"
DEPTH: 74' - 7"
FOUNDATION: FINISHED BASEMENT

■ Here is a Sun Country classic complete with grand windows, columned entry, and a balcony overhead. Windows wrap the home with sunshine. The bright floor plan includes a grand room, perfect for formal occasions; a family room featuring a fireplace, ideal for quality family time; and an expansive kitchen complete with a pantry and island. The master suite includes a sitting room with a ribbon of windows, two walk-in closets, dual vanities, and private access to the rear covered terrace. The second floor showcases three suites, each with its own bath, and an office.

upper level

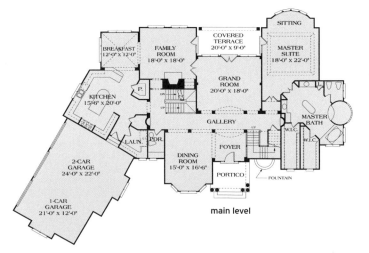

main level

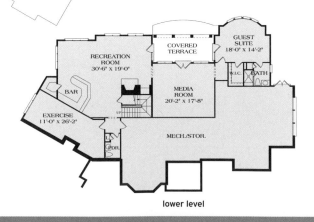

lower level

PHOTOGRAPHY BY RUSSELL KINGMAN
THIS HOME, AS SHOWN IN THE PHOTOGRAPH, MAY DIFFER FROM THE ACTUAL BLUEPRINTS. FOR MORE DETAILED INFORMATION, PLEASE CHECK THE FLOOR PLANS CAREFULLY.

PLAN: HPK1400104

STYLE: MEDITERRANEAN

MAIN LEVEL: 2,895 SQ. FT.

UPPER LEVEL: 905 SQ. FT.

LOWER LEVEL: 2,563 SQ. FT.

TOTAL: 6,363 SQ. FT.

BEDROOMS: 5

BATHROOMS: 6½

WIDTH: 73' - 4"

DEPTH: 89' - 0"

FOUNDATION: FINISHED BASEMENT

■ To the left of the facade, paired windows on a white wall effect a subtle but certain Mediterranean style to this grand design. The same appreciation for naturalistic forms can be seen in the rounded hallway from the main dining room to the nook and kitchen. A luxurious master suite occupies the left side of the plan, with private access to the covered patio. Guests will enjoy similar comforts in interestingly shaped rooms and full baths.

rear exterior

main level

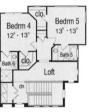

upper level

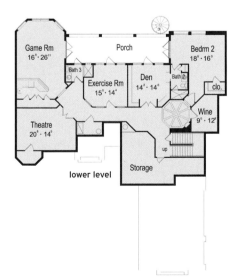

lower level

PLAN: HPK1400105

STYLE: MEDITERRANEAN

FIRST FLOOR: 2,450 SQ. FT.

SECOND FLOOR: 1,675 SQ. FT.

TOTAL: 4,125 SQ. FT.

BONUS SPACE: 1,568 SQ. FT.

BEDROOMS: 4

BATHROOMS: 3½

WIDTH: 65' - 10"

DEPTH: 85' - 2"

FOUNDATION: FINISHED
WALKOUT BASEMENT

■ Designed for sloping lots, this magnificent estate home offers windows that overlook the rear grounds from three separate levels. From the first floor, the foyer opens to a spacious dining room and grand room enriched by decorative columns and an abundance of windows. To the right is a large kitchen with an adjacent breakfast nook. The classic master suite claims the remainder of the first floor. Upstairs, three suites and a loft feature opportunities to survey the surrounding landscape. The lower level provides lots of space for family and friends. A gathering room and a game room share the warmth of a fireplace and access to a covered patio. An additional suite that's well suited for guests completes the plan.

rear exterior

PHOTO COURTESY OF LIVING CONCEPTS
THIS HOME, AS SHOWN IN THE PHOTOGRAPH, MAY DIFFER FROM THE ACTUAL BLUEPRINTS. FOR MORE DETAILED INFORMATION, PLEASE CHECK THE FLOOR PLANS CAREFULLY.

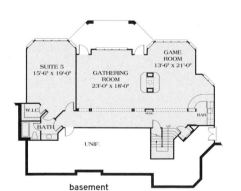

basement

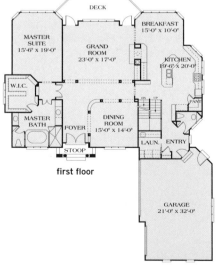

first floor

second floor

PLAN: HPK1400106

STYLE: COLONIAL

FIRST FLOOR: 1,140 SQ. FT.

SECOND FLOOR: 1,120 SQ. FT.

TOTAL: 2,260 SQ. FT.

BASEMENT: 964 SQ. FT.

BEDROOMS: 3

BATHROOMS: 2½

WIDTH: 38' - 0"

DEPTH: 44' - 0"

FOUNDATION: FINISHED

WALKOUT BASEMENT, SLAB

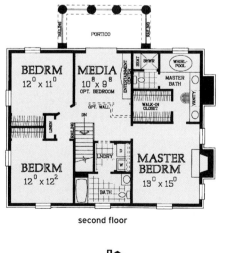

■ Take a step back to Southern Colonial America when you climb the stairs of the covered porch and enter the foyer of this casual family home. Three fireplaces spread a cozy mood throughout the plan, the first in the large living room. A second fireplace is the focal point of the large country kitchen with its snack bar/work island. The master bedroom houses the third fireplace—a romantic touch that creates a welcome retreat. The large master bath has a whirlpool tub and walk-in closet. Upstairs, two bedrooms share a full hall bath and an open lounge area that would make a perfect study.

rear exterior

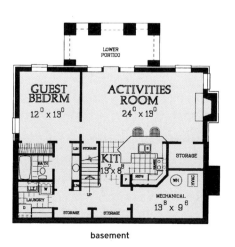

basement

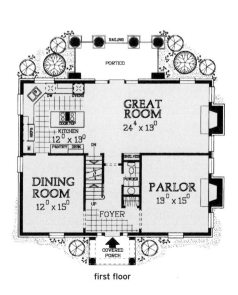

first floor

second floor

PLAN: HPK1400107

STYLE: COLONIAL

FIRST FLOOR: 1,567 SQ. FT.

SECOND FLOOR: 1,895 SQ. FT.

TOTAL: 3,462 SQ. FT.

BEDROOMS: 4

BATHROOMS: 3½

WIDTH: 63' - 0"

DEPTH: 53' - 6"

FOUNDATION: FINISHED WALKOUT BASEMENT

■ Although the facade may look like a quaint country cottage, this home's fine proportions contain formal living areas, including a dining room and a living room. At the back of the first floor you'll find a spacious kitchen and breakfast nook. A great room with a fireplace and bumped-out window makes everyday living very comfortable. A rear porch allows for outdoor dining and relaxation. Upstairs, four bedrooms include a master suite with lots of notable features. A boxed ceiling, lavish bath, large walk-in closet, and secluded sitting room (which would also make a nice study or exercise room) assure great livability.

PLAN: HPK1400108

STYLE: COLONIAL

FIRST FLOOR: 1,205 SQ. FT.

SECOND FLOOR: 1,160 SQ. FT.

TOTAL: 2,365 SQ. FT.

BONUS SPACE: 350 SQ. FT.

BEDROOMS: 3

BATHROOMS: 2½

WIDTH: 52' - 6"

DEPTH: 43' - 6"

FOUNDATION: FINISHED
WALKOUT BASEMENT

■ This charming exterior conceals a perfect family plan. The formal dining and living rooms reside on either side of the foyer. At the rear of the home is a family room with a fireplace and access to a deck and veranda. The modern kitchen features a sunlit breakfast area. The second floor provides four bedrooms, one of which may be finished at a later date and used as a guest suite. Note the extra storage space in the two-car garage.

first floor

second floor

PLAN: HPK1400109

STYLE: GEORGIAN

FIRST FLOOR: 2,081 SQ. FT.

SECOND FLOOR: 940 SQ. FT.

TOTAL: 3,021 SQ. FT.

BEDROOMS: 4

BATHROOMS: 3½

WIDTH: 69' - 9"

DEPTH: 65' - 0"

FOUNDATION: FINISHED WALKOUT BASEMENT

■ This Georgian country-style home displays an impressive appearance. The front porch and columns frame the elegant elliptical entrance. Georgian symmetry balances the living room and dining room off the foyer. The first floor continues into the two-story great room, which offers built-in cabinetry, a fireplace, and a large bay window that overlooks the rear deck. A dramatic tray ceiling, a wall of glass, and access to the rear deck complete the master bedroom. To the left of the great room, a large kitchen opens to a breakfast area with walls of windows. Upstairs, each of three family bedrooms features ample closet space as well as direct access to a bathroom.

first floor

second floor

PLAN: HPK1400110

STYLE: TRADITIONAL

SQUARE FOOTAGE: 2,752

BEDROOMS: 3

BATHROOMS: 2½

WIDTH: 90' - 0"

DEPTH: 72' - 10"

FOUNDATION: UNFINISHED BASEMENT

rear exterior

■ Columns introduce a welcoming covered porch that leads into the foyer. Here, still more columns define the formal dining room. The nearby family room is complete with a fireplace and built-ins and offers access to the sunroom/breakfast area. The lavish master suite is designed to pamper and will be a pleasant retreat for the homeowner. Two secondary bedrooms—or make one an office—share a full bath.

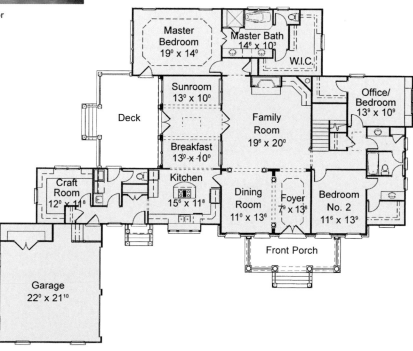

PLAN: HPK1400111

STYLE: TRANSITIONAL

MAIN LEVEL: 1,930 SQ. FT.

LOWER LEVEL: 1,211 SQ. FT.

TOTAL: 3,141 SQ. FT.

BEDROOMS: 3

BATHROOMS: 2½

WIDTH: 57' - 4"

DEPTH: 51' - 6"

FOUNDATION: FINISHED
WALKOUT BASEMENT

■ This delightful one-story home is designed to provide the homeowner with elegant surroundings in a convenient, relaxed package. A formal dining room defined by columns is visually open to the great room, showcasing a corner fireplace and triple windows overlooking the rear deck. A triple slider just off the breakfast room offers access to the delightful screened porch. An open stair rail to the lower level adds dimension to the family eating area and invites the lower level to be part of the living area. A master bedroom suite with a deluxe bath and spacious walk-in closet treats the homeowner to opulent surroundings. A finished lower level for this plan offers two additional bedrooms and a large recreation room with a wet bar.

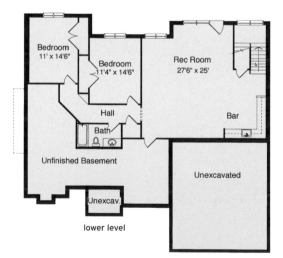

lower level

main level

PLAN: HPK1400112

STYLE: TRADITIONAL

FIRST FLOOR: 2,892 SQ. FT.

SECOND FLOOR: 1,120 SQ. FT.

TOTAL: 4,012 SQ. FT.

BEDROOMS: 4

BATHROOMS: 4½

WIDTH: 74' - 0"

DEPTH: 70' - 0"

FOUNDATION: FINISHED
WALKOUT BASEMENT

rear exterior

■ This handsome territorial-style home will catch your fancy if you have an active family that likes its activities and socializing to spill outdoors. A wrap-around front porch and three rear porches, one of them screened, offer lots of space for barbecues or just sitting and reading in the sunshine. Inside, a magnificent kitchen with an island counter and loads of counter and shelf space will immediately catch your eye. It opens to a large, informal dining area and the hearth-warmed keeping room with French doors to one of the back porches. A study has French-door access to the front porch. The master bedroom with a lavish bath has private access to a small rear porch. Three upstairs bedrooms have their own baths; two enjoy walk-in closets.

basement

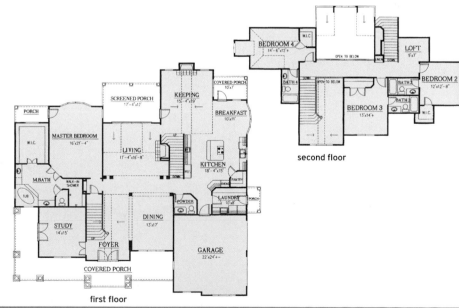

second floor

first floor

PLAN: HPK1400113

STYLE: FARMHOUSE
FIRST FLOOR: 1,840 SQ. FT.
SECOND FLOOR: 950 SQ. FT.
TOTAL: 2,790 SQ. FT.
BEDROOMS: 4
BATHROOMS: 3½
WIDTH: 58' - 6"
DEPTH: 62' - 0"
FOUNDATION: FINISHED
WALKOUT BASEMENT

■ The appearance of this Early American home brings the past to mind with its wraparound porch, wood siding, and flower-box detailing. Inside, columns frame the great room and the dining room. Left of the foyer lies the living room with a warming fireplace. The angular kitchen joins a sunny breakfast nook. The master bedroom has a spacious private bath and a walk-in closet. Stairs to the second level lead from the breakfast area to an open landing overlooking the great room. Three family bedrooms—two with walk-in closets and all three with private access to a bath—complete this level.

first floor

second floor

PLAN: HPK1400114

STYLE: COLONIAL

FIRST FLOOR: 1,897 SQ. FT.

SECOND FLOOR: 777 SQ. FT.

TOTAL: 2,674 SQ. FT.

BONUS SPACE: 705 SQ. FT.

BEDROOMS: 4

BATHROOMS: 4

WIDTH: 55' - 0"

DEPTH: 49' - 0"

FOUNDATION: FINISHED BASEMENT

■ This Early American Colonial is a design plan you'll be proud to call home. A series of windows and vertical columns majestically dots the front of the exterior, while a two-car garage—carefully hidden to the side—preserves symmetry. The interior is studded with columns as well, framing the entrance. A study is to the left, through double doors, and features a fireplace, wet bar, and bookcases. The master bedroom is uniquely angled, and features a hub of spoked windows. Double doors take you to the bath, where you will find it hard to tear yourself away. The treasure in this house is perhaps the two-story living room, lined with pillars. A snack bar in the kitchen seats four, and you can escape for a breath of the great outdoors via the breakfast area. A guest room is strategically located by the rear deck.

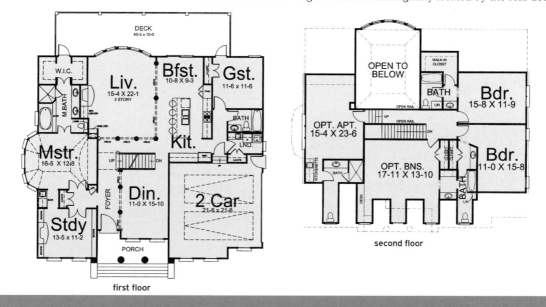

first floor

second floor

PLAN: HPK1400115

STYLE: TRADITIONAL

FIRST FLOOR: 3,413 SQ. FT.

SECOND FLOOR: 2,076 SQ. FT.

TOTAL: 5,489 SQ. FT.

BASEMENT: 430 SQ. FT.

BEDROOMS: 4

BATHROOMS: 3½

WIDTH: 90' - 6"

DEPTH: 63' - 6"

FOUNDATION: UNFINISHED BASEMENT

■ Classic design combined with dynamite interiors make this executive home a real gem. Inside, a free-floating curved staircase rises majestically to the second floor. The enormous living room, great for formal entertaining, features a dramatic two-story window wall. The family room, breakfast room, and kitchen are conveniently grouped. A large pantry and a companion butler's pantry serve both the dining room and kitchen. Privately located, the master suite includes a sitting area and a sumptuous master bath. The second floor contains Bedroom 2, which has a private bath. Bedrooms 3 and 4 share a bath that includes two private dressing areas. A large game room is accessed from a rear stair.

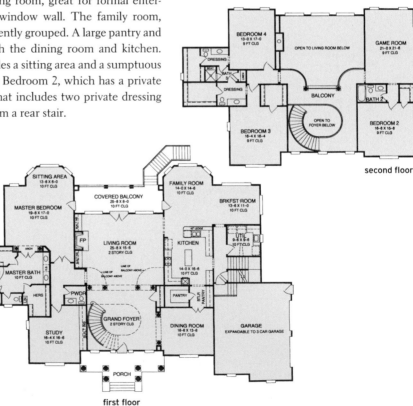

second floor

basement

first floor

PLAN: HPK1400116

STYLE: COLONIAL

FIRST FLOOR: 1,960 SQ. FT.

SECOND FLOOR: 905 SQ. FT.

TOTAL: 2,865 SQ. FT.

BONUS SPACE: 297 SQ. FT.

BEDROOMS: 4

BATHROOMS: 3½

WIDTH: 61' - 0"

DEPTH: 70' - 6"

FOUNDATION: FINISHED WALKOUT BASEMENT

■ Traditionalists will appreciate the classic styling of this Colonial home. The foyer opens to both a banquet-sized dining room and formal living room with a fireplace. Just beyond is the two-story great room. The entire right side of the main level is taken up by the enchanting master suite. The other side of the main level includes a large kitchen and a breakfast room just steps away from the detached garage. Upstairs, each bedroom features ample closet space and direct access to a bath. The detached garage features an unfinished office or studio on its second level.

first floor

second floor

STYLE: GEORGIAN

FIRST FLOOR: 1,828 SQ. FT.

SECOND FLOOR: 1,552 SQ. FT.

TOTAL: 3,380 SQ. FT.

BEDROOMS: 4

BATHROOMS: 3½

WIDTH: 54' - 3"

DEPTH: 70' - 3"

FOUNDATION: FINISHED

WALKOUT BASEMENT

■ A stately appearance and lots of living space give this home appeal. The foyer introduces formal living and dining rooms. For more casual occasions, a great room opens to the back porch. The breakfast room has convenient proximity to these informal areas. The kitchen has plenty of work space. Four bedrooms on the second floor enjoy complete privacy. In the master bedroom suite, a short hallway flanked by closets leads to a lovely bath with a spa tub, a compartmented toilet, a separate shower, and dual lavatories.

first floor

second floor

PLAN: HPK1400118

STYLE: GEORGIAN

FIRST FLOOR: 1,455 SQ. FT.

SECOND FLOOR: 1,649 SQ. FT.

TOTAL: 3,104 SQ. FT.

BEDROOMS: 4

BATHROOMS: 3½

WIDTH: 54' - 4"

DEPTH: 46' - 0"

FOUNDATION: FINISHED WALKOUT BASEMENT

QUOTE ONE®

■ The double wings, twin chimneys, and center portico of this home work in concert to create a classic architectural statement. The two-story foyer is flanked by the spacious dining room and formal living room, each containing their own fireplaces. A large family room with a full wall of glass opens conveniently to the kitchen and breakfast room. The master suite features a tray ceiling and French doors that open to a covered porch. A grand master bath completes the master suite. Two family bedrooms share a bath, and another has a private bath. Bedroom 4 features a nook for sitting or reading.

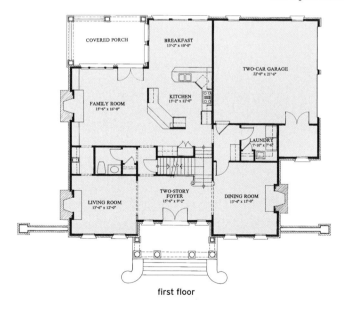

first floor

second floor

Interior Dreams

Your search for a new home begins with a perfect floor plan

An intelligent approach to the interior of your home can make any design feel spacious and provide plenty of room for a family. Part of that sense of space comes from interior design, but it begins with selecting a well-designed floor plan.

A few elements go into this selection process. As you flip through the pages of this book, use your imagination to make the floor plans come to life. Picture yourself in certain rooms, or the foyer, and consider the views through the house. Does the living room connect easily to the kitchen? How about the upstairs? These are ways designers can make a smaller space feel larger.

Measuring a room in your existing house or apartment may help you picture the space available in a floor plan. Most of us can imagine rooms more accurately in relation to another space, rather than simply interpreting dimensions from a floor plan.

All of this will help you narrow down your choices for the home plan that will fit you and your family perfectly.

An open floor plan, like the design that connects the kitchen to the living room in this home (page 163), can create a family-friendly living space.

PHOTOGRAPHY : JANNISS VANN & ASSOCIATES, INC.

Open Design

Early American homes featured small, box-like rooms that were designed that way, at least in part, because they were easy to heat. For years most new home design stuck to that approach.

More recently consumers have demanded more versatility and functionality in their floor plans, resulting in open, flowing spaces in the main living areas. The kitchen is often the centerpiece of these fresh designs, no longer closed off in a corner of the first floor. That gives families a sense of togetherness, even if they are engaging in different activities. Everyone can be within eyeshot, even with one person preparing dinner, one playing video games, one reading a book, and another working on a laptop. As busy as families can be these days, that bit of togetherness—even when everyone's doing their own thing—can mean a lot.

Above: A work island that doubles as a snack bar can provide the ideal transition between an open kitchen and a great room.

As much as these open floor plans fit with today's lifestyles, they provide an added benefit of maximizing living space in your home's total square footage. By connecting rooms you take advantage of more space—less is wasted on hallways and walls—and a smaller home will feel much larger.

Kitchen-Centric

Among the biggest demands for an open floor plan is that the design creates what some families call a "kitchen-centric" layout. That doesn't necessarily mean it will fall smack-dab in the middle of the first floor—but it does mean that the common living areas should fall just steps from the kitchen counter.

Most American families—or party hosts, for that matter—will tell you that everyone's activity flows through the kitchen. It follows that your new home should be designed to facilitate that activity. In the best plans, that means that the kitchen will include a snack bar and a small work desk, and will feature easy

access to the living room (or great room, hearth room, or keeping room), the dining room, and an outdoor space (either a deck, patio, lanai, or porch).

Flexible Rooms

Another family-friendly feature you'll find in many new home plans is bonus space, which offers flexibility as your family grows. These areas can be left unfinished

QUIET TIME

Creating an open design that connects your kitchen with other living spaces in your home can help bring families together and simplify your floor plan. But all that togetherness can have an unintended consequence—noise, while the great room television fights a sound war with the dishwasher and radio in the kitchen.

Recent advances in kitchen appliances can help, with more and more quiet appliances available. When shopping for items like dishwashers and garbage disposals for use in an open floor plan, focus on items with decibel levels around 44 db.

Take care with ceiling and wall treatments as well to help absorb noise. A vaulted or coffered ceiling in the great room or family room can help keep a bit of that noise in that space—preserving the open quality of the design without creating a battle of the bands between rooms in your home.

during the building process, saving money initially, but will be ready to finish off relatively easily if you find the need for an additional bedroom.

Alternatively, finish these areas when you build and use them for a kid's playroom, exercise room, or home office. They are typically perfect places for these types of rooms, offering privacy and convenience near the upstairs bedrooms. They can also keep the clutter—whether it's a child's toys or a parent's computer—out of the main living areas of the home. ■

A pair of two-car garages flank the home's entrance.

PHOTOGRAPHY COURTESY OF ARCHIVAL DESIGNS - JOANNE LOFTUS

Classic Elegance

This historic home has distinctive charm, and lets its hair down with a lower level designed for fun

This Georgian home is filled with historic touches. Its pair of two-car garages offer a hint of George Washington's Mt. Vernon, and the formal dining room and library at the front of the home are a first sign of the luxury within.

It's a very livable design as well, and nowhere is that more apparent than the lower level. Stepping down through the split foyer, a pair of French doors open to a spa-cious entertainment room. There you'll find space for extravagant gatherings, and at one end a large fireplace that creates a comfort-able setting for smaller groups. The bar can be the center of attention, and much more—it includes a range to save steps in food preparation when entertaining.

The main level features a beautiful open design between the grand room, morning

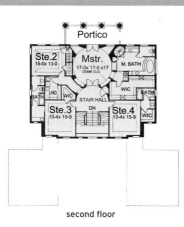

second floor

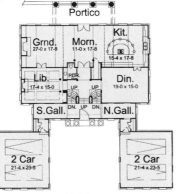

first floor

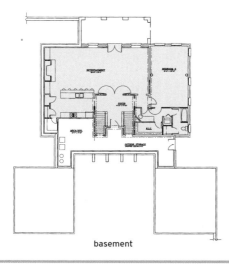

basement

SMART DESIGN *Creating a large entertaining space in the walkout basement allows for a more traditional layout upstairs.*

PLAN: HPK1400119

STYLE: GEORGIAN

FIRST FLOOR: 2,175 SQ. FT.

SECOND FLOOR: 1,927 SQ. FT.

TOTAL: 4,102 SQ. FT.

BASEMENT: 1,927 SQ. FT.

BEDROOMS: 4

BATHROOMS: 3½

WIDTH: 74' - 0"

DEPTH: 82' - 0"

FOUNDATION: FINISHED WALKOUT BASEMENT

area, and island kitchen, including access to a portico overlooking the backyard. The kitchen's unique design offers plenty of space for both serving and preparation, allowing family and friends to congregate comfortably without disturbing the cook.

Upstairs, a luxurious master suite is the center of attention, with the bedroom located beneath a dome ceiling. One additional bedroom has a private bath, while a large laundry room enjoys a prime location—no more lugging clothes up and down the stairs. ■

Above: The grand room includes a niche for a television above the fireplace.

Island Delight

This sunny design features a well-thought-out floor plan in a narrow footprint

Left: This sweet-faced country design inspires lazy days spent relaxing on the porches and balconies. **Above:** While the front porch is welcoming, the back offers privacy.

PHOTO BY: DOUG THOMPSON

SMART DESIGN

The room off the master suite could be a study or a bedroom, as your family's needs change.

Key West Conch style blends Old World charm with New World comfort in this picturesque design. A glass-paneled entry lends a warm welcome and complements a captivating front balcony. Once inside, step up to the main living area—a design that makes this plan work perfectly for a lot that slopes from back to front.

The balanced floor plan works well within a narrow footprint—reminiscent of the Caribbean "shotgun" houses. Two sets of French doors open the great room to wide views and extend the living areas to the back covered porch. A gourmet kitchen is pre-

pared for any occasion with a prep sink, plenty of counter space, an ample pantry, and an eating bar.

The mid-level landing leads to two additional bedrooms, a full bath, and a windowed art niche. Double French doors open the upper-level master suite to a sundeck and offer powerful views from the bedroom. Circle-head windows and a vaulted ceiling maintain a light and airy atmosphere. The master bath has a windowed soaking tub and a glass-enclosed walk-in shower. Sunsets may be viewed from the privacy of the deck, a remarkable vantage point in moonlight as well. ■

PLAN: HPK1400120

STYLE:	CONTEMPORARY
FIRST FLOOR:	876 SQ. FT.
SECOND FLOOR:	1,245 SQ. FT.
TOTAL:	2,121 SQ. FT.
BEDROOMS:	4
BATHROOMS:	2½
WIDTH:	27' - 6"
DEPTH:	64' - 0"
FOUNDATION:	CRAWLSPACE, PIER (SAME AS PILING)

Arch-topped French doors welcome natural light into the great room.

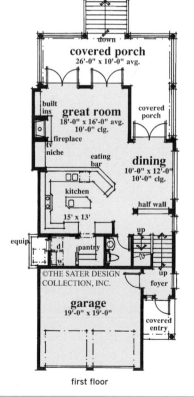

first floor

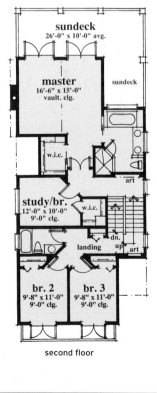

second floor

PLAN: HPK1400121

STYLE: COLONIAL

SQUARE FOOTAGE: 1,033 SQ. FT.

BASEMENT: 1,000 SQ. FT.

BEDROOMS: 3

BATHROOMS: 1½

WIDTH: 52' - 6"

DEPTH: 26' - 0"

FOUNDATION: UNFINISHED BASEMENT

■ Build this home with full livability on one level, with the option of expanding to the lower level in the future. Double doors open to the entry where a few steps lead up to the main level. The living room overlooks the cathedral entry and also sports a fireplace. An L-shaped country kitchen has space for a breakfast table and is open to the family room. A single entrance leads to a small deck in back. The right side of the plan is reserved for bedrooms—two family bedrooms and a master bedroom. All have adequate wall closets and share a full bath.

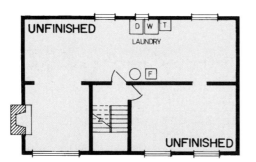

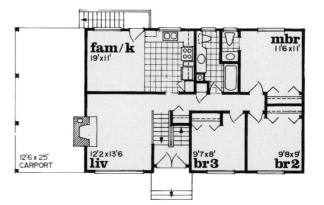

PLAN: HPK1400122

STYLE: COLONIAL

MAIN LEVEL: 1,282 SQ. FT.

LOWER LEVEL: 1,122 SQ. FT.

TOTAL: 2,404 SQ. FT.

BEDROOMS: 3

BATHROOMS: 2

WIDTH: 47' - 0"

DEPTH: 27' - 0"

FOUNDATION: UNFINISHED BASEMENT

■ Bold horizontal siding and clean lines make a pleasing exterior for this hillside home. The living room and dining room flow together for a spacious entertaining area. The living room is warmed by a hearth; the dining room has buffet space. The country kitchen is an ideal gathering spot and allows access to a rear deck. The master bedroom is tucked into a window bay and features a private bath. Two additional bedrooms share a full bath. The suggested lower level holds laundry space, plus two additional bedrooms, a den and a large family room with a fireplace—an additional 1,122 square feet—when finished. A warm sun deck graces the lower level.

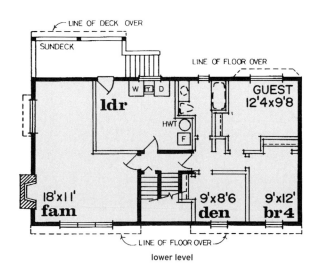

lower level

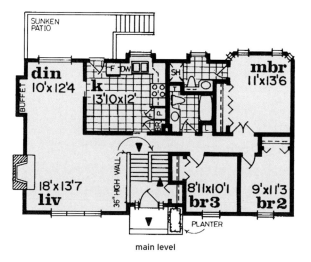

main level

PLAN: HPK1400123

STYLE: COUNTRY COTTAGE

SQUARE FOOTAGE: 1,509 SQ. FT.

BONUS SPACE: 100 SQ. FT.

BEDROOMS: 3

BATHROOMS: 2

WIDTH: 49' - 0"

DEPTH: 34' - 4"

FOUNDATION: UNFINISHED

WALKOUT BASEMENT

■ Inside this well-planned traditional home, an elegant sunlit foyer leads up a short flight of stairs to an immense vaulted great room with a fireplace. Arched openings lead to the open bayed breakfast area and kitchen. The master suite is tucked to one side with plenty of amenities—entrance to a private covered porch, plenty of storage, and decorative built-in plant shelves. Two family bedrooms occupy the opposite side of the home and share a full bath and more closet space. An unfinished basement provides for future lifestyle needs.

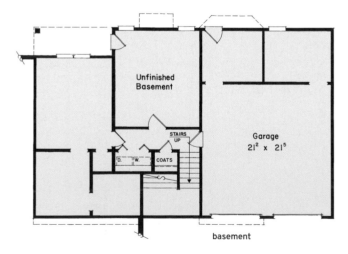

basement

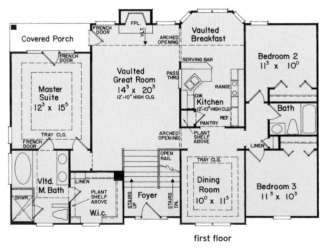

first floor

PLAN: HPK1400124

STYLE: TRADITIONAL

SQUARE FOOTAGE: 1,770

BEDROOMS: 3

BATHROOMS: 2½

WIDTH: 48' - 0"

DEPTH: 47' - 5"

FOUNDATION: FINISHED

WALKOUT BASEMENT

■ Wood frame, weatherboard siding, and stacked stone give this home its country cottage appeal. The entry opens to a great room with a cathedral ceiling and to a formal dining room with a 10-foot ceiling. The spacious kitchen features a corner sink and shares a snack bar with the breakfast area. The bedroom wing has convenient laundry access. Choose the formal dining room or, if needed, make this room into a fourth bedroom. The master suite opens with French doors. Amenities here include a volume ceiling, walk-in closet, and sunny whirlpool bath.

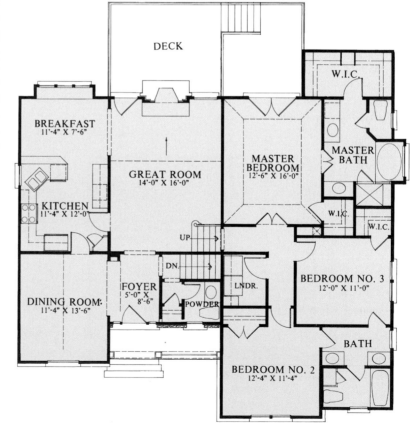

PLAN: HPK1400125

STYLE: COUNTRY COTTAGE

SQUARE FOOTAGE: 1,492

BASEMENT: 1,010 SQ. FT.

BEDROOMS: 3

BATHROOMS: 2

WIDTH: 46' - 6"

DEPTH: 38' - 0"

FOUNDATION: UNFINISHED
WALKOUT BASEMENT

■ Great for an uneven lot, this country home has a mid-level entry: go down to a garage, storage and an unfinished basement, or up to the main level. The vaulted great room greets you at the top of the stairs. A fireplace warms this space and is viewed from all other common areas. A galley kitchen easily serves the breakfast nook and formal dining room. The right side of the home is dedicated to the sleeping quarters. Secondary bedrooms share a full bath; the master suite is a private sanctuary with a vaulted bath and walk-in closet.

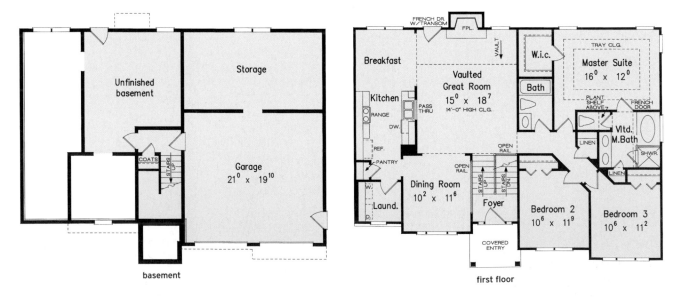

basement

first floor

PLAN: HPK1400126

STYLE: COLONIAL

SQUARE FOOTAGE: 1,235

BASEMENT: 1,152 SQ. FT.

BEDROOMS: 3

BATHROOMS: 2

WIDTH: 44' - 0"

DEPTH: 28' - 6"

FOUNDATION: UNFINISHED BASEMENT

■ Horizontal siding and brick lead to an entry that boasts a half-round window over its door. A cathedral ceiling is found in the foyer, which leads upstairs to the main living level. Amenities include a living room with a masonry fireplace, a dining room with buffet space and sliding glass doors to the rear terrace, and a U-shaped kitchen open to the dinette. The master bedroom features a large wall closet and private bath. Family bedrooms sit to the front and share a bath. The lower level has 1,161 square feet of unfinished space for future expansion.

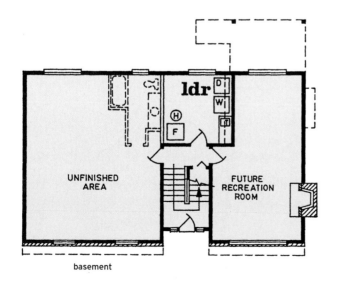

UNFINISHED AREA

ldr

FUTURE RECREATION ROOM

basement

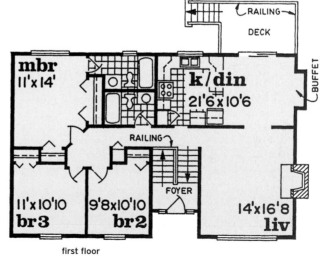

mbr
11' x 14'

k/din
21'6 x 10'6

BUFFET

RAILING

DECK

RAILING

FOYER

11' x 10'10
br3

9'8 x 10'10
br2

14' x 16'8
liv

first floor

PLAN: HPK1400127

STYLE: TRADITIONAL
MAIN LEVEL: 1,626 SQ. FT.
ENTRY LEVEL: 36 SQ. FT.
TOTAL: 1,662 SQ. FT.
BASEMENT: 1,060 SQ. FT.
BEDROOMS: 3
BATHROOMS: 2
WIDTH: 52' - 0"
DEPTH: 35' - 10"
FOUNDATION: CRAWLSPACE,
UNFINISHED WALKOUT
BASEMENT

■ Enjoy all the charm of a traditional country cottage in any neighborhood with this versatile family home. A lower-level entry leads down to the two-car garage, storage, and unfinished basement, or up to the main living spaces. Here, a vaulted great room immediately greets family and guests. The rear extended-hearth fireplace and bright windows make a wonderful impression. To the right, a sunny dining room and a breakfast nook with rear-property access are easily served by the angled gourmet kitchen. The master suite features a pampering spa bath with a vaulted ceiling, radius window, and garden tub. The far left holds two family bedrooms that share a full bath.

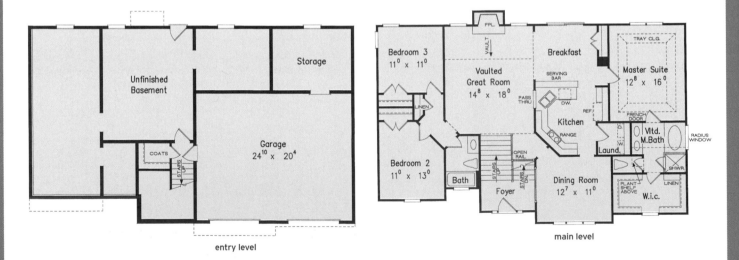

entry level

main level

PLAN: HPK1400128

STYLE: COLONIAL

SQUARE FOOTAGE: 1,048

BONUS SPACE: 480 SQ. FT.

BEDROOMS: 3

BATHROOMS: 1

WIDTH: 54' - 0"

DEPTH: 26' - 0"

FOUNDATION: UNFINISHED
BASEMENT, CRAWLSPACE

■ In traditional split-level styling, this simple design makes an efficient use of space in a smaller footprint. The main level features living and dining spaces that include a large living room, a dining room with sliding glass doors to the rear yard and a U-shaped kitchen. The single-car garage is accessed through the kitchen. Bedrooms are a few steps up: a master bedroom and two family bedrooms all share a full bath. The lower level holds space for a family room with fireplace and a mechanical area where the laundry and storage space are located. For the growing family, this is a most practical plan.

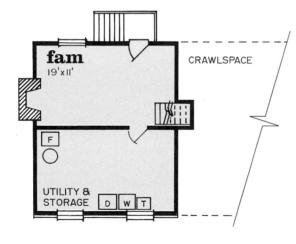

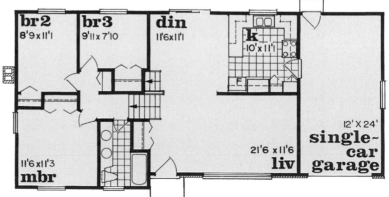

PLAN: HPK1400129

STYLE: TRADITIONAL
MAIN LEVEL: 1,504 SQ. FT.
LOWER LEVEL: 68 SQ. FT.
TOTAL: 1,572 SQ. FT.
BEDROOMS: 3
BATHROOMS: 2½
WIDTH: 51' - 2"
DEPTH: 32' - 4"
FOUNDATION: UNFINISHED
WALKOUT BASEMENT

■ Built-in views! Get a cut above the rest in this multilevel home. A flight of stairs leads to the foyer, where another short flight reveals a wonderful floor plan. An intricate ceiling and arched windows in the activity room create a sense of drama as a fireplace gently soothes. The kitchen and bayed dining area are bright and open, accessing the rear sundeck. The master suite is elegant and luxurious, and includes a vaulted resort-style bath. Two additional bedrooms share a full bath and hall linen closet.

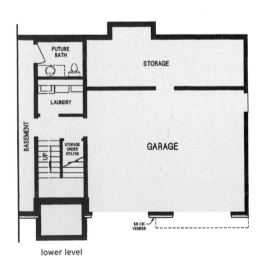

lower level

main level

PLAN: HPK1400130

STYLE: TRADITIONAL
MAIN LEVEL: 1,480 SQ. FT.
ENTRY LEVEL: 36 SQ. FT.
TOTAL: 1,516 SQ. FT.
BEDROOMS: 3
BATHROOMS: 2
WIDTH: 51' - 6"
DEPTH: 31' - 0"
FOUNDATION: UNFINISHED
WALKOUT BASEMENT

■ This lovely brick-and-siding home will be a welcome addition to any neighborhood. The illusion of two stories elevates this traditional home, with the garage and unfinished basement/storage area below and a well-planned layout above. A vaulted family room invites family and friends to delight in an extended-hearth fireplace. To the left, a gourmet country kitchen has a convenient serving bar to the sunny breakfast nook. Two bedrooms share a hall bath; on the far right, the master suite is secluded for privacy, with a pampering vaulted bath and plenty of natural light.

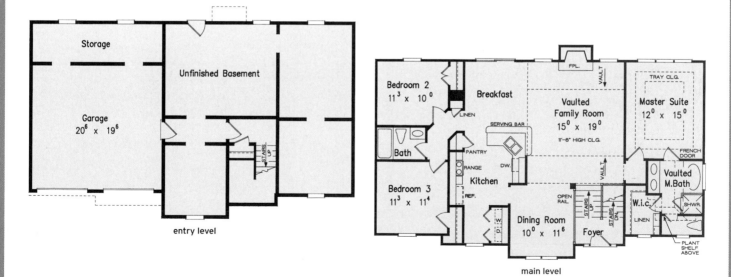

entry level

main level

PLAN: HPK1400131

STYLE: TRADITIONAL

MAIN LEVEL: 1,257 SQ. FT.

ENTRY LEVEL: 36 SQ. FT.

TOTAL: 1,293 SQ. FT.

BONUS SPACE: 476 SQ. FT.

BEDROOMS: 3

BATHROOMS: 2

WIDTH: 48' - 0"

DEPTH: 30' - 0"

FOUNDATION: UNFINISHED BASEMENT

■ Stucco and brick combine with classic styling to give this three-bedroom home plenty of curb appeal. Split-level, with the lower level available for future development, this is a house your family will love to call home. Inside and up a few steps is the living and dining area, with the efficient kitchen nearby. To the right is the sleeping zone, which is complete with two family bedrooms, a full hall bath, and a spacious master bedroom suite. On the lower level, a large room waits for future finishing, and the two-car garage shelters the family fleet.

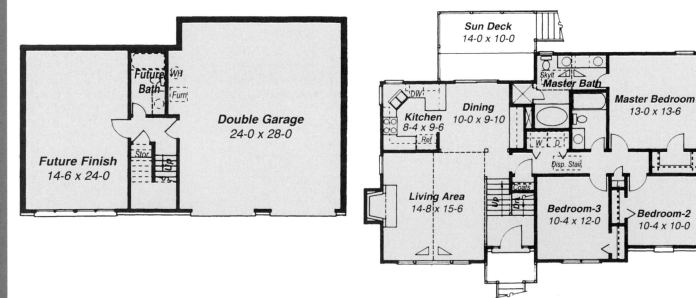

PLAN: HPK1400132

STYLE: TRADITIONAL

SQUARE FOOTAGE: 1,557

BONUS SPACE: 377 SQ. FT.

BEDROOMS: 3

BATHROOMS: 2

WIDTH: 46' - 0"

DEPTH: 40' - 0"

FOUNDATION: UNFINISHED
WALKOUT BASEMENT

■ This split-foyer plan has the charm of a bungalow with its stone and shake facade. The visual impact is impressive as you stand in the foyer looking into the living and dining rooms, both voluminous with modified cathedral ceilings. The master suite features all the amenities of a large plan with separate tub and shower and double vanities. The oversized linen closet can convert to a washer/dryer closet if the ground-level location is not used. The third bath on the ground level allows for a fourth bedroom/rec room to be finished as the family grows. The best feture of this small home is the triple side-entrance garage. As with all split foyers, it can also be built with a front-entry garage.

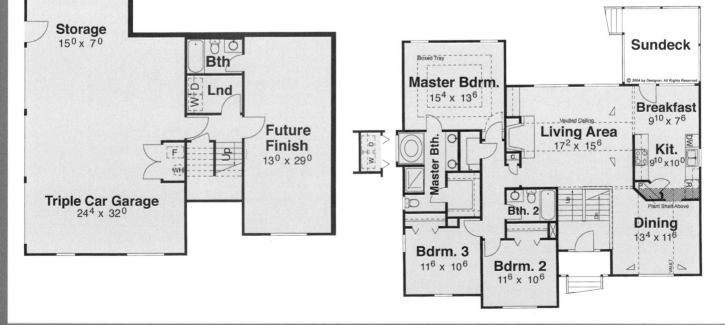

PLAN: HPK1400133

STYLE: TRADITIONAL
MAIN LEVEL: 646 SQ. FT.
LOWER LEVEL: 565 SQ. FT.
TOTAL: 1,211 SQ. FT.
BASEMENT: 942 SQ. FT.
BEDROOMS: 3
BATHROOMS: 1½
WIDTH: 38' - 0"
DEPTH: 42' - 5"
FOUNDATION: CRAWLSPACE, UNFINISHED BASEMENT

■ Adorned with horizontal siding and brick, the exterior of this home sports details for a rustic, country appeal. The entry is deep-set for weather protection and opens directly to the open living and dining area of the home. A fireplace and box-bay window here are added features. The kitchen's L-shaped configuration is designed for convenience and allows space for a breakfast table. Up a few steps are a full bath and the bedrooms—two family bedrooms and a master suite with a powder room. Space on the lower level can be developed into a family room with double-door access to a rear patio, a den, a recreation room with a fireplace, or extra bedrooms.

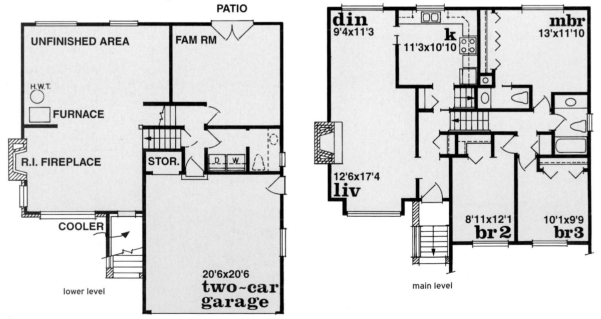

PLAN: HPK1400134

STYLE: TRADITIONAL

MAIN LEVEL: 1,194 SQ. FT.

LOWER LEVEL: 1,156 SQ. FT.

TOTAL: 2,350 SQ. FT.

BEDROOMS: 5

BATHROOMS: 3

WIDTH: 44' - 0"

DEPTH: 30' - 0"

FOUNDATION: FINISHED
BASEMENT

■ This traditional design offers not only a great exterior, but plenty of room for expansion in the future. The main level contains an open living room and dining room, warmed by a fireplace and open to the rear deck through sliding glass doors. The kitchen and breakfast room are reached easily from either the living room or dining room and also share access to the deck. The master bedroom and two family bedrooms reside on the left side of the plan. The master suite contains its own bath; family bedrooms share a full bath. The lower level offers unfinished space for two additional bedrooms, a den, a full bath, and a family room with a fireplace. The laundry room is also on this level.

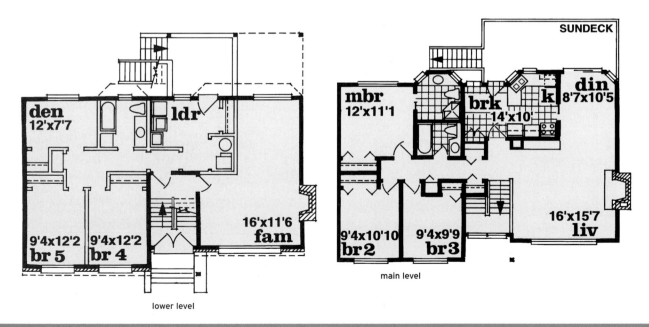

lower level

den 12'x7'7

ldr

9'4x12'2 br 5

9'4x12'2 br 4

16'x11'6 fam

main level

mbr 12'x11'1

brk 14'x10'

din 8'7x10'5

k

SUNDECK

9'4x10'10 br 2

9'4x9'9 br 3

16'x15'7 liv

PLAN: HPK1400135

STYLE: TRADITIONAL

SQUARE FOOTAGE: 1,257

BONUS SPACE: 1,092 SQ. FT.

BEDROOMS: 3

BATHROOMS: 1

WIDTH: 55' - 0"

DEPTH: 43' - 9"

FOUNDATION: UNFINISHED
BASEMENT

■ Brick and siding grace the exterior of this split-level design. The recessed entry leads to a skylit foyer that directs traffic to all areas of the plan. The living room has a bay window and fireplace and connects to a formal dining room with kitchen access. The kitchen is L-shaped and saves space for a breakfast table. Bedrooms revolve around a full hall bath with soaking tub. The unfinished lower level can be developed later into a family room, additional bedrooms, a bathroom, and a laundry.

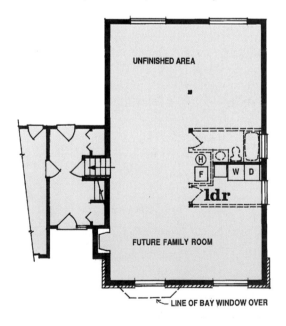

UNFINISHED AREA

ldr

FUTURE FAMILY ROOM

— LINE OF BAY WINDOW OVER

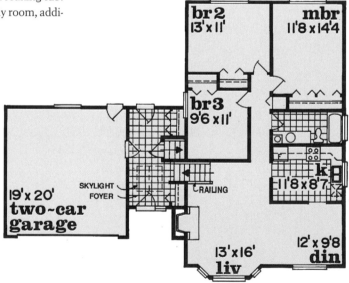

br 2
13'x11'

mbr
11'8 x14'4

br 3
9'6 x11'

19'x 20'
two~car
garage

SKYLIGHT
FOYER

RAILING

k
11'8 x8'7

13'x16'
liv

12' x 9'8
din

PLAN: HPK1400136

STYLE: TRADITIONAL

MAIN LEVEL: 1,247 SQ. FT.

LOWER LEVEL: 552 SQ. FT.

TOTAL: 1,799 SQ. FT.

BEDROOMS: 3

BATHROOMS: 2

WIDTH: 40' - 0"

DEPTH: 46' - 0"

FOUNDATION: UNFINISHED
BASEMENT, CRAWLSPACE

■ Choose this design and you'll have plenty of room to expand in the future. The lower level offers space for a laundry room, connecting powder room, family room, and additional bedrooms if needed. The main level features a front veranda that opens to spacious living and dining rooms. Double doors in the dining room lead to a sundeck, and the living room is warmed by a fireplace. The kitchen leaves space for a breakfast table and chairs. The master suite is at the rear of the plan and includes a walk-in closet and private bath. Two family bedrooms share a full bath.

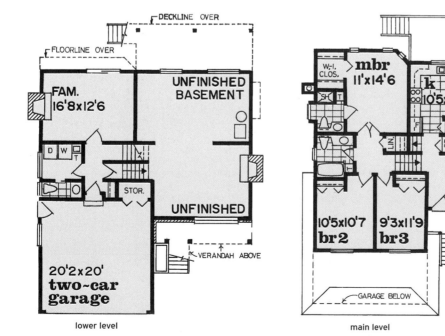

lower level

main level

PLAN: HPK1400137

STYLE: TRADITIONAL

SQUARE FOOTAGE: 1,047

BONUS SPACE: 712 SQ. FT.

BEDROOMS: 3

BATHROOMS: 2

WIDTH: 38' - 0"

DEPTH: 28' - 6"

FOUNDATION: UNFINISHED BASEMENT

■ This split-level design offers a single-car garage on the lower level along with space for a family room, extra bedrooms, or an in-law suite. The main level has a living room that overlooks the vaulted foyer, contains a cozy fireplace, and stretches to a dining area. Sliding glass doors lead out to a sundeck at the back. The kitchen features a counter pass-through to the dining room. Bedrooms on the left side of the plan include a master bedroom with a full bath and two bedrooms with a shared bath.

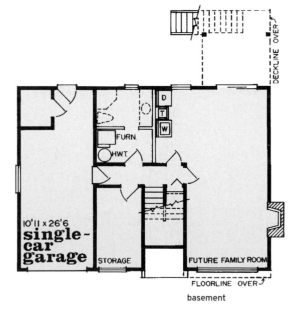

basement

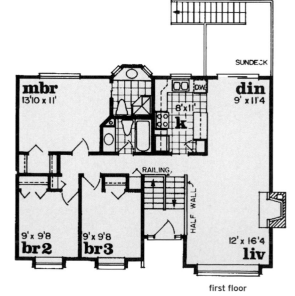

first floor

PLAN: HPK1400138

STYLE: TRADITIONAL

SQUARE FOOTAGE: 1,100

BONUS SPACE: 770 SQ. FT.

BEDROOMS: 3

BATHROOMS: 1

WIDTH: 40' - 0"

DEPTH: 34' - 0"

FOUNDATION: UNFINISHED
BASEMENT

■ Room on the lower level for future expansion makes this split-level as practical as it is appealing. Sharing this level with the two-car garage and laundry room is space for a recreation room, half-bath, and fourth bedroom. On the main level, living space includes a living room with fireplace and a bayed dining room with deck overlook. A door in the kitchen accesses the rear deck. The master bedroom is tucked away in a windowed bay at the opposite end of the home. It shares a bath with two family bedrooms with box-bay windows.

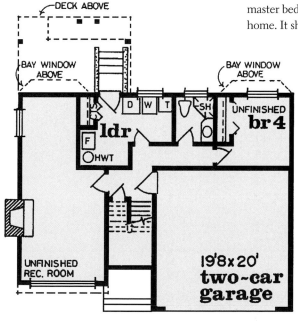

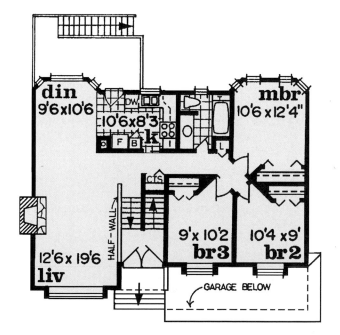

PLAN: HPK1400139

STYLE: TRADITIONAL

SQUARE FOOTAGE: 1,007

BONUS SPACE: 1,007 SQ. FT.

BEDROOMS: 3

BATHROOMS: 1

WIDTH: 26' - 0"

DEPTH: 39' - 4"

FOUNDATION: UNFINISHED BASEMENT

■ To accommodate a very narrow lot, this plan can be built without the deck and the garage, though the plan includes the options for both. The lower floor can be finished later into a family room and additional bedrooms and a bath, if you choose. The cathedral entry offers steps up to the main living areas. The living room has a fireplace and leads to the L-shaped kitchen. Here you'll find abundant counter and cupboard space and room for a breakfast table. Sliding glass doors open to the optional deck. Bedrooms include a master suite and two family bedrooms.

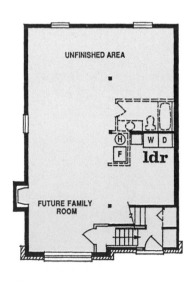

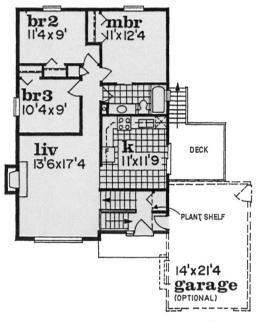

PLAN: HPK1400140

STYLE: TRADITIONAL

MAIN LEVEL: 1,197 SQ. FT.

LOWER LEVEL: 522 SQ. FT.

TOTAL: 1,719 SQ. FT.

BEDROOMS: 3

BATHROOMS: 2

WIDTH: 44' - 0"

DEPTH: 30' - 0"

FOUNDATION: UNFINISHED BASEMENT

■ Perfect for a hillside lot, this design combines brick and horizontal siding to lovely effect. Double doors with a transom overhead create a fine entry. The living room has a fireplace, and the dining room has sliding glass doors to the rear deck. The kitchen and attached breakfast room are nearby and also open to the deck. Three bedrooms are found on the left side of the plan. The master suite has a private bath with a garden sink and corner shower. Family bedrooms share a full bath.

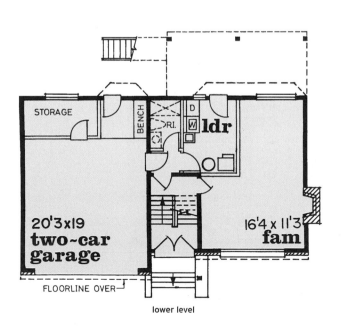

lower level

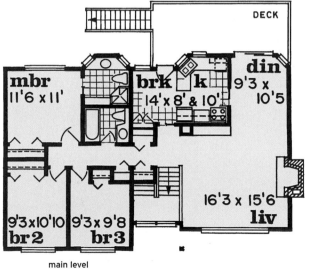

main level

PLAN: HPK1400141

STYLE: TRADITIONAL

SQUARE FOOTAGE: 1,161

BONUS SPACE: 891 SQ. FT.

BEDROOMS: 3

BATHROOMS: 1½

WIDTH: 38' - 0"

DEPTH: 42' - 5"

FOUNDATION: UNFINISHED
BASEMENT

■ This spacious split-level home is well suited to a medium-to-narrow-frontage lot. Steps lead up to a covered front porch at the entry with a single door into the foyer and double doors into the living room. The living room and dining room are part of one large open area, warmed by a fireplace. The kitchen is L-shaped and saves room for a breakfast table. The kitchen can be isolated by pocket doors at each entrance. A few steps up take you to the upper-level sleeping quarters. The master bedroom sits to the back and features a walk-in closet and half-bath. Family bedrooms sit to the front and share a full bath. Unfinished space in the basement provides 891 square feet for future development that might include a family room with fireplace and an additional bedroom with half-bath. The two-car garage offers storage and work-bench space.

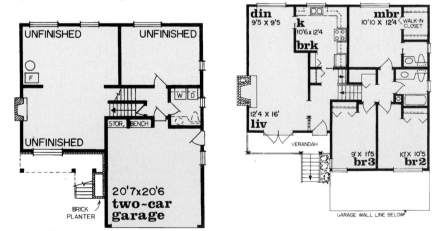

PLAN: HPK1400142

STYLE: COLONIAL

SQUARE FOOTAGE: 1,200

BONUS SPACE: 858 SQ. FT.

BEDROOMS: 3

BATHROOMS: 2

WIDTH: 52' - 0"

DEPTH: 32' - 0"

FOUNDATION: UNFINISHED
BASEMENT, CRAWLSPACE

■ This well-planned, split-level design leaves room for expansion in the future The foyer opens to the living room with a window seat and a railing that separates it from the dining room above. Reach the sundeck through sliding glass doors in the dining room on the main level. The L-shaped kitchen is nearby and has an island work space. Three bedrooms include a master suite with a full bath and walk-in closet and two family bedrooms with a shared bath. The bonus area has 858 square feet of unfinished space.

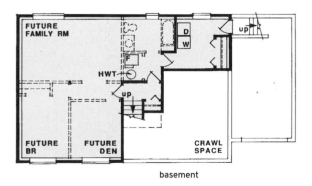

basement

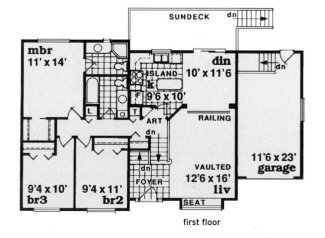

first floor

PLAN: HPK1400143

STYLE: COUNTRY COTTAGE

MAIN LEVEL: 620 SQ. FT.

LOWER LEVEL: 468 SQ. FT.

TOTAL: 1,088 SQ. FT.

BONUS SPACE/BASEMENT:
620/468 SQ. FT.

BEDROOMS: 3

BATHROOMS: 2

WIDTH: 38' - 0"

DEPTH: 31' - 0"

FOUNDATION: UNFINISHED
BASEMENT, CRAWLSPACE

■ Craftsman styling and a welcoming porch create marvelous curb appeal for this design. A compact footprint allows economy in construction. A volume ceiling in the living and dining rooms and the kitchen make this home live larger than its modest square footage. The kitchen features generous cabinet space and flows directly into the dining room (note the optional buffet) to create a casual country feeling. The master bedroom offers a walk-in closet, a full bath, and a bumped-out window overlooking the rear yard. The lower level provides room for an additional bedroom, den, family room, and full bath.

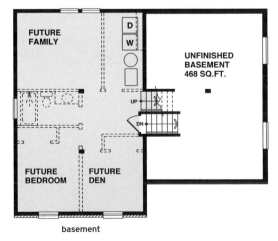

basement

main level/upper level

PLAN: HPK1400237

STYLE: COUNTRY COTTAGE

FIRST FLOOR: 1,388 SQ. FT.

SECOND FLOOR: 1,835 SQ. FT.

TOTAL: 3,223 SQ. FT.

BEDROOMS: 4

BATHROOMS: 3½

WIDTH: 37' - 6"

DEPTH: 78' - 5"

FOUNDATION: UNFINISHED
WALKOUT BASEMENT

rear exterior

■ Brick and siding blend seamlessly to inspire abundant curb appeal in this Craftsman home. Inside, the layout is equally seamless, incorporating a smart design. The kitchen easily serves the adjoining keeping room and breakfast nook. The screen porch and patio are ideal for entertaining and alfresco meals. Upstairs, the master suite, enhanced by stepped ceilings, boasts a lavish master bath, and a private sitting area. Two additional family bedrooms are separated by a Jack-and-Jill bath. A computer station is conveniently located on this level. An exercise/media/guest room completes this plan.

first floor

second floor

PLAN: HPK1400144

STYLE: COLONIAL
SQUARE FOOTAGE: 1,215
BONUS SPACE: 609 SQ. FT.
BEDROOMS: 3
BATHROOMS: 2
WIDTH: 62' - 0"
DEPTH: 34' - 2"
FOUNDATION: CRAWLSPACE,
UNFINISHED BASEMENT

■ The main entry to this home is well protected by a columned front porch. The vaulted living room has a warming fireplace. The vaulted ceiling carries over to the country-style kitchen, which features a work island and a generously sized eating area. A deck just beyond is the perfect spot for outdoor dining. The bedrooms up a few stairs include a master suite with a walk-in closet and full bath. Two additional bedrooms have wall closets and share the use of a main bath in the hallway. The lower level may be developed later as needs grow. It features space for a family room, two bedrooms—or one bedroom and a den—and a full bath. The laundry room is also on this level.

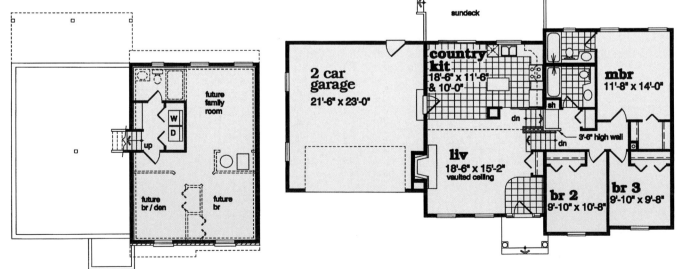

PLAN: HPK1400145

STYLE: BUNGALOW

SQUARE FOOTAGE: 1,040

BONUS SPACE: 1,013 SQ. FT.

BEDROOMS: 3

BATHROOMS: 1

WIDTH: 52' - 0"

DEPTH: 31' - 0"

FOUNDATION: UNFINISHED BASEMENT

■ Affordable, yet appealing, this three-bedroom home is an ideal starter home. Unfinished space in the lower level adds a family room and additional bedrooms with a full bath. The main level includes all the right spaces—a living room with a fireplace, a U-shaped kitchen with room for a table and chairs, and three bedrooms with a full bath. The single-car garage is accessed from the outside and may be built as a detached garage if needed for a narrow lot. Special features include a hall coat closet, a linen closet, and abundant windows.

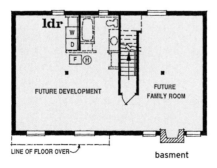

basement

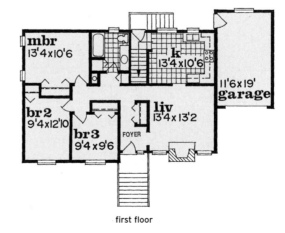

first floor

PLAN: HPK1400146

STYLE: COUNTRY COTTAGE

MAIN LEVEL: 581 SQ. FT.

UPPER LEVEL: 264 SQ. FT.

LOWER LEVEL: 722 SQ. FT.

TOTAL: 1,567 SQ. FT.

BEDROOMS: 3

BATHROOMS: 2

WIDTH: 44' - 0"

DEPTH: 27' - 6"

FOUNDATION: SLAB

■ This compact country home has a rustic brick exterior accentuated by roundels and a tall bay with multipaned windows. Inside, space seems to stretch in all directions despite the plan's modest 1,567 square feet. To the right of the entry, the living room with a fireplace flows into the dining area, which has easy access to the kitchen and box-bay breakfast niche. Also on the first level are the great room and laundry. Upstairs, two bedrooms share a bath; a master suite, with a tub and shower, twin vanities, and a vaulted ceiling, offers relaxation.

upper level

main level

PLAN: HPK1400147

STYLE: TRADITIONAL

MAIN LEVEL: 1363 SQ. FT.

LOWER ENTRY LEVEL: 179 SQ. FT.

TOTAL: 1,542 SQ. FT.

BONUS SPACE: 669 SQ. FT.

BEDROOMS: 3

BATHROOMS: 2

WIDTH: 44' - 0"

DEPTH: 43' - 0"

FOUNDATION: UNFINISHED
BASEMENT

■ A columned, covered entry charms the exterior of this three-bedroom, split-entry home. Inside, a 1 ½-story foyer boasts a dual staircase—one up to the main-floor living area and the other down to the basement. The living area includes a gas fireplace and windows on all walls, ensuring natural light. The adjacent dining room with a buffet alcove exits through a sliding glass door to the rear patio. The roomy kitchen has a raised snack bar, built-in pantry, and access to a bayed eating area surrounded by windows. A skylight brightens the hall to the three bedrooms. Look for His and Hers closets and a private bath in the master suite. Future expansion is reserved for space on the lower level.

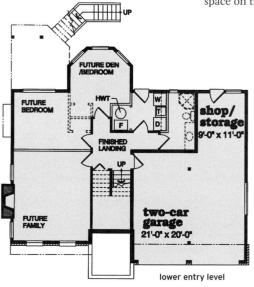

lower entry level

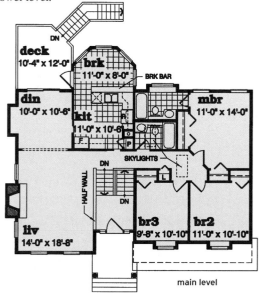

main level

PLAN: HPK1400148

STYLE: VACATION

FIRST FLOOR: 2,024 SQ. FT.

SECOND FLOOR: 717 SQ. FT.

TOTAL: 2,741 SQ. FT.

BEDROOMS: 3

BATHROOMS: 2½

WIDTH: 55' - 4"

DEPTH: 57' - 8"

FOUNDATION: SLAB

L

■ As you enter this charming country home, you are greeted with warmth and livability. The dining room, to the left of the entry, includes a window seat and connects to the kitchen with its snack bar to the breakfast area and to the sunken family room beyond. The family room features a central fireplace and access to the back terrace. Beyond the formal living room are two family bedrooms with access to the terrace, a covered patio, and a shared full bath. The luxurious master bedroom is located on the second floor for privacy and features a separate study and sitting area, a private deck, and an amenity-filled master bath.

second floor

first floor

PLAN: HPK1400149

STYLE: BUNGALOW

SQUARE FOOTAGE: 1,184

BONUS SPACE: 902 SQ. FT.

BEDROOMS: 3

BATHROOMS: 2

WIDTH: 38' - 6"

DEPTH: 60' - 4"

FOUNDATION: UNFINISHED BASEMENT

■ This affordable home is not only appealing, but is well suited to a narrow lot. The entry level hosts a skylit foyer and a spacious living room with a box-bay window, a fireplace, and multipane windows. Up a few steps is the L-shaped kitchen with a pantry, the breakfast room, island work center, and French doors to a rear patio. The master bedroom at the rear of the plan has a private bath and linen closet; the two family bedrooms share a full bath. Lower-level space can be developed to include a recreation room or game room, an additional bedroom, and a full bath.

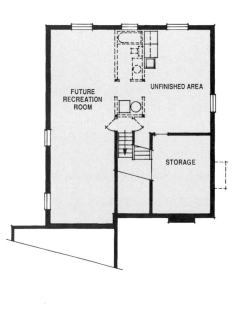

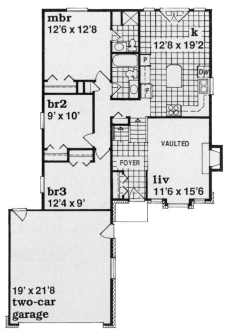

PLAN: HPK1400150

STYLE: TRADITIONAL

SQUARE FOOTAGE: 1,299

BONUS SPACE: 617 SQ. FT.

BEDROOMS: 3

BATHROOMS: 2

WIDTH: 42' - 0"

DEPTH: 40' - 0"

FOUNDATION: UNFINISHED BASEMENT

■ Semicircular transom windows and decorative columns adorn the front entry of this traditional home. A railing separates the cathedral entry and the living room, which has a bay window. Open space in the formal area, warmed by a fireplace, offers room for entertaining. A buffet nook helps to define the dining room, which is easily served by the nearby kitchen. The lower level offers 617 square feet of space for future expansion.

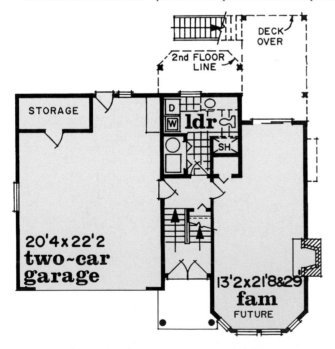

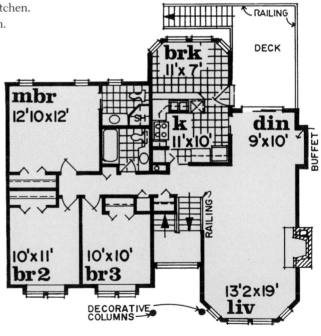

PLAN: HPK1400151

STYLE: TRADITIONAL

SQUARE FOOTAGE: 1,325

BONUS SPACE: 1,272 SQ. FT.

BEDROOMS: 3

BATHROOMS: 2

WIDTH: 38' - 0"

DEPTH: 56' - 0"

FOUNDATION: UNFINISHED
BASEMENT

■ A lovely bay window and a recessed entry, complemented by vertical wood siding, enhance the exterior of this split-level design. Skylights brighten the entry and the staircase to the main level. Three bedrooms line the left side of the plan, and the master suite has a walk-in closet. The lower level contains 1,272 square feet of unfinished space that can be developed into two additional bedrooms, a full bath, a den, and a recreation room.

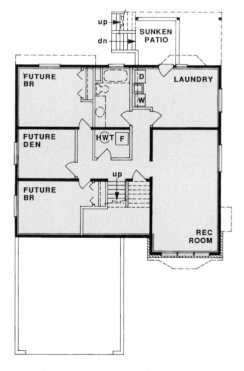

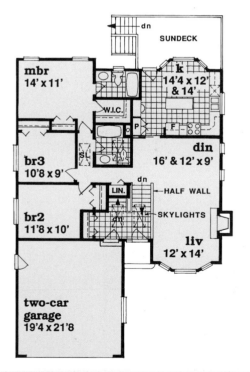

PLAN: HPK1400152

STYLE: NW CONTEMPORARY

SQUARE FOOTAGE: 1,276

BONUS SPACE: 967 SQ. FT.

BEDROOMS: 3

BATHROOMS: 2

WIDTH: 40' - 0"

DEPTH: 38' - 0"

FOUNDATION: UNFINISHED BASEMENT

■ If you'd like to start small and expand later as your family grows, this plan offers that option. The basement is unfinished but can be developed into a family room, bedroom, and full bath in addition to the laundry room and two-car garage at this level. A large living/dining area is found on the main level. It is graced by a fireplace, buffet space, and sliding glass doors to the rear deck. The L-shaped kitchen is efficiently designed and holds space for a breakfast table. Three bedrooms and two full baths include a master suite with walk-in closet.

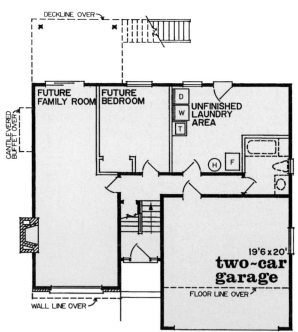

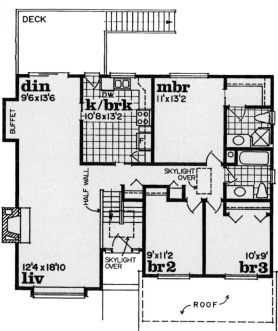

PLAN: HPK1400153

STYLE: CONTEMPORARY

MAIN LEVEL: 1,861 SQ. FT.

LOWER LEVEL: 1,181 SQ. FT.

TOTAL: 3,042 SQ. FT.

BEDROOMS: 4

BATHROOMS: 3

WIDTH: 54' - 0"

DEPTH: 40' - 4"

FOUNDATION: UNFINISHED BASEMENT

■ A Spanish-style bi-level? Why not? This one has lots going for it upstairs and down. Up top, note the living room and formal dining room; they share a fireplace, and each leads to a cozy deck out back. In addition, the kitchen and breakfast area are centers of attention; the latter has a wonderful over-sized pantry. Zoned to the left of the entry are three bedrooms (two if you make one a study). Down below is a potpourri of space: family room, lounge with raised-hearth fireplace, large laundry room (note the bay window), another bedroom, full bath, and plenty of storage in the garage.

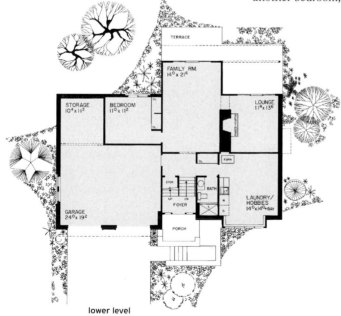

lower level

main level

The Benefits of Basements

A perfect element in hillside homes, basements can expand the enjoyment of your home

EXPOSURES UNLIMITED, RON & DONNA KOLB

Building a hillside home creates opportunities that can be equal to or greater than their challenges—and chief among those is the chance to build a living basement.

A basement can deliver huge dividends if you crave a private retreat like a recreation room, home theater, or home office. Even if those rooms aren't on your wish list—or your budget—at the moment, selecting a plan with a full basement foundation can leave the option open to finish the space in the future.

Full basement foundations are typically more expensive and more time-consuming to build than their slab or crawlspace alternatives, but that's often not the case on a sloped lot. In many cases, the contour of the land will make a basement your most affordable foundation option, and basements almost always cost less than adding an additional above-ground story.

Even if a basement leads to additional cost, it can be well worth it. Remodelers report that besides kitchen and bath renovations, finished basements provide the biggest return on homeowners' investments, and you can make it even more worthwhile by planning on a finished basement from the start of your home-building project.

But never mind the long-term financial benefits basements provide. Consider the other ways your basement can pay you back:

• Climate: Basements are cooler in the summer and warmer in the winter. Because they are naturally insulated by the earth, you'll spend less on heating and cooling costs and find yourself drawn there on particularly hot or cold days.

• Peace and Quiet: If you long for an escape from the hectic comings-and-goings upstairs, get away to the basement. On the other hand, if your children's playroom or your spouse's exercise room makes too much of a racket where it is, move it to the basement and reclaim the quiet upstairs.

• More Space: Maybe you were planning on using that extra bedroom as a home office before a new addition to the family created the need for a nursery. With a basement, you could always move the office downstairs. With less and less space available around homes, expanding down is usually a more attractive option than expanding out.

Endless Options

Obviously, we've come a long way since the dark, dreary basement you were probably scared of as a little kid. Because parts or all of basement walls are underground, in the past they were prone to moisture problems. But advancements in moisture prevention have made basements more livable than ever before. Waterproofing membranes don't take long to apply during the construction process and can even be added later, although at greater cost.

Thanks to these waterproofing techniques, the possibilities for your basement are almost endless—including something as simple as an extra bedroom or as extraordinary as a sauna. But because of the qualities inherent in a finished basement, some rooms are perfectly suited for the space:

• Media Room: Since it's quiet and secluded, the basement can be a perfect place to escape and watch a movie in an entertainment room or home theater. If your basement is dark, it can be ideal for a media room—simply install indirect lighting on a dimmer switch for once the show is over. You'll want to take special care with wall and floor coverings, as well as furnishings, to preserve the sound quality.

• Activity Room: Whether it's a home workshop for the do-it-yourselfer in the family, an art studio, or a child's playroom, you can find a home for it in the basement. It's easily accessible yet out of the way, and will free up space upstairs.

• Laundry Room: Consumers are asking home designers for more and more out of their laundry rooms, and the basement is one spot where it's easy to deliver. It offers space that is usually hard to come by on a house's main level, and easy access to necessary components like water and drainage.

• Wine Cellar: There's a reason you've never heard of a "wine attic." The temperate climate of a basement is perfectly suited for storing wine. If you are a connoisseur—or would like to be—think about including a wine cellar in the plans for your new basement.

• Rec Room: Entertaining can be a blast in a fully outfitted rec room, complete with a pool table or other fun accessories. Decorate however you would like, and have fun with it—homeowners often feel more comfortable taking chances with decorating themes in their basements that they might be hesitant to try upstairs. A walk-out basement can be even more suited for entertaining in warm weather if it opens up to a patio or backyard.

• Home Spa: If you want to really indulge—and enjoy the peace and quiet of the basement—consider adding a whirlpool or sauna to your basement.

With all those options, it's no surprise that more and more homeowners are discovering the benefits of basements. As you search for the perfect plan for you, keep the possibility of a full or walkout basement in mind if you can—consider it deep thinking. ■

Opposite page: This home features a walkout basement, a modern appeal, and an appreciation of the outdoors. For details, see page 183. Right: This striking home, found on page 181, features a home theater in the basement.

Comfortable Fit

Beautiful views and an appreciation of the outdoors are just two ways this home suits its surroundings

With a quaint country design that would fit in just about anywhere, this home doesn't strike a garish pose from the street. Instead, it fits right in, offering comfort and a friendly layout that is designed for today's lifestyles.

A great room anchors the main level, and its cathedral ceilings include windows that welcome plenty of natural light. It connects easily to the entryway and kitchen, which has an L shape around a center island. There's plenty of storage space, accentuated by the built-in cabinets in the adjacent dining room and the nearby pantry. The main level also features four porches—one on each side—including a private porch located off the beautiful master suite. Cathedral ceilings, a spacious bath, and a nearby den are added touches to the homeowners' retreat.

It's the full basement that allows this home to fit perfectly into the rolling landscape. In this setting it also incorporates a patio off the back porch. The basement itself houses two bedrooms, each with a walk-in closet, as well as plenty of storage space.

Left: The home's attention to detail can be seen in the front door and the stairway to the basement. Above: With traditional good looks, this home would fit in any neighborhood.

PHOTO BY DONNA L. AHMANN

main level

lower level

PLAN: HPK1400154

STYLE: EUROPEAN COTTAGE

MAIN LEVEL: 2,551 SQ. FT.

LOWER LEVEL: 2,028 SQ. FT.

TOTAL: 4,579 SQ. FT.

BEDROOMS: 4

BATHROOMS: 3

WIDTH: 89' - 4"

DEPTH: 67' - 0"

FOUNDATION: FINISHED BASEMENT

A large rec room at the heart of the basement will draw a crowd, and in includes one space that's practically built for a pool table. A media room is closed off by double doors to allow for theater-quality sound, while a nearby wet bar includes an enclosed wine room. ■

Soft green hues create a comforting feel in the master bath (above) and bedroom (right).

Triumphant Arches

This impressive facade gives way to a comfortable floor plan

Arches and columns adorn the front windows and doors on this elegant home, lending a European flair to its distinctive design. That continues inside, where comfort and style coexist beautifully on both the main and lower levels.

A see-through fireplace becomes a focal point in both the great room and the hearth room on the main level. A beamed ceiling—complete with recessed lighting—is just part of the beautiful woodwork in the great room, which includes a flat-screen television installed above the fireplace. On the other side of the fire, the hearth room provides a

Above: A dignified facade offers plenty of curb appeal. Top: The hearth room provides a casual gathering spot that connects easily to the kitchen.

SMART DESIGN

Media rooms, wine cellars, and exercise rooms are ideal uses for basement space, and this home has all three.

lower level

main level

PLAN: HPK1400155

STYLE: EUROPEAN COTTAGE

MAIN LEVEL: 2,262 SQ. FT.

LOWER LEVEL: 2,195 SQ. FT.

TOTAL: 4,457 SQ. FT.

BEDROOMS: 4

BATHROOMS: 3½

WIDTH: 76' - 0"

DEPTH: 59' - 4"

FOUNDATION: FINISHED BASEMENT

The basement rec room is an inviting retreat, with a bar located in front of the wine cellar.

comfortable transition to the kitchen, which includes a built-in breakfast nook. An adjacent deck is the ideal place to enjoy outdoor meals.

The master suite occupies most of the right side of the main level, with a den alongside it. The bedroom enjoys beautiful backyard views, and the large master bath is filled with amenities—the best of which, perhaps,

being the corner whirlpool tub.

Downstairs, three bedrooms share two full baths. There's plenty of space for friends and family to relax as well. A bar extends in front of a spacious wine cellar, serving a rec room that includes a fireplace. Nearby, you can step down into the media room and enjoy a movie, or enter the exercise room for a workout. ■

PLAN: **HPK1400156**

STYLE: CRAFTSMAN

SQUARE FOOTAGE: 2,326

BONUS SPACE: 358 SQ. FT.

BEDROOMS: 3

BATHROOMS: 2½

WIDTH: 64' - 0"

DEPTH: 72' - 4"

FOUNDATION: FINISHED BASEMENT

■ Fine details like the shed dormer, open millwork accents, arched entry, and a standing-seam roof will make this home a neighborhood favorite. A split-bedroom floor plan positions the family bedrooms to the left with a compartmented bath between them. The family room, with fireplace and built-ins, is a generous and open space that works with the huge island kitchen, bright sunroom, and breakfast nook. A more formal dining space is found to the right of the foyer. Seclusion is just one amenity the master suite boasts; others include a oversized walk-in closet, super bath, and French doors to the deck.

PLAN: HPK1400157

STYLE: NW CONTEMPORARY

FIRST FLOOR: 2,120 SQ. FT.

SECOND FLOOR: 1,520 SQ. FT.

THIRD FLOOR: 183 SQ. FT.

TOTAL: 3,823 SQ. FT.

BONUS/HOME OFFICE:
377/526 SQ. FT.

BEDROOMS: 5

BATHROOMS: 4½ + ½

WIDTH: 76' - 0"

DEPTH: 81' - 0"

FOUNDATION: FINISHED
WALKOUT BASEMENT, SLAB,
CRAWLSPACE

■ The rustic chic of Craftsman details makes this an unusual example of estate architecture. But, extravagant floor planning leaves no doubt that luxury is what this home is about. The first floor has open spaces for living: a reading room and dining room flanking the foyer, a huge family room with built-ins and fireplace plus covered deck access, and an island kitchen and nook with built-in table. The first-floor master suite is graced with a beamed ceiling. Its attached bath is well appointed and spacious. On the second floor are four bedrooms and three baths. Third-floor attic space can be used for whatever suits you best. Don't miss the home theater that can be developed in the basement and home-office space over the garage.

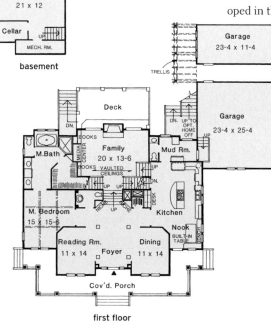

basement

first floor

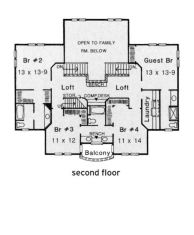

second floor

third floor

optional layout

PLAN: HPK1400158

STYLE: CRAFTSMAN

MAIN LEVEL: 3,793 SQ. FT.

LOWER LEVEL: 1,588 SQ. FT.

TOTAL: 5,381 SQ. FT.

BEDROOMS: 4

BATHROOMS: 3½

WIDTH: 99' - 8"

DEPTH: 68' - 8"

FOUNDATION: FINISHED

WALKOUT BASEMENT

PHOTO BY: EXPOSURES UNLIMITED, RON & DONNA KOLB. THIS HOME, AS SHOWN IN THE PHOTOGRAPH, MAY DIFFER FROM THE ACTUAL BLUEPRINTS. FOR MORE DETAILED INFORMATION, PLEASE CHECK THE FLOOR PLANS CAREFULLY.

■ The richness of the exterior showcases an excellent Craftsman design. The wraparound foyer presents a luxurious entrance in addition to providing an efficient traffic flow. Columns at the entrance to the great room, dining room, and kitchen combine to create a warm, inviting space. Split bedrooms provide privacy while the master suite, with access to the rear deck, is complemented by a spacious dressing room and His and Hers walk-in closets. Various ceiling treatments throughout add to the enchanting atmosphere. Angled stairs lead to a finished lower level with a nine-foot ceiling and a walkout to the rear yard. This space is perfect for a home theater, exercise room, guest quarters, or summer expansion space.

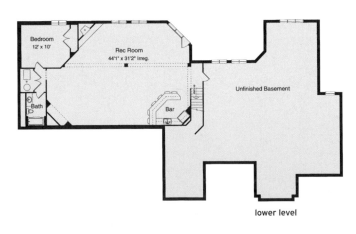

lower level

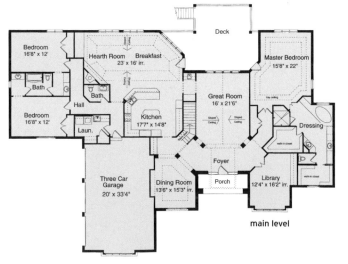

main level

PLAN: HPK1400159

STYLE: CONTEMPORARY

MAIN LEVEL: 1,227 SQ. FT.

UPPER LEVEL: 1,575 SQ. FT.

LOWER LEVEL: 1,069 SQ. FT.

TOTAL: 3,871 SQ. FT.

BEDROOMS: 3

BATHROOMS: 3½

WIDTH: 41' - 10"

DEPTH: 73' - 0"

FOUNDATION: FINISHED
WALKOUT BASEMENT

■ This beautiful home is artistically designed to become an integral part of a hillside lot that showcases a spectacular view. Exterior spaces combine with indoor living areas to focus attention on the beauty of integrating design, comfort, and luxury into an exquisite package. The entry at the side of the home introduces a foyer, library, and spectacular master bedroom suite with deluxe amenities and a wall of glass to the outdoors. Split stairs adorned with wrought iron and wood trim directs you to the lower level where a fun game room, media area, and wet bar cluster around the wall of windows; or to the upper level where you will be dazzled by the beauty of the great room, dining room, and gourmet kitchen. An elevator is located to the rear for ease of movement between floors. An Arts & Crafts motif reflects clean lines reminiscent of turn-of-the-Century styling; and the use of space and flow maintain the character of relaxed elegance.

lower level

main level

upper level

PLAN: HPK1400160

STYLE: BUNGALOW

MAIN LEVEL: 2,160 SQ. FT.

LOWER LEVEL: 919 SQ. FT.

TOTAL: 3,079 SQ. FT.

BEDROOMS: 3

BATHROOMS: 2½

WIDTH: 68' - 3"

DEPTH: 60' - 11"

FOUNDATION: FINISHED BASEMENT

■ An eye-catching shed dormer is both lovely and functional, bringing light into the foyer. A mud room is the perfect casual entry off the garage, right next to the main-level laundry and optional third-car garage. The open kitchen works with the keeping, breakfast, and grand rooms. A study—or living room—and formal dining room flank the foyer for entertaining guests.

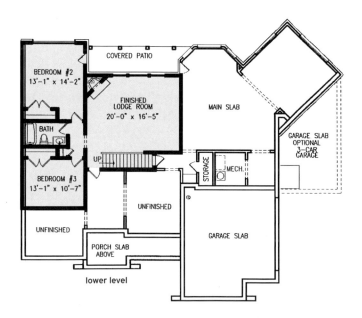

lower level

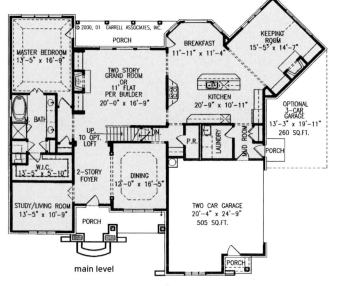

main level

PLAN: HPK1400161

STYLE: VICTORIAN

MAIN LEVEL: 1,092 SQ. FT.

LOWER LEVEL: 1,128 SQ. FT.

TOTAL: 2,220 SQ. FT.

BEDROOMS: 3

BATHROOMS: 2½

WIDTH: 42' - 0"

DEPTH: 46' - 8"

FOUNDATION: BASEMENT

■ Beautiful Craftsman accents are evident in this design, perfect for a sloping lot. A double-door entry opens off a covered porch to an impressive vaulted foyer. Living areas are to the back and manifest in vaulted living and dining rooms. The living room boasts a bay window and fireplace. Access to the deck sits between the living and dining rooms. The L-shaped kitchen features an island work space and vaulted breakfast bay with deck access. The laundry area is to the front of the house and contains a half bath. Stairs to the lower level are found in the foyer. Sleeping quarters are found below— two family bedrooms and a master suite. The master suite has a walk-in closet and bath with separate tub and shower. Family bedrooms share a full bath.

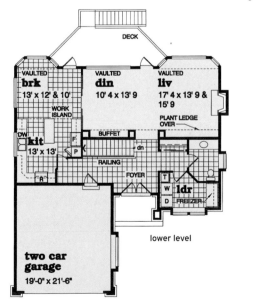

lower level

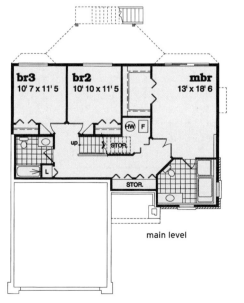

main level

© 2000 Donald A. Gardner, Inc.

PLAN: HPK1400162

STYLE: CONTEMPORARY

MAIN LEVEL: 1,682 SQ. FT.

UPPER LEVEL: 577 SQ. FT.

LOWER LEVEL: 690 SQ. FT.

TOTAL: 2,949 SQ. FT.

BONUS SPACE: 459 SQ. FT.

BEDROOMS: 4

BATHROOMS: 3½

WIDTH: 79' - 0"

DEPTH: 68' - 2"

FOUNDATION: FINISHED BASEMENT

■ Stone and siding combine to give this Craftsman design striking curb appeal. A portico sets the tone with a gentle arch and four stately columns. A clerestory above the front entrance floods the two-story foyer with natural light. Inside, Old World charm gives way to an open, family-efficient floor plan. The kitchen partitions the dining room and breakfast area and easily accesses a screened porch for outdoor entertaining. The great room features a two-story fireplace and French doors that lead to the rear porch. A family room also sports a fireplace and patio access. The master bedroom is crowned by a tray ceiling, and a balcony with a curved alcove separates two additional bedrooms upstairs.

upper level

main level

lower level

PLAN: HPK1400163

STYLE: CRAFTSMAN

FIRST FLOOR: 2,782 SQ. FT.

SECOND FLOOR: 1,027 SQ. FT.

TOTAL: 3,809 SQ. FT.

BASEMENT: 1,316 SQ. FT.

BEDROOMS: 4

BATHROOMS: 4½

WIDTH: 78' - 2"

DEPTH: 74' - 6"

FOUNDATION: FINISHED
WALKOUT BASEMENT

rear exterior

■ Filled with specialty rooms and abundant amenities, this countryside house is the perfect dream home. Double doors open into an angled foyer, flanked by a music room and a formal great room warmed by a fireplace. The music room leads to the master wing of the home, which includes a spacious bath with a dressing area and double walk-in closet. The great room is the heart of the home—its central position allows access to the island kitchen, formal dining room, and library. Stairs behind the kitchen lead upstairs to a balcony accessing three family bedrooms. The lower level features a billiard room, hobby room, media room, and future possibilities.

basement

first floor

second floor

PLAN: HPK1400164

STYLE: NW CONTEMPORARY
FIRST FLOOR: 3,162 SQ. FT.
SECOND FLOOR: 1,595 SQ. FT.
TOTAL: 4,757 SQ. FT.
BONUS SPACE: 2,651 SQ. FT.
BEDROOMS: 3
BATHROOMS: 3 + 3 HALF BATHS
WIDTH: 110' - 2"
DEPTH: 68' - 11"
FOUNDATION: FINISHED
BASEMENT, SLAB

■ Victorian and Craftsman styles blend and create an inviting and detailed home. A two-story turret houses a second-floor reading room and first-floor master sitting bay. The dining and living areas are open and convenient to the rear porch and gourmet kitchen. An interior fountain divides the breakfast area and the spacious family room. The first-floor master suite features a corner fireplace and private bath. Family quarters, including two bedrooms and a large library, can be found on the second floor. Storage for holiday items and large keepsakes is also provided. On the lower level, a magnificent auto gallery, complete with a special car elevator, is perfect for the auto enthusiast in the family.

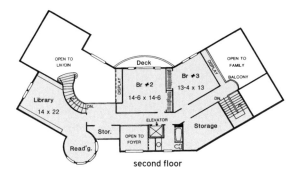

second floor

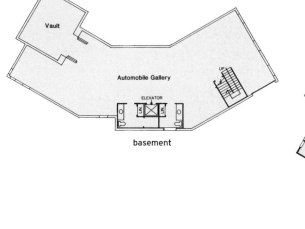

basement

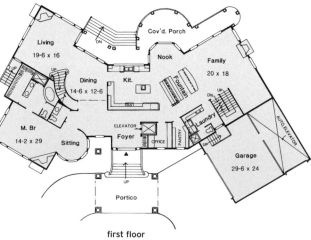

first floor

PLAN: HPK1400165

STYLE: CRAFTSMAN

FIRST FLOOR: 3,649 SQ. FT.

SECOND FLOOR: 1,302 SQ. FT.

TOTAL: 4,951 SQ. FT.

BEDROOMS: 4

BATHROOMS: 3½ + ½

WIDTH: 88' - 4"

DEPTH: 82' - 9"

FOUNDATION: FINISHED BASEMENT, UNFINISHED BASEMENT

■ The air of an English Country manor is re-created throughtout this home. Repeating interior arches, stone walls, and beamed ceilings are reminiscent of a home created a half century ago. Highlights include an inviting outdoor summer living room with stone floor, fireplace, wood-beamed ceiling, and the magnificent view it offers. Other exciting features include a large gathering space with kitchen/breakfast room, butler/wine gallery, pub, and hearth room. Views from the entry include the great room, formal dining room, and a library with double doors and built-ins. The first-floor master bedroom pampers with luxury; three upper-level bedrooms—each with private access to a bath and large walk-in closets—make this home the perfect fit for your family.

first floor

second floor

PLAN: HPK1400166

STYLE: TRADITIONAL
SQUARE FOOTAGE: 1,792
BASEMENT: 1,792 SQ. FT.
BEDROOMS: 3
BATHROOMS: 2
WIDTH: 71' - 0"
DEPTH: 49' - 0"
FOUNDATION: FINISHED
BASEMENT

■ This charming ranch home includes many features normally found in larger homes. From the three-car garage to the large master bedroom with walk-in closet and large bathroom, your family will enjoy the spaciousness of this home. The open kitchen and dining floor plan makes this a perfect place for family gatherings, and you'll love the arched opening into the spacious great room complete with fireplace. Two additional bedrooms on the main floor make this the perfect home for any size family.

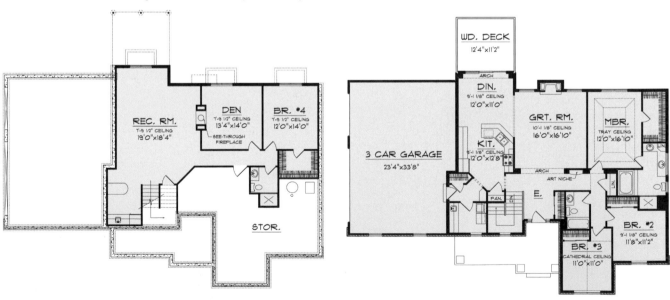

PLAN: HPK1400167

STYLE: TRADITIONAL

SQUARE FOOTAGE: 1,587

BASEMENT: 970 SQ. FT.

BEDROOMS: 3

BATHROOMS: 2½

WIDTH: 54' - 0"

DEPTH: 61' - 0"

FOUNDATION: FINISHED
BASEMENT

■ This traditional-style narrow-lot home makes it the perfect home for any size family. Inside you'll find that the kitchen, dining, and living rooms all work together to create an open floor that makes this home feel spacious, yet comfortable. The master suite has a large walk-in closet and bathroom with a shower. And you'll love the extra garage stall that tucks up behind the kitchen, making this a highly functional home.

basement

first floor

PLAN: HPK1400168

STYLE: FRENCH COUNTRY	
SQUARE FOOTAGE: 2,640	
BONUS SPACE: 2,640 SQ. FT.	
BEDROOMS: 3	
BATHROOMS: 2½	
WIDTH: 50' - 0"	
DEPTH: 70' - 4"	

■ Escape to the French countryside in your private cottage. A hipped dormer anchoring a pitched roof announces this house of distinction. Sunlight graces the entryway, upon which you enter through French doors, and are rewarded with a view to the gathering room with fireplace down the main hallway. A split staircase leads to the combination game/rec room with bar, exercise room, an extra bedroom with attached bath, and plentiful storage space. Bedrooms 2 and 3 are tucked away to the right of the entry on the main floor. Upon touring the kitchen—complete with separate dining and eating areas, and pantry—be sure not to miss the master suite with dual vanity, spa tub, separately compartmented shower and toilet, and two closets.

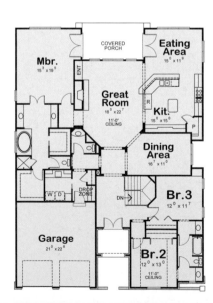

PLAN: HPK1400169

STYLE: TRADITIONAL

SQUARE FOOTAGE: 1,758

BASEMENT: 997 SQ. FT.

BEDROOMS: 2

BATHROOMS: 2

WIDTH: 48' - 0"

DEPTH: 63' - 0"

FOUNDATION: FINISHED
BASEMENT

■ Designed for a narrow lot, this one-story home offers an open great room with a cozy fireplace and dining area with excellent views to the backyard, rear deck, and delightful screened porch—great for the summer. The conveniently located kitchen enjoys an island cooktop and plenty of cabinet and counter space. A library/bedroom is found at the entrance of the house while a secluded master bedroom is found to the rear left for extra privacy. This master retreat boasts a dressing area, dual vanities, an angled soaking tub, and a large walk-in closet. The future space in the basement holds a spacious recreation room for family entertainment, a large family bedroom, and another library/bedroom all sharing a full bath.

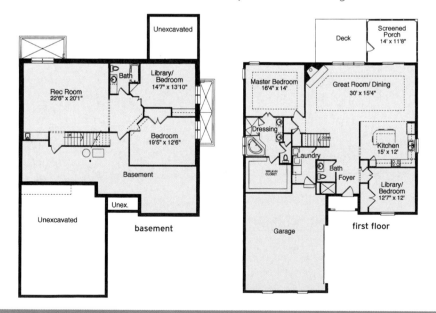

PLAN: HPK1400170

STYLE: EUROPEAN COTTAGE

FIRST FLOOR: 1,488 SQ. FT.

SECOND FLOOR: 602 SQ. FT.

TOTAL: 2,090 SQ. FT.

BONUS SPACE: 1,321 SQ. FT.

BEDROOMS: 2

BATHROOMS: 2

WIDTH: 60' - 0"

DEPTH: 44' - 0"

FOUNDATION: FINISHED BASEMENT

■ A truly original angle at the entrance of this country home belies a much more traditionally designed floor plan. There are two sets of stairs in the foyer, one leading to the second level and the other to the basement. The island kitchen and dining room enjoy the glow of the living room fireplace. The master suite with walk-in closet and bathroom are on the main level and situated next to the two-car garage. Up the short flight of stairs you'll find a convenient home office—or make it a sitting room to create a truly lavish second bedroom with a roomy closet and private bath. Finish the bonus space as a third bedroom if you wish.

second floor

basement

first floor

PLAN: HPK1400171

STYLE: CONTEMPORARY

FIRST FLOOR: 2,292 SQ. FT.

SECOND FLOOR: 925 SQ. FT.

TOTAL: 3,217 SQ. FT.

BEDROOMS: 3

BATHROOMS: 3½

WIDTH: 70' - 0"

DEPTH: 71' - 0"

FOUNDATION: CRAWLSPACE, FINISHED BASEMENT, SLAB

rear exterior

■ An abundance of windows provides a wealth of natural light throughout this Contemporary home. A covered patio offers French-door access to the two-story dining room. The great room sits at the heart of the home with a corner fireplace and built-in media center. The home office is appropriately placed adjacent to the lavish master suite. The rear patio boasts a built-in BBQ pit ideal for outdoor entertaining. Upstairs houses two additional family bedrooms with full baths and a library with built-in amenities.

first floor

second floor

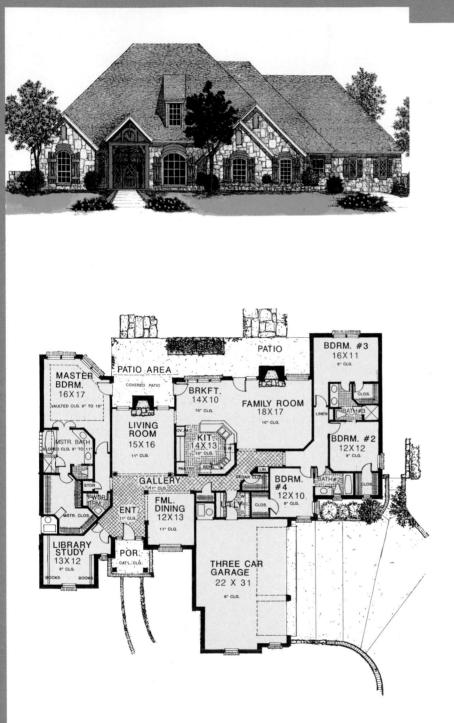

PLAN: HPK1400172

STYLE: TRADITIONAL

SQUARE FOOTAGE: 3,079

BEDROOMS: 4

BATHROOMS: 3½

WIDTH: 80' - 0"

DEPTH: 74' - 10"

FOUNDATION: CRAWLSPACE, FINISHED BASEMENT, SLAB

■ A stone facade and hipped rooflines present this handsome home as both sturdy and comfortable. Linked by a gallery hallway the impressive living room with a gas fireplace, the elegant dining room, and the study/library work harmoniously to ensure refined entertaining. The kitchen, filled with counter space, meshes well with the sunlit breakfast area and the family room, which enjoys another fireplace. Three family bedrooms are located on the right side of the home, and a dazzling master suite, filled with comforts to make your fantasies come true, enjoys privacy on the left. An extensive rear patio is perfect for family relaxation and larger social activities.

PLAN: HPK1400173

STYLE: TRANSITIONAL

SQUARE FOOTAGE: 2,269

BASEMENT: 830 SQ. FT.

BEDROOMS: 3

BATHROOMS: 2

WIDTH: 63' - 0"

DEPTH: 67' - 8"

FOUNDATION: UNFINISHED
BASEMENT, FINISHED
BASEMENT

■ This handsome brick facade, highlighted with stone accents and a turret-style bay, will bring European style to any neighborhood. Enter to find a well-planned design with heightened ceilings and elegant touches. The great room boasts a wall of windows for great views, and an extended-hearth fireplace framed by built-in shelving. The kitchen features a serving bar that can comfortably seat four. A sloped ceiling defines the dining room, sunny and cheerful with a wall of windows. Exquisite in every detail, the master suite indulges in a spa bath with a step-up tub, a separate shower, and a massive walk-in closet. To the far right, a bayed library and a bedroom open to a full hall bath. Basement space can include a recreation room and hobby room, or finish it to suit your needs.

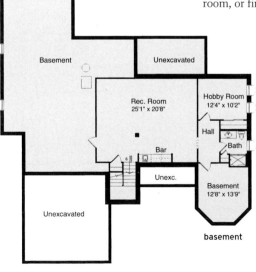

basement

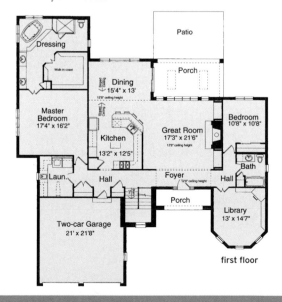

first floor

PLAN: HPK1400174

STYLE: TRADITIONAL

MAIN LEVEL: 3,570 SQ. FT.

LOWER LEVEL: 2,367 SQ. FT.

TOTAL: 5,937 SQ. FT.

BEDROOMS: 4

BATHROOMS: 4½

WIDTH: 84' - 6"

DEPTH: 69' - 4"

FOUNDATION: FINISHED

WALKOUT BASEMENT

■ The stone and brick exterior with multiple gables and a side-entry garage create a design that brags great curb appeal. The gourmet kitchen with an island and snack bar combine with the spacious breakfast room and hearth room to create a warm and friendly atmosphere for family living. The luxurious master bedroom with a sitting area and fireplace is complemented by a deluxe dressing room and walk-in closet. The lower level contains an office, media room, billiards room, exercise area, and plenty of storage.

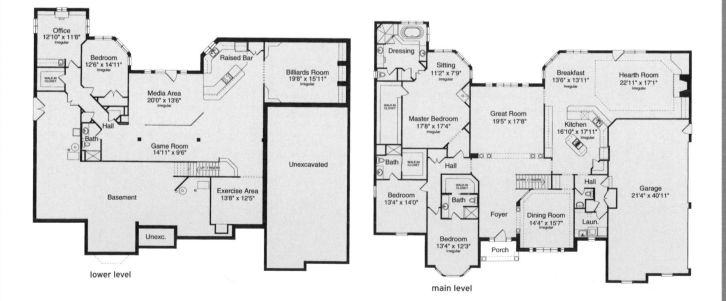

lower level

main level

PLAN: HPK1400175

STYLE: EUROPEAN COTTAGE

MAIN LEVEL: 2,582 SQ. FT.

LOWER LEVEL: 1,746 SQ. FT.

TOTAL: 4,328 SQ. FT.

BEDROOMS: 3

BATHROOMS: 3½

WIDTH: 70' - 8"

DEPTH: 64' - 0"

FOUNDATION: FINISHED BASEMENT

■ Stone accents provide warmth and character to the exterior of this home. An arched entry leads to the interior, where elegant window styles and dramatic ceiling treatments create an impressive showplace. The gourmet kitchen and breakfast room offer a spacious area for chores and family gatherings, and provide a striking view through the great room to the fireplace. An extravagant master suite and a library with built-in shelves round out the main level. On the lower level, two additional bedrooms, a media room, a billiards room, and an exercise room complete the home.

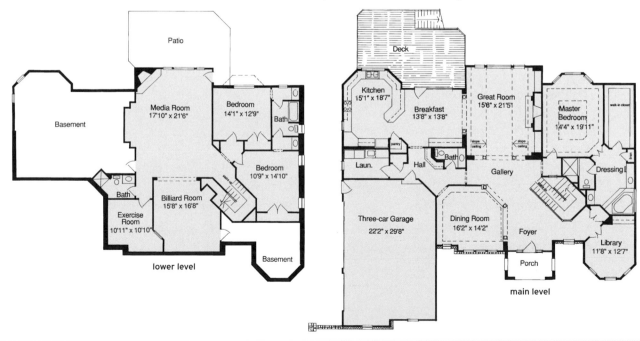

PLAN: HPK1400176

STYLE: FRENCH	
FIRST FLOOR: 2,117 SQ. FT.	
SECOND FLOOR: 740 SQ. FT.	
TOTAL: 2,857 SQ. FT.	
BONUS SPACE: 1,380 SQ. FT.	
BEDROOMS: 4	
BATHROOMS: 2½	
WIDTH: 74' - 8"	
DEPTH: 71' - 8"	
FOUNDATION: FINISHED BASEMENT	

■ Designed for a sloping lot, but adaptable to any location, this traditional home enjoys hints of European style for a truly wonderful plan. Inside, the entry leads to a columned living room with a stunning bowed window. French doors open to a nearby den, and the gourmet kitchen is just steps away. Here, a cooktop island serving bar overlooks the breakfast nook and family room, topped by a cathedral ceiling. A four-season room at the rear provides just the right combination of nature and protection from the elements. The right wing is devoted to the master suite, with a step-up tub and a massive walk-in closet. Three upper-level bedrooms share a spacious bath. Future space is available in the basement, accommodating a toy room, recreation room, fifth bedroom, and a wet bar.

second floor

basement

first floor

PLAN: HPK1400177

STYLE: NORMAN

FIRST FLOOR: 3,056 SQ. FT.

SECOND FLOOR: 1,307 SQ. FT.

TOTAL: 4,363 SQ. FT.

BONUS SPACE: 692 SQ. FT.

BEDROOMS: 4

BATHROOMS: 4½

WIDTH: 94' - 4"

DEPTH: 79' - 2"

FOUNDATION: CRAWLSPACE,

UNFINISHED BASEMENT,

FINISHED BASEMENT

■ This fantasy begins as soon as you step from the porch into the two-story vaulted foyer. To the right sits the columned elegance of the formal dining room and to the right a personal library awaits. Steps away, the entrance to the master suite beckons with promises of a sitting area, morning kitchen, L-shaped walk-in closet, garden tub, separate shower, and dual vanities. The three family bedrooms upstairs each have a full bath and ample closet space. In addition to the bedrooms, the option of a game room/billiards room provides plenty of space for casual entertainment. A three-car garage completes this plan.

basement

first floor

second floor

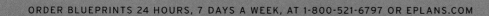

PLAN: HPK1400178

STYLE: FRENCH

FIRST FLOOR: 3,880 SQ. FT.

SECOND FLOOR: 3,635 SQ. FT.

TOTAL: 7,515 SQ. FT.

BASEMENT: 2,531 SQ. FT.

BEDROOMS: 5

BATHROOMS: 5½ + ½

WIDTH: 101' - 4"

DEPTH: 110' - 4"

FOUNDATION: FINISHED BASEMENT

■ Amenities abound in this opulent French Country design, which includes a separate apartment or guest house and a two-story pool house. Entertaining is easy, with a central grand room and the formal dining room located right off the foyer. The heart of your gatherings, though, will be in the combination kitchen, breakfast nook, and gathering room, where a fireplace and a private screened porch make this area warm and comfortable. Another favorite area will be the upper-level recreation room that opens, via French doors, to a home theater with a platform. While the sumptuous master suite is located on the first floor for privacy, four guest suites are available on the second floor. A skylit loft is tucked away on the third floor.

rear exterior

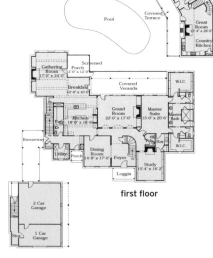

basement

optional layout

first floor

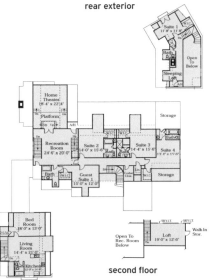

second floor

PLAN: HPK1400179

STYLE: COUNTRY COTTAGE

FIRST FLOOR: 4,654 SQ. FT.

SECOND FLOOR: 1,950 SQ. FT.

TOTAL: 6,604 SQ. FT.

BASEMENT: 1,934 SQ. FT.

BEDROOMS: 4

BATHROOMS: 6½

WIDTH: 122' - 4"

DEPTH: 97' - 0"

FOUNDATION: FINISHED BASEMENT, FINISHED WALKOUT BASEMENT

■ Stately elegance and affluent taste create a rich stone-and-brick facade, met by a floor plan that caters to formality and fun for the family who wants it all! The design begins with a grand foyer, opening through French doors to the study, or under arches to the dining room and gracious living room. The kitchen is created with conversation in mind; nearby, the cheerful nook and family room are ready for casual gatherings. The main-level master suite is highlighted by a romantic fireplace, private porch and an opulent bath. Upstairs, three bedroom suites join a study loft. The lower level can be completed to include exercise, recreation, game, and hobby rooms; a wet bar; and tons of storage.

basement

second floor

first floor

PLAN: HPK1400180

STYLE: TRANSITIONAL
FIRST FLOOR: 2,614 SQ. FT.
SECOND FLOOR: 892 SQ. FT.
TOTAL: 3,506 SQ. FT.
BASEMENT: 1,319 SQ. FT.
BEDROOMS: 4
BATHROOMS: 5
WIDTH: 74' - 1"
DEPTH: 103' - 9"
FOUNDATION: FINISHED
BASEMENT

rear exterior

■ Stone accents and eclectic architecture give this traditional family home a European feel. The covered entry opens directly onto the vaulted living room/family room combination; a fireplace warms the space as large windows and rear-porch access celebrate nature. A bedroom suite to the left would make an outstanding second master suite. A bayed outdoor room with a fireplace is accessed from the master suite and the gourmet island kitchen. Two bedrooms with private baths reside upstairs, along with a playroom. The lower level is all fun and games, with a vast recreation room, media room, studio, and work room that is perfect for hobbies.

basement

first floor

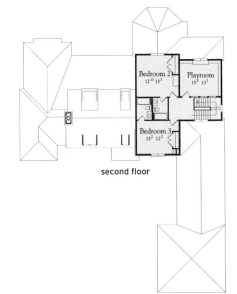

second floor

PLAN: HPK1400181

STYLE: NORMAN

FIRST FLOOR: 3,121 SQ. FT.

SECOND FLOOR: 1,278 SQ. FT.

TOTAL: 4,399 SQ. FT.

BONUS SPACE: 351 SQ. FT.

BEDROOMS: 4

BATHROOMS: 3½ + ½

WIDTH: 86' - 7"

DEPTH: 81' - 4"

FOUNDATION: FINISHED BASEMENT, UNFINISHED BASEMENT

■ A brick/stone facade creates the solid exterior of this French Country design. Inside, a library in the front is warmed by a fireplace, but the heart of the house is found in a large, open great room with a second fireplace. The spacious gourmet kitchen enjoys warmth from the grand room to the left and a third fireplace in the adjoining family room on the right. Access to a rear covered porch and deck/patio can be gained from the family room. There are three bedrooms upstairs and a bonus room/optional fifth bedroom. Each bedroom boasts a walk-in closet and convenient access to a full bath.

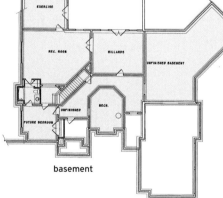

basement

first floor

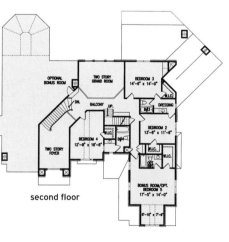

second floor

PLAN: HPK1400182

STYLE: GEORGIAN

FIRST FLOOR: 3,463 SQ. FT.

SECOND FLOOR: 1,924 SQ. FT.

TOTAL: 5,387 SQ. FT.

BEDROOMS: 4

BATHROOMS: 5½

WIDTH: 88' - 6"

DEPTH: 98' - 0"

FOUNDATION: CRAWLSPACE,
FINISHED BASEMENT,
UNFINISHED BASEMENT

■ This magnificent home offers 4 bedrooms, 5½ baths, and curb appeal to beat the band. The elegant foyer opens to the library, the formal dining room, and the breathtaking living room. To the right find the kitchen, breakfast nook and the cozy keeping room. The master suite finds privacy on the far left. The second floor holds three additional bedrooms, four full baths and a rec room.

first floor

second floor

PLAN: HPK1400183

STYLE: MEDITERRANEAN
FIRST FLOOR: 3,340 SQ. FT.
SECOND FLOOR: 1,540 SQ. FT.
THIRD FLOOR: 850 SQ. FT.
TOTAL: 5,730 SQ. FT.
BEDROOMS: 4
BATHROOMS: 4½
WIDTH: 106' - 0"
DEPTH: 82' - 0"
FOUNDATION: FINISHED
BASEMENT

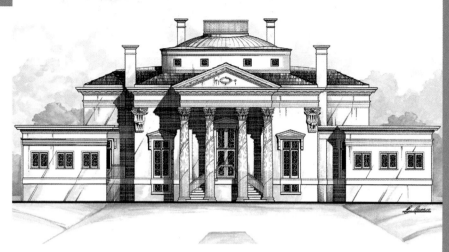

■ This is a grand design—there is no denying it. Symmetrical, ornate, historical, and complex, it speaks to those with the discretion to investigate a very particular kind of estate home. Interior spaces are adorned with distinctive details. The entry and gallery focus on circular stairs with double access to the second-floor landing. Each of the living areas has a unique and decorative ceiling treatment. Even the master bath is enhanced beyond the ordinary. Aspects to appreciate: a formal library, two walk-in pantries, a master bedroom vestibule, double garages, a private master bedroom porch, an elevator, and a gigantic storage area on the second floor.

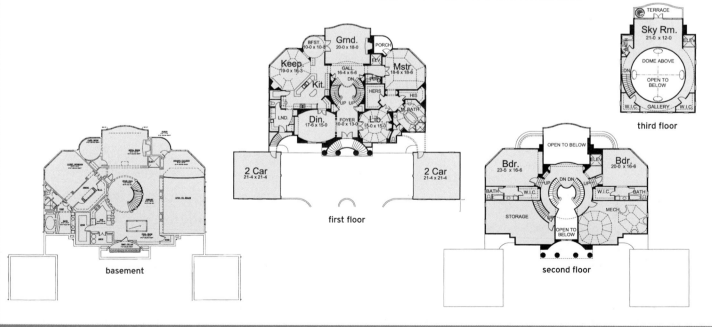

basement

first floor

second floor

third floor

Solid Foundation

Selecting the right hillside home begins with your foundation choice

One theme in this book has been the idea that the opportunities presented by a hillside lot far outweigh the supposed challenges. In fact, by choosing the right foundation for your lot from the start, you can virtually eliminate those challenges—and get on to enjoying your dream home.

The selection process begins with an assessment of your land. For example, some soil conditions may make a finished basement impractical or impossible. In those scenarios, a home with a raised foundation—like those found in this chapter—can be the perfect solution.

Elsewhere, a full or walkout basement may be more suitable. These options, as can be seen in this book, can significantly increase the living space in a home while helping a design adapt to most sloping lots. Walkout basements are especially effective on lots that slope from the front to back. That preserves the architecture of the front of the house, while creating a basement exit in back. Other plans that call for a full basement may need a simple modification to be used as a walkout basement on a hillside lot.

Raised Expectations

Raised foundations offer the flexibility to suit nearly any sloped lot. Long a staple of waterfront areas, raised foundations are equally effective on a mountainside setting. A raised foundation can be especially suited to a site where soil conditions make a fin-ished basement impractical or impossible.

What's more, a raised foundation can help preserve the architectural integrity of a classic home design. A quintessential European design, for example, may not typically fit on a hillside lot. By raising the foundation slightly—with, for example, the design found on page 257—you can achieve that look on virtually any plot of land. Additional examples in this chapter include a classic Southern farmhouse (page 246) or a Neoclassical design with a wrap-around porch (page 239).

Many hillside lots offer cooling breezes and spectacular views. A home with a raised foundation can amplify those gorgeous views ever so slightly, putting you on a stage from which you can enjoy the scenery. ■

Opposite page: Raised or pier foundations are common on beach homes like this one, on page 241, and are also effective on hillside lots. Above: An impressive entryway welcomes you to this raised foundation home, found on page 216.

MAKE IT YOURS

As you search for the perfect home plan, you may find one that very nearly fits your wish list—but falls just short. If that's the case, consider customizing the plan to make it perfect.

Customization could involve changing a garage from two cars to three, altering an exterior building material, or even changing the foundation to better fit your lot. Whatever the case, Hanley Wood's Customization Service can help evaluate your possibilities and make the necessary changes directly to your blueprints. Turn to page 264 for more details.

With customization, you could add a private sitting area overlooking the backyard to this master suite, found on page 237.

Character Building

This design brings a hint of an old barn to a hillside lot

This farmhouse gets all the details right, beginning with the gambrel roof over the garage that seems plucked from a barn along a country dirt road. Porches strike a welcoming pose at both the front and back of the home, and a raised foundation allows it to fit perfectly on this side-sloping lot.

Above: The wraparound porch is an essential part of this home's country appeal. Right: A charming dining room connects easily to the gourmet kitchen.

BRYAN WILLY PHOTOGRAPHY

SMART DESIGN
A raised foundation can make a lot like this one, which slopes from right to left, easily buildable.

Inside you'll find a spacious layout that's consistent with a classic farmhouse, with plenty of room for the entire family. The first floor mixes traditional formal rooms at the front of the room with an open floor plan connecting the more casual spaces. The huge grand room, breakfast area, and country kitchen all connect together easily, and with architectural details that you'll fall in love with—like a window seat flanked by built-in shelves and a wine rack in the breakfast area.

The sunken grand room has a curved wall overlooking the backyard, a view that's shared on the covered porch off the breakfast nook.

Five bedrooms reside upstairs, including the luxurious master suite. It features tray ceilings in the bedroom and bath, plus a sitting area and two walk-in closets. Three of the four other bedrooms have walk-in closets and window seats. Yet another smart detail is found in one of the upstairs bathrooms: a laundry chute. ∎

The two-story foyer has the welcoming feel of an 18th Century farmhouse.

first floor

second floor

PLAN: HPK1400184

STYLE: EUROPEAN COTTAGE
FIRST FLOOR: 1,839 SQ. FT.
SECOND FLOOR: 2,320 SQ. FT.
TOTAL: 4,159 SQ. FT.
BEDROOMS: 5
BATHROOMS: 3½
WIDTH: 61' - 6"
DEPTH: 61' - 0"
FOUNDATION: UNFINISHED WALKOUT BASEMENT, CRAWLSPACE

Three dormers and full-width front porch create a welcoming facade.

Southern Hospitality

Step up to comfort and charm in this picture-perfect Southern farmhouse

Natural light floods the breakfast area and kitchen.

PHOTO BY CHRIS A. LITTLE OF ATLANTA

Just as raised foundation homes offer versatility for location—with applications on mountainsides, beachfront property, or gently sloping hills—they provide almost limitless options for architectural styles as well. Here, a traditional Southern Country home, complete with a full-width front porch, is elevated on a raised foundation that makes it suitable for any sloping lot.

Porches at front and back not only domi-

SMART DESIGN *The raised foundation gives the porches at the front and back of this home beautiful views.*

nate the facade of this home, but create an indoor/outdoor lifestyle as well. No fewer than 12 doors—some of them pairs of French doors—open to the porches, with at least one doorway in every room on the first floor. The result is a home that feels much larger than its already generous 3,200 square feet.

A spacious living room is the centerpiece of the first floor, opening up to the back porch, breakfast area, and kitchen. A dining room, guest bedroom, and large utility room are also on the first floor, as well as the luxurious master suite. With doors opening to both front and back porches, the master suite stretches the entire depth of the house, featuring two walk-in closets and a garden tub.

Upstairs, two more bedrooms each have a walk-in closet and views through the dormers at the front of the house. A third room is designated as an exercise room, but could easily be used as a home office, media room, or fifth bedroom. ■

Above Right: The living room enjoys an open floor plan and access to the back porch.

second floor

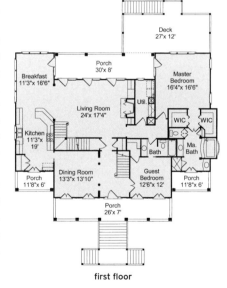

first floor

PLAN: HPK1400185

STYLE: COUNTRY COTTAGE

FIRST FLOOR: 2,213 SQ. FT.

SECOND FLOOR: 1,010 SQ. FT.

TOTAL: 3,223 SQ. FT.

BEDROOMS: 4

BATHROOMS: 4

WIDTH: 61' - 4"

DEPTH: 67' - 0"

FOUNDATION: PIER
(SAME AS PILING)

PLAN: HPK1400186

STYLE: SPANISH COLONIAL

SQUARE FOOTAGE: 2,846

BEDROOMS: 3

BATHROOMS: 3½

WIDTH: 66' - 8"

DEPTH: 91' - 4"

FOUNDATION: PIER

(SAME AS PILING)

■ Looking a bit like a villa resort, this breathtaking Spanish Colonial beauty is designed to pamper every member of the family. Enter from the upper level, or take the garage elevator—great for heavy loads of groceries. The foyer reveals an elegant dining room and unique great room, each with outdoor access. An angled kitchen opens to the bright breakfast nook and is equipped with both a butler's and walk-in pantry. Two bedrooms to the right enjoy private baths. In the left wing, the master suite opens through French doors; past the extra storage closet, the bedroom is bathed in natural light, courtesy of sliding glass doors. An immense walk-in closet and decadent bath with a corner whirlpool tub are wonderful additions. A nearby study is accented with arched windows.

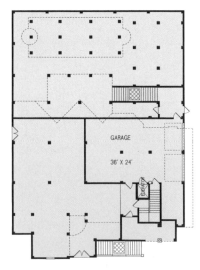

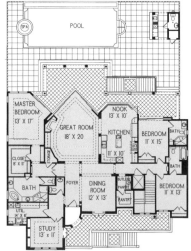

PLAN: HPK1400187

STYLE: SPANISH COLONIAL

SQUARE FOOTAGE: 3,596

BONUS SPACE: 444 SQ. FT.

BEDROOMS: 3

BATHROOMS: 2½ + ½

WIDTH: 97' - 0"

DEPTH: 140' - 6"

FOUNDATION: SLAB

■ What do you get when you cross a traditional family home with a Spanish Colonial villa? Everything! This outstanding plan is suited to any neighborhood, yet retains a strong Southwestern presence. A textured-stucco entry reveals a lush courtyard. To the right, two family bedrooms and a study enjoy privacy and quiet. A vintage-style beamed ceiling continues from the great room and dining room into the island kitchen. The secluded master suite celebrates luxury with a sitting room, private veranda, exercise area, and resplendent bath. A bonus room above the three-car garage provides space for a guest suite. Not to be missed: expanded courtyard/veranda areas and a cabana with a separate bath and outdoor fireplace.

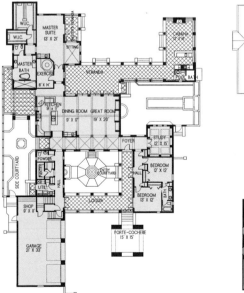

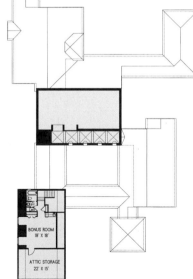

PLAN: HPK1400188

STYLE: TRADITIONAL

FIRST FLOOR: 2,249 SQ. FT.

SECOND FLOOR: 620 SQ. FT.

TOTAL: 2,869 SQ. FT.

BONUS SPACE: 308 SQ. FT.

BEDROOMS: 4

BATHROOMS: 3½

WIDTH: 69' - 6"

DEPTH: 52' - 0"

■ An impressive two-story entrance welcomes you to this stately home. Massive chimneys and pillars and varying rooflines add interest to the stucco exterior. The foyer, lighted by a clerestory window, opens to the formal living and dining rooms. The living room—which could also serve as a study—features a fireplace, as does the family room. Both rooms access the patio. The L-shaped island kitchen opens to a bay-windowed breakfast nook, which is echoed by the sitting area in the master suite. A room next to the kitchen could serve as a bedroom or a home office. The second floor contains two family bedrooms plus a bonus room for future expansion.

rear exterior

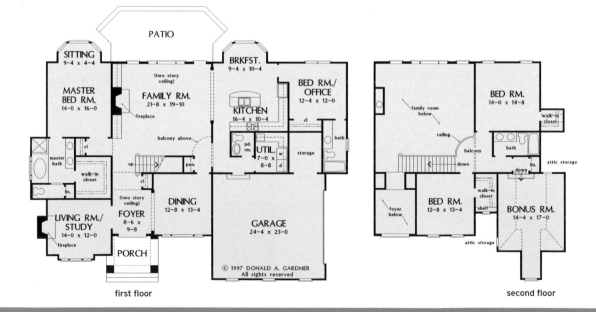

first floor

second floor

PLAN: HPK1400189

STYLE: TRADITIONAL

FIRST FLOOR: 3,226 SQ. FT.

SECOND FLOOR: 2,474 SQ. FT.

TOTAL: 5,700 SQ. FT.

BEDROOMS: 5

BATHROOMS: 4

WIDTH: 118' - 0"

DEPTH: 53' - 0"

FOUNDATION: CRAWLSPACE

■ Your grand entry begins through a double-doored entrance to the foyer, with immediate access to the library on the right, and the dining hall to the left. A gorgeous rounded staircase sprawls before you at the end of the hall. Double doors at the foot of the staircase take you to the resplendent master suite. A grand salon is at the very end of the hall, which leads through to the family room at one end (by the see-through fireplace). The institutional-sized kitchen is optimally designed for all of your culinary needs. The laundry, second staircase, second half-bath, and an elevator are accessible through the kitchen. A morning room is located adjacent to the family room, and accesses onto the veranda. The second floor holds four more bedrooms and a bonus room, a sitting room, studio, upper grand salon, and three more baths, with bookcases in the upper stair hall.

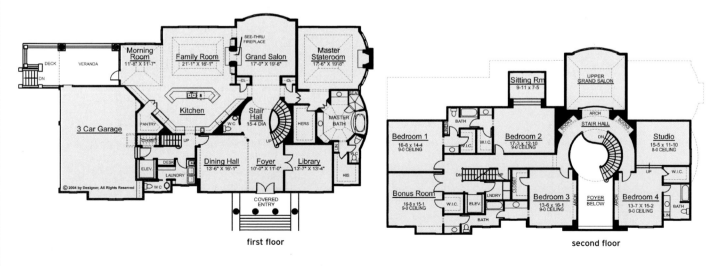

first floor

second floor

PLAN: HPK1400190

STYLE: ITALIANATE

FIRST FLOOR: 1,671 SQ. FT.

SECOND FLOOR: 846 SQ. FT.

TOTAL: 2,517 SQ. FT.

BONUS SPACE: 140 SQ. FT.

BEDROOMS: 3

BATHROOMS: 2

WIDTH: 44' - 0"

DEPTH: 55' - 0"

FOUNDATION: ISLAND

BASEMENT

■ This magnificent villa boasts a beautiful stucco exterior framing a spectacular entry. The heart of the home is served by a well-crafted kitchen with wrapping counter space and an island cooktop counter. The breakfast nook enjoys a view of the veranda and beyond, and brings natural light to the casual eating space. Archways supported by columns separate the dining room from the great room, which boasts a fireplace and built-in cabinetry. On the upper level, the master suite features a sitting area and a private veranda. The master bath provides a knee-space vanity, whirlpool tub, and walk-in closet.

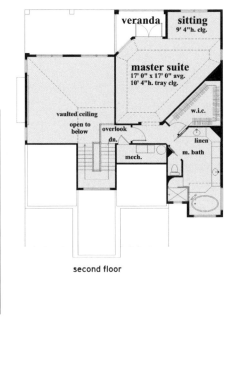

second floor

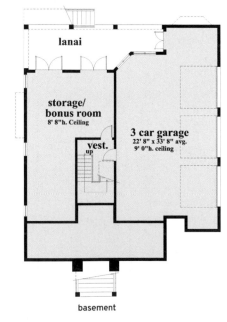

basement

first floor

PLAN: HPK1400191

STYLE: ITALIANATE

SQUARE FOOTAGE: 3,074

BEDROOMS: 3

BATHROOMS: 3½

WIDTH: 77' - 0"

DEPTH: 66' - 8"

FOUNDATION: ISLAND

BASEMENT

■ This stunning paradise achieves its casual European character by mixing Spanish and French influences. A fanlight transom caps the stately entry. The dazzling portico leads to a mid-level foyer and to the grand salon. Two guest suites provide accommodations for visiting relatives and friends. Each of the suites offers a private bath and walk-in closet. A gallery hall connects the suites and leads to a convenient laundry and lower-level staircase. The master wing opens to a private area of the rear covered porch. Nearby, a cabana-style powder room opens to the porch and to the homeowner's private hall. Pocket doors to the study provide a quiet place for reading, web surfing, and quiet conversations.

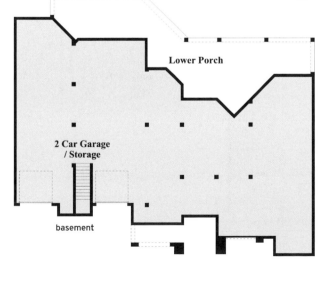

PLAN: HPK1400192

STYLE: BUNGALOW

FIRST FLOOR: 1,537 SQ. FT.

SECOND FLOOR: 812 SQ. FT.

TOTAL: 2,349 SQ. FT.

BONUS SPACE: 869 SQ. FT.

BEDROOMS: 3

BATHROOMS: 2½

WIDTH: 45' - 4"

DEPTH: 50' - 0"

FOUNDATION: ISLAND
BASEMENT

■ Dramatic rooflines complement a striking arched-pediment entry and a variety of windows on this refined facade. The entry porch leads to a landing that rises to the main-level living area—an arrangement well suited for unpredictable climates. A fireplace warms the great room, which sports a tray ceiling and opens to the rear porch through lovely French doors. The gourmet kitchen serves a stunning formal dining room, which offers wide views through a wall of windows. Separate sets of French doors let in natural light and fresh air and permit access to both of the rear porches.

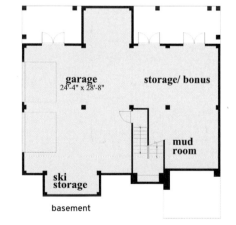

basement

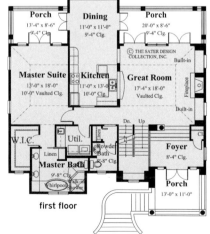

first floor

second floor

PLAN: HPK1400193

STYLE: ITALIANATE

FIRST FLOOR: 1,342 SQ. FT.

SECOND FLOOR: 511 SQ. FT.

TOTAL: 1,853 SQ. FT.

BEDROOMS: 3

BATHROOMS: 2

WIDTH: 44' - 0"

DEPTH: 40' - 0"

FOUNDATION: ISLAND

BASEMENT

■ Historic architectural details and timeless materials come together in this outrageously beautiful home. With a perfect Mediterranean spirit, arch-top windows create curb appeal and allow the beauty and warmth of nature within. To the rear of the plan, an elegant dining room easily flexes to serve traditional events as well as impromptu gatherings. An angled island counter accents the gourmet kitchen and permits wide interior vistas. The master bedroom features a spacious bedroom that leads outside to a private porch. On the upper level, an open deck extends the square footage of one of the secondary bedrooms.

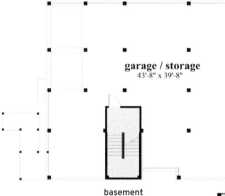

garage / storage
43'-8" x 39'-8"

basement

open deck
17'-0" x 10'-6"

bedroom
13'-8" x 12'-0"
12' clg.

open

loft

bath

bedroom
10'-0" x 13'-2"
12' clg.

second floor

© THE SATER DESIGN COLLECTION, INC.

Porch
17'-0" x 10'-6"

Dining
13'-8" x 12'-4"
8'-0" Clg.

Porch
12'-0" x 6'-6"

Fireplace

Kitchen
14'-0" x14'-2"
8'-0" Clg.

Master
12'-0" x 15'-0"
8'-0" Clg.

Great Room
17'-0" x 21'-4"

Pantry

Foyer

W.I.C.

Dn.

Up.

Utility
8'-0" Clg.

M. Bath
8'-0" Clg.

Up.

Porch
13'-2" x 6'-6"

Walk-in Shower

Whirlpool

first floor

PLAN: HPK1400194

STYLE: CRAFTSMAN

FIRST FLOOR: 1,896 SQ. FT.

SECOND FLOOR: 692 SQ. FT.

TOTAL: 2,588 SQ. FT.

BEDROOMS: 3

BATHROOMS: 2½

WIDTH: 60' - 0"

DEPTH: 84' - 10"

■ This fine three-bedroom home is full of amenities and will surely be a family favorite! A covered porch leads into the great room/dining room. Here, a fireplace reigns at one end, casting its glow throughout the room. A private study is tucked away, perfect for a home office or computer study. The master bedroom suite offers a bayed sitting area, large walk-in closet, and pampering bath. With plenty of counter and cabinet space and an adjacent breakfast area, the kitchen will be a favorite gathering place for casual mealtimes. The family sleeping zone is upstairs and includes two bedrooms, a full bath, a loft/study area, and a huge storage room.

first floor

second floor

PLAN: HPK1400195

STYLE: VACATION

SQUARE FOOTAGE: 1,404

BONUS SPACE: 256 SQ. FT.

BEDROOMS: 2

BATHROOMS: 2

WIDTH: 54' - 7"

DEPTH: 46' - 6"

FOUNDATION: CRAWLSPACE

■ This rustic Craftsman-style cottage provides an open interior with good flow to the outdoors. The front covered porch invites casual gatherings; inside, the dining area is set for both everyday and formal occasions. Meal preparations are a breeze with a cooktop/snack-bar island in the kitchen. A centered fireplace in the great room shares its warmth with the dining room. A rear hall leads to the master bedroom and a secondary bedroom; upstairs, a loft has space for computers.

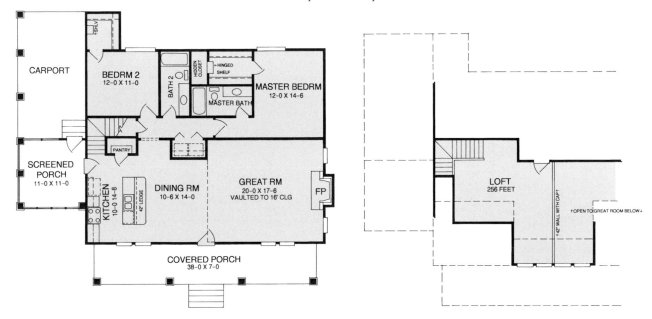

PLAN: HPK1400196

STYLE: BUNGALOW

SQUARE FOOTAGE: 1,120

BONUS SPACE: 1,056 SQ. FT.

BEDROOMS: 3

BATHROOMS: 1½

WIDTH: 44' - 0"

DEPTH: 26' - 0"

FOUNDATION: UNFINISHED BASEMENT

■ This economical three-bedroom, split-level design offers an efficient floor plan that can be expanded. Brick veneer and siding grace the outside, which is further enhanced by three bay windows. The living and dining rooms on the left side of the plan offer a fireplace and buffet alcove. The U-shaped kitchen has loads of cupboards and counter space and connects directly to the dining room. Bedrooms on the right side include a master suite with a half-bath and two family bedrooms sharing a full bath. The lower level includes space for a family room with a fireplace, one or two bedrooms, and a full bath.

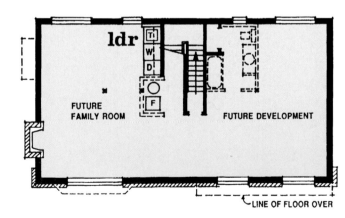

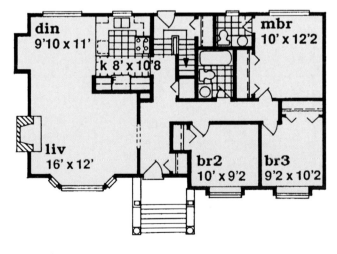

PLAN: HPK1400197

STYLE: SOUTHERN COLONIAL

SQUARE FOOTAGE: 2,240

BEDROOMS: 3

BATHROOMS: 2½

WIDTH: 71' - 10"

DEPTH: 76' - 10"

FOUNDATION: PIER
(SAME AS PILING)

■ Interesting rooflines, keystone arches atop fanlight windows, and a dramatic covered entry precede the masterful plan within. The foyer opens to the dining room on the right and the living room that boasts a wonderful view to the rear porch and deck straight ahead. A sunny breakfast nook adjoins the angled kitchen on the right. The master suite on the left delights with a cozy corner fireplace, access to the deck, and a lavish bath. Two additional bedrooms share a full bath.

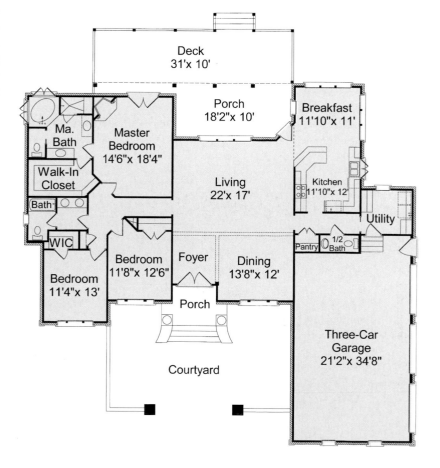

PLAN: HPK1400198

STYLE: SEASIDE

MAIN LEVEL: 2,061 SQ. FT.

UPPER LEVEL: 464 SQ. FT.

TOTAL: 2,525 SQ. FT.

BONUS SPACE: 452 SQ. FT.

BEDROOMS: 5

BATHROOMS: 4

WIDTH: 50' - 0"

DEPTH: 63' - 0"

FOUNDATION: PIER
(SAME AS PILING)

■ This waterfront home offers classic seaboard details with louvered shutters, covered porches, and an open floor plan. The lower level comprises two single-car garages, a game room with an accompanying full bath, and a utility room. The U-shaped staircase leads to the main living areas where the island kitchen is open to the dining room. The living room offers a wall of windows with access to the rear porch and deck. Two bedrooms lie to the left and share a full bath. On the right are the master suite and a fourth bedroom—each with private baths. Upstairs, a fifth bedroom with a bath completes the plan.

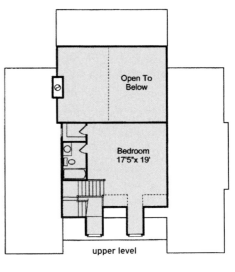

upper level

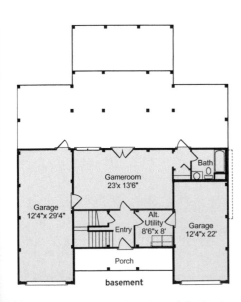

basement

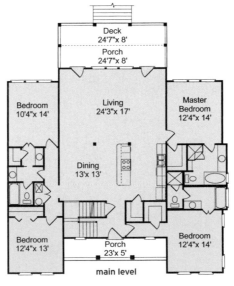

main level

PLAN: HPK1400199

STYLE: TIDEWATER

FIRST FLOOR: 1,855 SQ. FT.

SECOND FLOOR: 901 SQ. FT.

TOTAL: 2,756 SQ. FT.

BEDROOMS: 3

BATHROOMS: 3½

WIDTH: 66' - 0"

DEPTH: 50' - 0"

FOUNDATION: ISLAND BASEMENT

■ This Southern tidewater cottage is the perfect vacation hideaway. An octagonal great room with a multifaceted vaulted ceiling illuminates the interior. The island kitchen is brightened by a bumped-out window and a pass-through to the lanai. Two walk-in closets and a whirlpool bath await to indulge the homeowner in the master suite. A set of double doors opens to the vaulted master lanai for quiet comfort. The U-shaped staircase leads to a loft, which overlooks the great room and the foyer. Two additional family bedrooms offer private baths. A computer center and a morning kitchen complete the upper level.

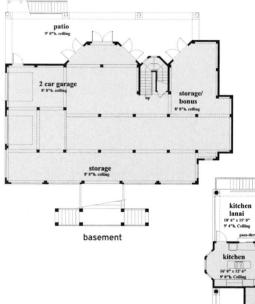

basement

first floor

second floor

PLAN: HPK1400200

STYLE: FLORIDIAN	
FIRST FLOOR: 942 SQ. FT.	
SECOND FLOOR: 571 SQ. FT.	
TOTAL: 1,513 SQ. FT.	
BEDROOMS: 2	
BATHROOMS: 2½	
WIDTH: 32' - 0"	
DEPTH: 53' - 0"	
FOUNDATION: PIER (SAME AS PILING)	

■ The modest detailing of Greek Revival style gave rise to this grand home. A mid-level foyer eases the trip from the ground level to the raised living area, while an arched vestibule announces the great room. The formal dining room offers French-door access to the covered porch. Built-ins, a fireplace, and two ways to access the porch make the great room truly great. A well-appointed kitchen serves a casual eating bar as well as the dining room. Upstairs, each of two private suites has a windowed tub, a vanity, and wardrobe space. A pair of French doors opens each of the bedrooms to an observation sun deck through covered porches.

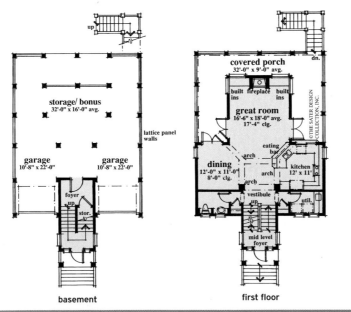
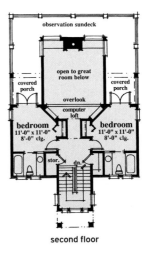

basement

first floor

second floor

PLAN: HPK1400201

STYLE: FLORIDIAN
FIRST FLOOR: 2,725 SQ. FT.
SECOND FLOOR: 1,418 SQ. FT.
TOTAL: 4,143 SQ. FT.
BEDROOMS: 4
BATHROOMS: 5½
WIDTH: 61' - 4"
DEPTH: 62' - 0"
FOUNDATION: ISLAND
BASEMENT

L

■ Florida living takes off in this inventive design. A grand room gains attention as a superb entertaining area. A see-through fireplace here connects this room to the dining room. In the study, quiet time is assured—or slip out the doors and onto the veranda for a breather. A full bath connects the study and Bedroom 2. Bedroom 3 sits on the opposite side of the house and enjoys its own bath. The kitchen features a large work island and a connecting breakfast nook. Upstairs, the master bedroom suite contains His and Hers baths, a see-through fireplace, and access to an upper deck. A guest bedroom suite is located on the other side of the upper floor.

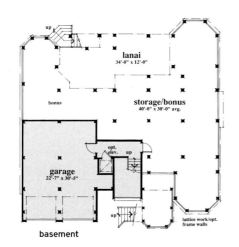

basement

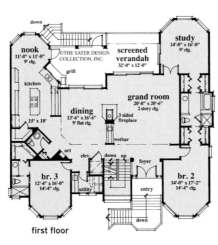

first floor

second floor

PLAN: HPK1400202

STYLE: FLORIDIAN

FIRST FLOOR: 1,136 SQ. FT.

SECOND FLOOR: 636 SQ. FT.

TOTAL: 1,772 SQ. FT.

BEDROOMS: 2

BATHROOMS: 2

WIDTH: 41' - 9"

DEPTH: 45' - 0"

FOUNDATION: SLAB, PIER
(SAME AS PILING)

■ This two-story home's pleasing exterior is complemented by its warm character and decorative "widow's walk." The covered entry—with its dramatic transom window—leads to a spacious great room highlighted by a warming fireplace. To the right, the dining room and kitchen combine to provide a delightful place for mealtimes, with access to a side sun deck through double doors. A study, bedroom, and full bath complete the first floor. The luxurious master suite on the second floor features an oversized walk-in closet and a separate dressing area. The pampering master bath enjoys a relaxing whirlpool tub, double-bowl vanity, and compartmented toilet.

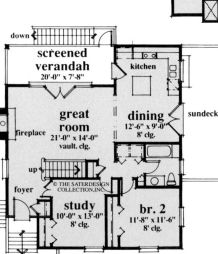

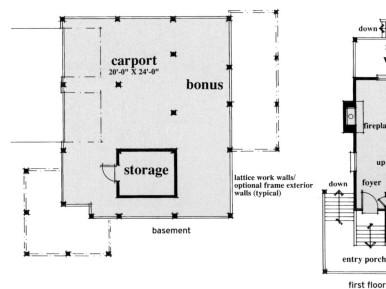

PLAN: HPK1400203

STYLE: FLORIDIAN

FIRST FLOOR: 1,302 SQ. FT.

SECOND FLOOR: 602 SQ. FT.

TOTAL: 1,904 SQ. FT.

BEDROOMS: 3

BATHROOMS: 2½

WIDTH: 48' - 0"

DEPTH: 45' - 0"

FOUNDATION: PIER
(SAME AS PILING)

L

■ An abundance of porches and a deck encourage year-round indoor/outdoor relationships in this classic two-story home. The spacious great room, with its cozy fireplace, and the adjacent dining room both offer access to the screened porch/deck area through French doors. The private master suite accesses both front and rear porches and leads into a relaxing private bath complete with dual vanities and a walk-in closet. An additional family bedroom and a loft/bedroom are also available.

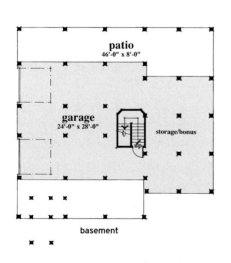

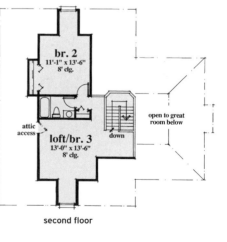

PLAN: HPK1400204

STYLE: COUNTRY COTTAGE
FIRST FLOOR: 1,050 SQ. FT.
SECOND FLOOR: 458 SQ. FT.
TOTAL: 1,508 SQ. FT.
BEDROOMS: 3
BATHROOMS: 2½
WIDTH: 35' - 6"
DEPTH: 39' - 9"
FOUNDATION: PIER
(SAME AS PILING)

■ This adorable abode could serve as a vacation cottage, guest house, starter home, or in-law quarters. The side-gabled design allows for a front porch with a "down-South" feel. Despite the small size, this home is packed with all the necessities. The first-floor master suite has a large bathroom and a walk-in closet. An open, functional floor plan includes a powder room, a kitchen/breakfast nook area, and a family room with a corner fireplace. Upstairs, two additional bedrooms share a bath. One could be used as a home office.

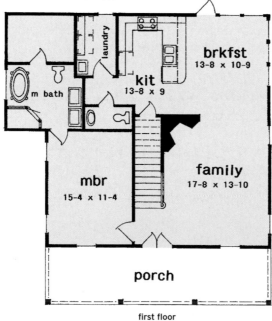

first floor

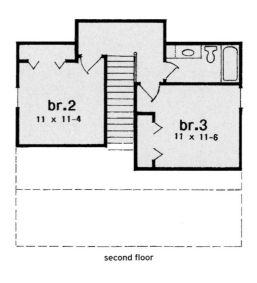

second floor

PLAN: HPK1400205

STYLE: COUNTRY COTTAGE

FIRST FLOOR: 1,045 SQ. FT.

SECOND FLOOR: 690 SQ. FT.

TOTAL: 1,735 SQ. FT.

BEDROOMS: 3

BATHROOMS: 2½

WIDTH: 40' - 4"

DEPTH: 32' - 0"

FOUNDATION: UNFINISHED BASEMENT

■ An oversized dormer with a sunburst window enhances the charm of the raised and covered porch of this three-bedroom home. Inside, the living room contains a fireplace that can also be viewed from the formal dining area. The U-shaped kitchen and sunny breakfast nook open to the rear sun deck, perfect for an outdoor barbecue grill. Privacy is ensured for the master suite with the split floor plan and a powder room for guests. A luxurious master bath ensures relaxation with a large soaking tub, separate shower, twin-vanity sinks, and a roomy walk-in closet. Two family bedrooms on the second floor share a full bath and a sitting area.

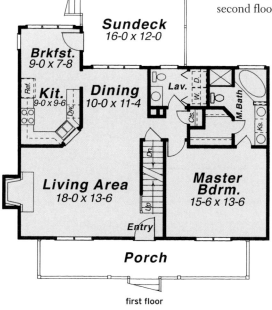

first floor

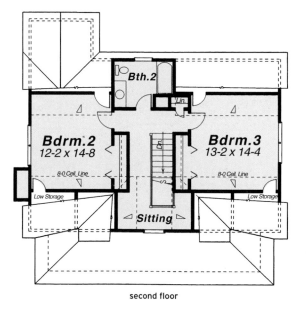

second floor

PLAN: HPK1400206

STYLE: FLORIDIAN

FIRST FLOOR: 1,073 SQ. FT.

SECOND FLOOR: 470 SQ. FT.

TOTAL: 1,543 SQ. FT.

BEDROOMS: 4

BATHROOMS: 2

WIDTH: 30' - 0"

DEPTH: 71' - 6"

FOUNDATION: PIER
(SAME AS PILING)

■ Holding the narrowest of footprints, this adorable little seaside plan is big on interior space—perfect for low-lying beachfront areas. The family room has three big windows and opens to the tiled U-shaped kitchen and breakfast nook, with access to the rear deck. The master bedroom, which includes a walk-in closet, and another bedroom share a full bath on this floor. Two more bedrooms and another bath are upstairs. A convenient utility room is located on the main level.

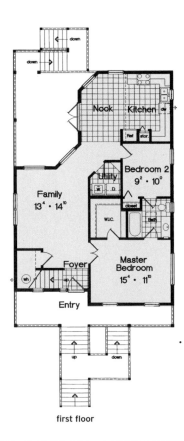

first floor

second floor

PLAN: HPK1400207

STYLE: RESORT LIFESTYLES

SQUARE FOOTAGE: 1,970

BEDROOMS: 3

BATHROOMS: 2

WIDTH: 34' - 8"

DEPTH: 83' - 0"

■ This slim design with triple gables, front and back porches, and a quartet of bay windows is an optimal home for waterfront properties. The great room, dining room, and kitchen are open to one another for a spacious, casual atmosphere. Numerous windows and volume ceilings enhance spaciousness throughout the home. Columns add just the right amount of definition to the open dining room. Up front, two bedrooms, one with access to a private front porch, share a full bath. The master suite is secluded at the rear of the home with back-porch access, dual walk-in closets, and a sumptuous bath with a garden tub and oversized shower.

©1998 Donald A. Gardner, Inc.

PLAN: HPK1400208

STYLE: CONTEMPORARY

FIRST FLOOR: 1,650 SQ. FT.

SECOND FLOOR: 712 SQ. FT.

TOTAL: 2,362 SQ. FT.

BEDROOMS: 3

BATHROOMS: 2½

WIDTH: 58' - 10"

DEPTH: 47' - 4"

■ Cedar shakes and striking gables with decorative scalloped insets adorn the exterior of this lovely coastal home. The generous great room is expanded by a rear wall of windows, with additional light from transom windows above the front door and a rear clerestory dormer. The kitchen features a pass-through to the great room. The dining room, great room, and study all access an inviting back porch. The master bedroom is a treat with a private balcony, His and Hers walk-in closets, and an impeccable bath. Upstairs, a room-sized loft with an arched opening overlooks the great room below. Two more bedrooms, one with its own private balcony, share a hall bath.

first floor

second floor

PLAN: HPK1400209

STYLE: COUNTRY COTTAGE

FIRST FLOOR: 2,129 SQ. FT.

SECOND FLOOR: 1,206 SQ. FT.

TOTAL: 3,335 SQ. FT.

BONUS SPACE: 422 SQ. FT.

BEDROOMS: 4

BATHROOMS: 4

WIDTH: 59' - 4"

DEPTH: 64' - 0"

FOUNDATION: FINISHED WALKOUT BASEMENT

rear exterior

■ French style embellishes this dormered country home. Stepping through French doors to the foyer, the dining area is immediately to the left. To the right is a set of double doors leading to a study or secondary bedroom. A lavish master bedroom provides privacy and plenty of storage space. The living room sports three doors to the rear porch and a lovely fireplace with built-ins. A secluded breakfast nook adjoins an efficient kitchen. Upstairs, two of the three family bedrooms boast dormer windows. Plans include a basement-level garage that adjoins a game room and two handy storage areas.

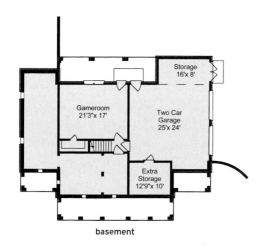

basement

first floor

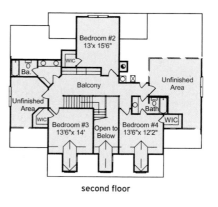

second floor

PLAN: HPK1400210

STYLE: COUNTRY COTTAGE

FIRST FLOOR: 2,086 SQ. FT.

SECOND FLOOR: 1,077 SQ. FT.

TOTAL: 3,163 SQ. FT.

BONUS SPACE: 403 SQ. FT.

BEDROOMS: 4

BATHROOMS: 3½

WIDTH: 81' - 10"

DEPTH: 51' - 8"

■ This beautiful farmhouse, with its prominent twin gables and bays, adds just the right amount of country style. The master suite is quietly tucked away downstairs with no rooms directly above. The family cook will love the spacious U-shaped kitchen and adjoining bayed breakfast nook. A bonus room awaits expansion on the second floor, where three large bedrooms share two full baths. Storage space abounds with walk-ins, half-shelves, and linen closets. A curved balcony borders a versatile loft/study, which overlooks the stunning two-story family room.

rear exterior

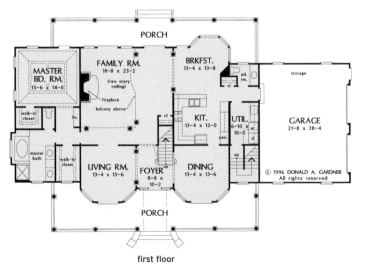

first floor

second floor

PLAN: HPK1400211

STYLE: NEOCLASSIC

FIRST FLOOR: 1,293 SQ. FT.

SECOND FLOOR: 1,138 SQ. FT.

TOTAL: 2,431 SQ. FT.

BONUS SPACE: 575 SQ. FT.

BEDROOMS: 4

BATHROOMS: 2½

WIDTH: 63' - 4"

DEPTH: 53' - 4"

FOUNDATION: UNFINISHED
BASEMENT, CRAWLSPACE, SLAB

■ Spacious rooms arranged around a central foyer, plus a charming, warm, and dignified exterior, result in a home for quality family living. Enter the house through a welcoming wraparound porch into an impressive two-story foyer. Formal living and dining rooms are presented on each side of the foyer. Rooms for the informal activities are placed in the rear; the family room merges with the dinette and is separated by a wet bar. An oversized master bedroom boasts a huge walk-in closet, a roomy bath with double basins, whirlpool tub, stall shower, and a decorative window. The efficient U-shaped kitchen is equipped with a pantry and an adjacent planning desk.

first floor

second floor

PLAN: HPK1400212

STYLE: VACATION

FIRST FLOOR: 1,623 SQ. FT.

SECOND FLOOR: 978 SQ. FT.

TOTAL: 2,601 SQ. FT.

BEDROOMS: 3

BATHROOMS: 2

WIDTH: 48' - 0"

DEPTH: 57' - 0"

FOUNDATION: PIER
(SAME AS PILING)

■ Offering a large wraparound porch, this fine two-story pier home is full of amenities. The living room has a warming fireplace and plenty of windows to enjoy the view. The galley kitchen features unique angles, with a large island/peninsula separating this room from the dining area. Two bedrooms share a bath and easy access to the laundry facilities. Upstairs, a lavish master suite is complete with a detailed ceiling, a private covered porch, a walk-in closet, and a pampering bath. A nearby study—or make it a secondary bedroom—features a walk-in closet.

first floor

second floor

PLAN: HPK1400213

STYLE: SEASIDE

FIRST FLOOR: 1,056 SQ. FT.

SECOND FLOOR: 807 SQ. FT.

TOTAL: 1,863 SQ. FT.

BEDROOMS: 4

BATHROOMS: 3

WIDTH: 33' - 0"

DEPTH: 54' - 0"

FOUNDATION: CRAWLSPACE,
PIER (SAME AS PILING)

■ Run up a flight of stairs to an attractive four-bedroom home! The living room features a fireplace and easy access to the L-shaped kitchen. Here, a work island makes meal preparation a breeze. Two family bedrooms share a full bath and access to the laundry facilities. Upstairs, a third bedroom offers a private bath and two walk-in closets. The master suite is complete with a pampering bath, two walk-in closets, and a large private balcony.

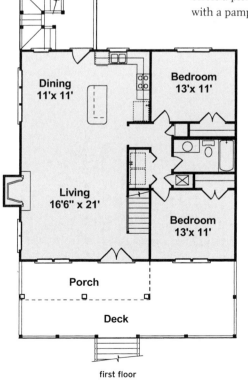

first floor

second floor

PLAN: HPK1400214

STYLE: PLANTATION

FIRST FLOOR: 2,193 SQ. FT.

SECOND FLOOR: 1,136 SQ. FT.

TOTAL: 3,329 SQ. FT.

BONUS SPACE: 347 SQ. FT.

BEDROOMS: 4

BATHROOMS: 4

WIDTH: 41' - 6"

DEPTH: 71' - 4"

FOUNDATION: PIER
(SAME AS PILING)

■ This farmhouse is far from old-fashioned with a computer loft/library and future game room designed into the second floor. Two wrapping porches grace the exterior, offering expanded outdoor living spaces. The breakfast nook, dining room, and family room radiate off the central island kitchen. The study/bedroom at the front is situated with an adjacent full bath, making this ideal for a guest room. Three bedrooms share two baths on the second floor while the master suite, with its elaborate private bath, finds seclusion on the first floor.

first floor

second floor

PLAN: HPK1400215

STYLE: RESORT LIFESTYLES

FIRST FLOOR: 1,500 SQ. FT.

SECOND FLOOR: 1,112 SQ. FT.

TOTAL: 2,612 SQ. FT.

BEDROOMS: 4

BATHROOMS: 3

WIDTH: 42' - 0"

DEPTH: 49' - 6"

© 2000 Donald A. Gardner, Inc.

■ Porches front and back, a multitude of windows, and a narrow facade make this elevated pier foundation perfect for beach property or any waterfront lot. The main living areas are positioned at the rear of the home for the best views of the water. The great room features a vaulted ceiling, fireplace, and back porch access. The kitchen is open, sharing space with a bayed breakfast area and lovely sun room. The first floor includes a bedroom/study and full bath, while the master suite and two more family bedrooms can be found upstairs. The master suite boasts a private porch and sitting room with bay window.

first floor

second floor

PLAN: HPK1400216

STYLE: PLANTATION

FIRST FLOOR: 1,742 SQ. FT.

SECOND FLOOR: 1,624 SQ. FT.

TOTAL: 3,366 SQ. FT.

BEDROOMS: 4

BATHROOMS: 3

WIDTH: 42' - 10"

DEPTH: 77' - 6"

FOUNDATION: PIER
(SAME AS PILING)

■ Porches abound upon this grand, two-story home—perfect for nature enthusiasts. The first floor holds the entertaining spaces with the island kitchen acting as a hub around which all activity revolves. The den, with a cozy corner fireplace, and the breakfast nook are ideal for more intimate situations. On the second floor, the master suite pampers with a luxurious bath and a private porch. Two additional bedrooms share a full bath on this floor; the first-floor bedroom works well as a guest bedroom.

first floor

second floor

PLAN: HPK1400217

STYLE: COUNTRY COTTAGE

FIRST FLOOR: 1,901 SQ. FT.

SECOND FLOOR: 1,874 SQ. FT.

TOTAL: 3,775 SQ. FT.

BEDROOMS: 4

BATHROOMS: 3½

WIDTH: 50' - 0"

DEPTH: 70' - 0"

FOUNDATION: PIER
(SAME AS PILING)

■ This elegant Charleston townhouse is enhanced by Southern grace and three levels of charming livability. Covered porches offer outdoor living space at every level. The first floor offers a living room warmed by a fireplace, an island kitchen serving a bayed nook, and a formal dining room. A first-floor guest bedroom is located at the front of the plan, along with a laundry and powder room. The second level offers a sumptuous master suite boasting a private balcony, a master bath, and enormous walk-in closet. Two other bedrooms sharing a Jack-and-Jill bath are also on this level. The basement level includes a three-car garage and game room warmed by a fireplace.

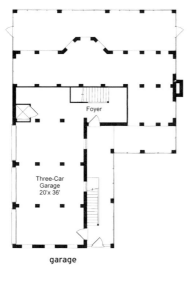

garage

first floor

second floor

PLAN: HPK1400218

STYLE: PLANTATION
FIRST FLOOR: 2,236 SQ. FT.
SECOND FLOOR: 1,208 SQ. FT.
TOTAL: 3,444 SQ. FT.
BONUS SPACE: 318 SQ. FT.
BEDROOMS: 4
BATHROOMS: 4
WIDTH: 42' - 6"
DEPTH: 71' - 4"
FOUNDATION: PIER
(SAME AS PILING)

■ This spacious home offers a front porch and a second-floor balcony as well as a wraparound porch in the rear. The elegant foyer, with its grand staircase, is flanked by the dining room on the left and the study on the right. The island kitchen adjoins the family room and the sunny breakfast nook. The master suite, with an elaborate private bath, is secluded in the back for privacy. Three additional bedrooms—one with a sitting room—share two full baths on the second floor.

first floor

second floor

PLAN: HPK1400219

STYLE: VICTORIAN

FIRST FLOOR: 1,182 SQ. FT.

SECOND FLOOR: 838 SQ. FT.

TOTAL: 2,020 SQ. FT.

BEDROOMS: 4

BATHROOMS: 3

WIDTH: 34' - 0"

DEPTH: 52' - 0"

FOUNDATION: PIER
(SAME AS PILING)

■ This two-story coastal home finds its inspiration in a Craftsman style that's highlighted by ornamented gables. Open planning is the key with the living and dining areas sharing the front of the first floor with the U-shaped kitchen and stairway. Both the dining room and the living room access the second porch. The master suite boasts a walk-in closet, private vanity, and angled tub. The utility room is efficiently placed between the kitchen and bath. Bedrooms 2 and 3 share a bath while Bedroom 4 enjoys a private bath.

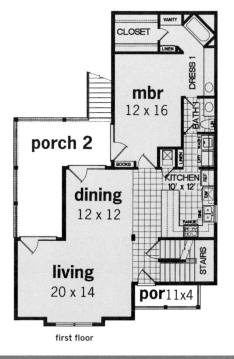

first floor

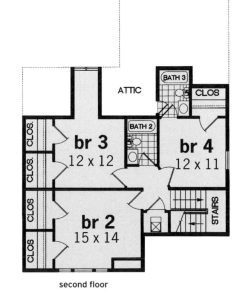

second floor

PLAN: HPK1400220

STYLE: PLANTATION

FIRST FLOOR: 2,578 SQ. FT.

SECOND FLOOR: 1,277 SQ. FT.

TOTAL: 3,855 SQ. FT.

BEDROOMS: 4

BATHROOMS: 4

WIDTH: 53' - 6"

DEPTH: 97' - 0"

FOUNDATION: PIER
(SAME AS PILING)

■ This charming Charleston design is full of surprises! Perfect for a narrow footprint, the raised foundation is ideal for a waterfront location. An entry porch introduces a winding staircase. To the right is a living room/library that functions as a formal entertaining space. A large hearth and two sets of French doors to the covered porch enhance the great room. The master suite is positioned for privacy and includes great amenities that work to relax the homeowners. Upstairs, three family bedrooms, two full baths, an open media room, and a future game room create a fantastic casual family space.

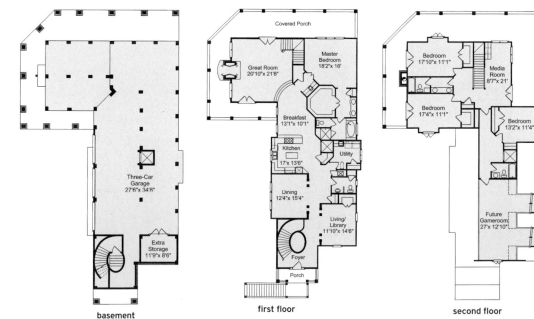

basement

first floor

second floor

PLAN: HPK1400221

STYLE: COUNTRY COTTAGE

FIRST FLOOR: 832 SQ. FT.

SECOND FLOOR: 278 SQ. FT.

TOTAL: 1,110 SQ. FT.

BEDROOMS: 2

BATHROOMS: 2

WIDTH: 32' - 0"

DEPTH: 34' - 0"

FOUNDATION: PIER
(SAME AS PILING)

■ Designed for the relaxing coastal lifestyle, this casual beach house aims to please, with three well-planned levels. The lower level has French doors to the front for privacy and opens to reveal a carport, covered porch, tons of storage (great for sandy surfboards), and an enclosed entry/utility area. The main level features a two-story living room with a wonderful porch that stretches the length of the house. The kitchen is efficient and easily serves the dining area. The master bedroom has an ample walk-in closet and is conveniently adjacent to a full bath. Upstairs, an additional bedroom has a semiprivate bath and accesses the observation room for amazing ocean sunset views.

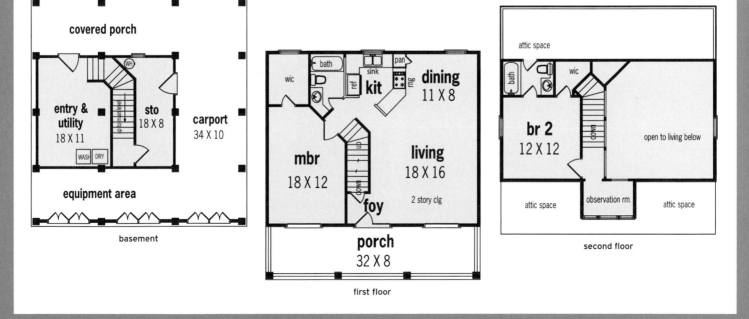

PLAN: HPK1400222

STYLE: FLORIDIAN

SQUARE FOOTAGE: 2,190

BONUS SPACE: 875 SQ. FT.

BEDROOMS: 3

BATHROOMS: 2

WIDTH: 58' - 0"

DEPTH: 54' - 0"

FOUNDATION: SLAB

■ A strikingly simple staircase leads to the dramatic entry of this contemporary design. The foyer opens to a grand room with a fireplace and a built-in entertainment center. An expansive lanai opens from the living area and offers outdoor relaxation. For traditional occasions, a front-facing dining room offers a place for elegant entertaining. The master suite features a lavish bath with two walk-in closets, a whirlpool tub, and twin lavatories. Double doors open from the gallery hall to a study that is convenient to the master bedroom. Two additional bedrooms share a private hall and a full bath on the opposite side of the plan.

QUOTE ONE®

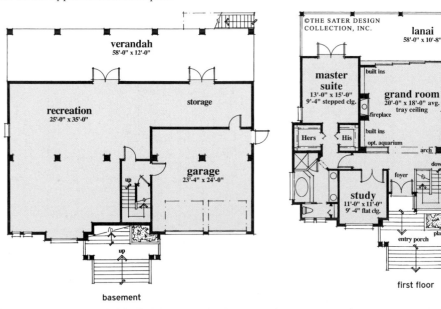

PLAN: HPK1400223

STYLE: COUNTRY COTTAGE

FIRST FLOOR: 2,390 SQ. FT.

SECOND FLOOR: 1,200 SQ. FT.

TOTAL: 3,590 SQ. FT.

BEDROOMS: 4

BATHROOMS: 3

WIDTH: 61' - 0"

DEPTH: 64' - 4"

FOUNDATION: PIER
(SAME AS PILING)

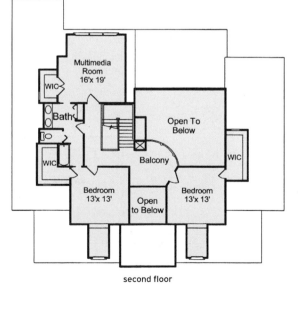

rear exterior

■ This luxurious waterfront design sings of southern island influences. A front covered porch opens to a foyer, flanked by a study and dining room. The living room, warmed by a fireplace and safe from off-season ocean breezes, overlooks the rear covered porch. The island kitchen extends into a breakfast room. Beyond the covered porch, the wood deck is also accessed privately from the master suite. This suite includes a private whirlpool bath and huge walk-in closet. A guest suite is located on the first floor, while two additional bedrooms and a multimedia room are located on the second level.

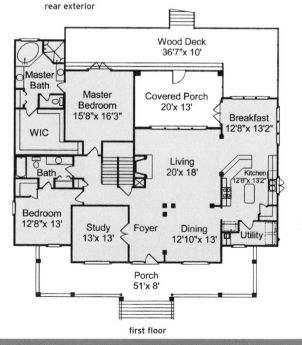

first floor

second floor

PLAN: HPK1400224

STYLE: FLORIDIAN
FIRST FLOOR: 1,736 SQ. FT.
SECOND FLOOR: 640 SQ. FT.
TOTAL: 2,376 SQ. FT.
BONUS SPACE: 840 SQ. FT.
BEDROOMS: 3
BATHROOMS: 2
WIDTH: 54' - 0"
DEPTH: 44' - 0"
FOUNDATION: SLAB

■ Lattice door panels, shutters, a balustrade, and a metal roof add character to this delightful coastal home. Double doors flanking a fireplace open to the side sundeck from the spacious great room. Access to the rear veranda is also provided from this room. An adjacent dining room provides views of the rear grounds and space for formal and informal entertaining. The glassed-in nook shares space with the L-shaped kitchen containing a center work island. Bedrooms 2 and 3, a full bath, and a utility room complete this floor. Upstairs, a sumptuous master suite awaits. Double doors extend to a private deck from the master bedroom. His and Hers walk-in closets lead the way to a grand bath featuring an arched whirlpool tub, a double-bowl vanity, and a separate shower.

second floor

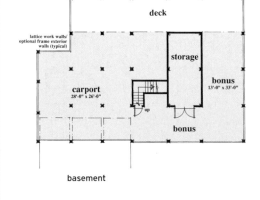

basement

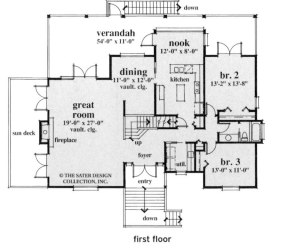

first floor

PLAN: HPK1400225

STYLE: TIDEWATER

SQUARE FOOTAGE: 3,074

BEDROOMS: 3

BATHROOMS: 3½

WIDTH: 77' - 0"

DEPTH: 66' - 8"

FOUNDATION: ISLAND BASEMENT

■ The individual charm and natural beauty of this sensational home reside in its pure symmetry and perfect blend of past and future. A steeply pitched roof caps a collection of Prairie-style windows and elegant columns. The portico leads to a midlevel foyer, which rises to the grand salon. A wide-open leisure room hosts a corner fireplace that's ultra cozy. The master wing sprawls from the front portico to the rear covered porch, rich with luxury amenities and plenty of secluded space.

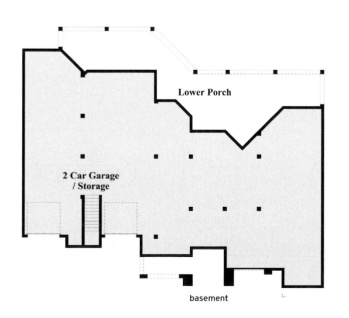

basement

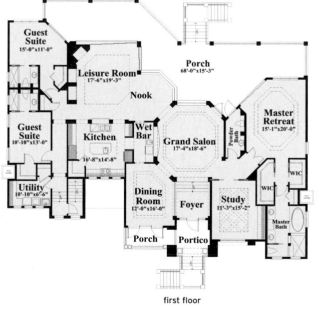

first floor

Homes With Raised Foundations

PLAN: HPK1400226

STYLE: COUNTRY COTTAGE
FIRST FLOOR: 2,036 SQ. FT.
SECOND FLOOR: 1,230 SQ. FT.
TOTAL: 3,266 SQ. FT.
BEDROOMS: 5
BATHROOMS: 3½
WIDTH: 57' - 4"
DEPTH: 59' - 0"
FOUNDATION: PIER
(SAME AS PILING)

■ The standing-seam metal roof adds character to this four- (or five-) bedroom home. The covered front porch, screened porch, and rear deck add outdoor living spaces for nature enthusiasts. A flexible room is found to the left of the foyer and the dining room is to the right. The galley kitchen is accessed through an archway with a sunny breakfast nook adjoining at the back. The lavish master suite is on the left with a private bath that includes access to the laundry room. The second floor holds three bedrooms and a multimedia room where the family can spend quality time in a casual atmosphere.

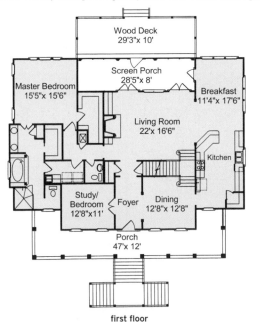

first floor

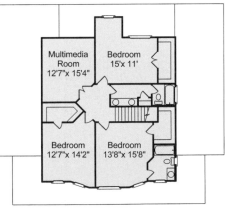

second floor

CHRIS A. LITTLE FROM ATLANTA; COURTESY OF CHATHAM HOME PLANNING, INC. THIS HOME, AS SHOWN IN THE PHOTOGRAPH, MAY DIFFER FROM THE ACTUAL BLUEPRINTS. FOR MORE DETAILED INFORMATION, PLEASE CHECK THE FLOOR PLANS CAREFULLY.

PLAN: HPK1400227

STYLE: RESORT LIFESTYLES

FIRST FLOOR: 1,620 SQ. FT.

SECOND FLOOR: 770 SQ. FT.

TOTAL: 2,390 SQ. FT.

BEDROOMS: 3

BATHROOMS: 3½

WIDTH: 49' - 0"

DEPTH: 58' - 8"

© 2000 Donald A. Gardner, Inc.

■ Multiple gables, a center dormer with arched clerestory window, and a striking front staircase create visual excitement for this three-bedroom coastal home. Vaulted ceilings in the foyer and great room highlight a dramatic second-floor balcony that connects the two upstairs bedrooms, each with its own bath and private porch. The great room is generously proportioned with built-ins on either side of the fireplace. Private back porches enhance the dining room and the master suite, which boasts His and Her walk-in closets and a magnificent bath with dual vanities, a garden tub, and separate shower.

first floor

second floor

PLAN: HPK1400228

STYLE: SEASIDE

FIRST FLOOR: 1,552 SQ. FT.

SECOND FLOOR: 653 SQ. FT.

TOTAL: 2,205 SQ. FT.

BEDROOMS: 3

BATHROOMS: 2

WIDTH: 60' - 0"

DEPTH: 50' - 0"

FOUNDATION: PIER
(SAME AS PILING)

■ A split staircase adds flair to this European-style coastal home, where a fireplace brings warmth on chilly evenings. The foyer opens to the expansive living/dining area and island kitchen. A multitude of windows fills the interior with sunlight and ocean breezes. The wraparound rear deck finds access near the kitchen. The utility room is conveniently tucked between the kitchen and the two first-floor bedrooms. The second-floor master suite offers a private deck and a luxurious bath with a garden tub, shower, and walk-in closet.

rear exterior

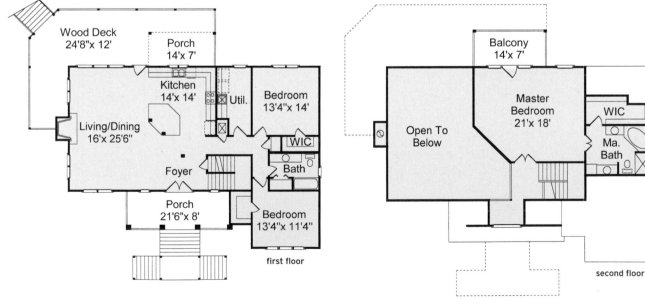

first floor

second floor

PHOTO COURTESY OF CHATHAM HOME PLANNING, INC.CHRIS A. LITTLE OF ATLANTA (PHOTOGRAPHER) THIS HOME, AS SHOWN IN THE PHOTOGRAPH, MAY DIFFER FROM THE ACTUAL BLUEPRINTS. FOR MORE DETAILED INFORMATION, PLEASE CHECK THE FLOOR PLANS CAREFULLY.

PLAN: HPK1400229

STYLE: EUROPEAN COTTAGE

SQUARE FOOTAGE: 2,413

BEDROOMS: 3

BATHROOMS: 3

WIDTH: 66' - 4"

DEPTH: 62' - 10"

© 2000 Donald A. Gardner, Inc.

■ An impressive hipped roof and unique, turret-style roofs top the two front bedrooms of this extraordinary coastal home. An arched window in an eyebrow dormer crowns the double-door front entrance. A remarkable foyer creates quite a first impression and leads to the generous great room via a distinctive gallery with columns and a tray ceiling. The great room, master bedroom, and master bath also boast tray ceilings—as well as numerous windows and back-porch access. The master bedroom not only provides a substantial amount of space in the walk-in closet, but also features a garden tub and massive shower. A delightful breakfast area and bay window complement the kitchen.

PLAN: HPK1400230

STYLE: LAKEFRONT

SQUARE FOOTAGE: 1,114

BEDROOMS: 2

BATHROOMS: 1

WIDTH: 39' - 8"

DEPTH: 36' - 4"

FOUNDATION: UNFINISHED
BASEMENT

■ Lakeside or curbside, this 1,114-square-foot design soars to new heights for relaxed living. A second-story portico and walls of light-loving windows surround the exterior. The master bedroom with full bath and family room with fireplace enjoy lofty cathedral ceilings. A spacious second bedroom, rounded kitchen with sprawling lunch counter, and gracious dining room complement this outstanding space.

PLAN: HPK1400231

STYLE: SEASIDE
FIRST FLOOR: 1,383 SQ. FT.
SECOND FLOOR: 595 SQ. FT.
TOTAL: 1,978 SQ. FT.
BONUS SPACE: 617 SQ. FT.
BEDROOMS: 3
BATHROOMS: 2
WIDTH: 48' - 0"
DEPTH: 42' - 0"
FOUNDATION: ISLAND
BASEMENT

■ This fabulous Key West home blends interior space with the great outdoors. Designed for a balmy climate, this home boasts expansive porches and decks—with outside access from every area of the home. A sun-dappled foyer leads via a stately midlevel staircase to a splendid great room, which features a warming fireplace tucked in beside beautiful built-in cabinetry. Highlighted by a wall of glass that opens to the rear porch, this two-story living space opens to the formal dining room and a well-appointed kitchen. Spacious secondary bedrooms on the main level open to outside spaces and share a full bath. Upstairs, a 10-foot tray ceiling highlights a private master suite, which provides French doors to an upper-level porch.

basement

first floor

second floor

PLAN: HPK1400232

STYLE: LAKEFRONT
FIRST FLOOR: 967 SQ. FT.
SECOND FLOOR: 1,076 SQ. FT.
THIRD FLOOR: 349 SQ. FT.
TOTAL: 2,392 SQ. FT.
BEDROOMS: 5
BATHROOMS: 3½
WIDTH: 39' - 8"
DEPTH: 36' - 8"
FOUNDATION: PIER
(SAME AS PILING)

■ Three levels of beach living at its finest! From the shore this house will stand out with its spectacular porches, balconies, and staircases. Starting from the top you'll find a guest room with its own bathroom, secluded for privacy. The second level holds a kitchen with an island for informal meals and a dining room for more formal entertaining occasions. The dining room and family room both enjoy access to a balcony. The master suite is also on this level and includes an expansive closet leading to the master bath. Three more bedrooms, a full bath, and the living room occupy the first level, along with a laundry room—necessary for keeping beach clothes sand-free.

third floor

first floor

second floor

PLAN: HPK1400233

STYLE: FLORIDIAN

FIRST FLOOR: 2,066 SQ. FT.

SECOND FLOOR: 809 SQ. FT.

TOTAL: 2,875 SQ. FT.

BONUS SPACE: 1,260 SQ. FT.

BEDROOMS: 3

BATHROOMS: 3½

WIDTH: 64' - 0"

DEPTH: 45' - 0"

FOUNDATION: PIER
(SAME AS PILING)

■ If entertaining is your passion, then this is the design for you. With a large, open floor plan and an array of amenities, every gathering will be a success. The foyer embraces living areas accented by a glass fireplace and a wet bar. The grand room and dining room each access a screened veranda for outside enjoyments. The gourmet kitchen delights with its openness to the rest of the house. A morning nook here also adds a nice touch. Two bedrooms and a study radiate from the first-floor living areas. Upstairs is a masterful master suite. It contains a huge walk-in closet, a whirlpool tub, and a private sundeck with a spa.

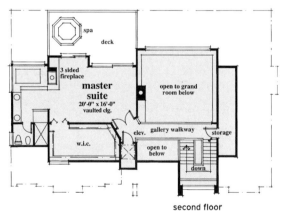

second floor

hanley▲wood
SELECTION, CONVENIENCE, SERVICE!

With more than 50 years of experience in the industry and millions of blueprints sold, Hanley Wood is a trusted source of high-quality, high-value pre-drawn home plans.

Using pre-drawn home plans is a **reliable, cost-effective way** to build your dream home, and our vast selection of plans is second-to-none. The nation's finest designers craft these plans that builders know they can trust. Meanwhile, our friendly, knowledgeable customer service representatives can help you every step of the way.

WHAT YOU'LL GET WITH YOUR ORDER

The contents of each designer's blueprint package is unique, but all contain detailed, high-quality working drawings. You can expect to find the following standard elements in most sets of plans:

1. FRONT PERSPECTIVE

This artist's sketch of the exterior of the house gives you an idea of how the house will look when built and landscaped.

2. FOUNDATION AND BASEMENT PLANS

This sheet shows the foundation layout including concrete walls, footings, pads, posts, beams, and bearing walls, and foundation notes. If the home features a basement, the first-floor framing details may also be included on this plan. If your plan features slab construction rather than a basement, the plan shows footings and details for a monolithic slab. This page, or another in the set, may include a sample plot plan for locating your house on a building site. Additional sheets focus on foundation cross-sections and other details.

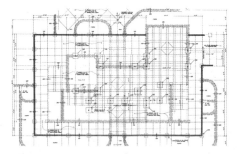

3. DETAILED FLOOR PLANS

These plans show the layout of each floor of the house. Rooms and interior spaces are carefully dimensioned, doors and windows located, and keys are given for cross-section details provided elsewhere in the plans.

4. HOUSE AND DETAIL CROSS-SECTIONS

Large-scale views show sections or cutaways of the foundation, interior walls, exterior walls, floors, stairways, and roof details. Additional cross-sections may show important changes in floor, ceiling, or roof heights, or the relationship of one level to another. These sections show exactly how the various parts of the house fit together and are extremely valuable during construction. Additional sheets may include enlarged wall, floor, and roof construction details.

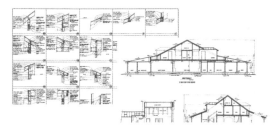

5. ROOF AND FLOOR STRUCTURAL SUPPORTS

The roof and floor framing plans provide detail for these crucial elements of your home. Each includes floor joist, ceiling joist, rafter and roof joist size, spacing, direction, span, and specifications. Beam and window headers, along with necessary details for framing connections, stairways, skylights, or dormers are also included.

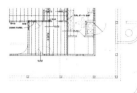

6. ELECTRICAL PLAN

The electrical plan offers a detailed outline of all wiring for your home, with notes for all lighting, outlets, switches, and circuits. A layout is provided for each level, as well as basements, garages, or other structures.

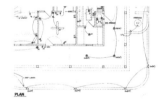

7. EXTERIOR ELEVATIONS

In addition to the front exterior, your blueprint set will include drawings of the rear and sides of your house as well. These drawings give notes on exterior materials and finishes. Particular attention is given to cornice detail, brick and stone accents, or other finish items that make your home unique.

BEFORE YOU CALL

You are making a terrific decision to use a pre-drawn house plan—it is one you can make with confidence, knowing that your blueprints are crafted by national-award-winning certified residential designers and architects, and trusted by builders.

Once you've selected the plan you want—or even if you have questions along the way—our experienced customer service representatives are available 24 hours a day, seven days a week to help you navigate the home-building process. To help them provide you with even better service, please consider the following questions before you call:

■ Have you chosen or purchased your lot?
If so, please review the building setback requirements of your local building authority before you call. You don't need to have a lot before ordering plans, but if you own land already, please have the width and depth dimensions handy when you call.

■ Have you chosen a builder?
Involving your builder in the plan selection and evaluation process may be beneficial. Luckily, builders know they can have confidence with pre-drawn plans because they've been designed for livability, functionality, and typically are builder-proven at successful home sites across the country.

■ Do you need a construction loan?
Construction loans are unique because they involve determining the value of something that is not yet constructed. Several lenders offer convenient contstruction-to-permanent loans. It is important to choose a good lending partner—one who will help guide you through the application and appraisal process. Most will even help you evaluate your contractor to ensure reliability and credit worthiness. Our partnership with IndyMac Bank, a nationwide leader in construction loans, can help you save on your loan, if needed.

■ How many sets of plans do you need?
Building a home can typically require a number of sets of blueprints—one for yourself, two or three for the builder and subcontractors, two for the local building department, and one or more for your lender. For this reason, we offer 5- and 8-set plan packages, but your best value is the Reproducible Plan Package. Reproducible plans are accompanied by a license to make modifications and typically up to 12 duplicates of the plan so you have enough copies of the plan for everyone involved in the financing and construction of your home.

■ Do you want to make any changes to the plan?
We understand that it is difficult to find blueprints for a home that will meet all of your needs. That is why Hanley Wood is glad to offer plan Customization Services. We will work with you to design the modifications you'd like to see and to adjust your blueprint plans accordingly—anything from changing the foundation; adding square footage, redesigning baths, kitchens, or bedrooms; or most other modifications. This simple, cost-effective service saves you from hiring an outside architect to make alterations. Modifications may only be made to Reproducible Plan Packages that include the license to modify.

■ Do you have to make any changes to meet local building codes?
While all of our plans are drawn to meet national building codes at the time they were created, many areas required that plans be stamped by a local engineer to certify that they meet local building codes. Building codes are updated frequently and can vary by state, county, city, or municipality. Contact your local building inspection department, office of planning and zoning, or department of permits to determine how your local codes will affect your construction project. The best way to assure that you can make changes to your plan, if necessary, is to purchase a Reproducible Plan Package.

■ Has everyone—from family members to contractors—been involved in selecting the plan?
Building a new home is an exciting process, and using pre-drawn plans is a great way to realize your dreams. Make sure that everyone involved has had an opportunity to review the plan you've selected. While Hanley Wood is the only plans provider with an exchange policy, it's best to be sure all parties agree on your selection before you buy.

CALL TOLL-FREE 1-800-521-6797

Source Key
HPK14

CUSTOMIZE YOUR PLAN –
HANLEY WOOD CUSTOMIZATION SERVICES

Creating custom home plans has never been easier and more directly accessible. Using state-of-the-art technology and top-performing architectural expertise, Hanley Wood delivers on a long-standing customer commitment to provide world-class home-plans and customization services. Our valued customers—professional home builders and individual home owners—appreciate the convenience and accessibility of this interactive, consultative service.

With the Hanley Wood Customization Service you can:
- Save valuable time by avoiding drawn-out and frequently repetitive face-to-face design meetings
- Communicate design and home-plan changes faster and more efficiently
- Speed-up project turn-around time

- Build on a budget without sacrificing quality
- Transform master home plans to suit your design needs and unique personal style

All of our design options and prices are impressively affordable. A detailed quote is available for a $50 consultation fee. Plan modification is an interactive service. Our skilled team of designers will guide you through the customization process from start to finish making recommendations, offering ideas, and determining the feasibility of your changes. This level of service is offered to ensure the final modified plan meets your expectations. If you use our service the $50 fee will be applied to the cost of the modifications.

You may purchase the customization consultation before or after purchasing a plan. In either case, it is necessary to purchase the Reproducible Plan Package and complete the accompanying license to modify the plan before we can begin customization.

Customization Consultation..$50

TOOLS TO WORK WITH YOUR BUILDER

**Two Reverse Options For Your Convenience –
Mirror and Right-Reading Reverse (as available)**
Mirror reverse plans simply flip the design 180 degrees—keep in mind, the text will also be flipped. For a minimal fee you can have one or all of your plans shipped mirror reverse, although we recommend having at least one regular set handy. Right-reading reverse plans show the design flipped 180 degrees but the text reads normally. When you choose this option, we ship each set of purchased blueprints in this format.

Mirror Reverse Fee (indicate the number of sets when ordering).........$55
Right Reading Reverse Fee (all sets are reversed).............................$175

A Shopping List Exclusively for Your Home – Materials List
A customized Materials List helps you plan and estimate the cost of your new home, outlining the quantity, type, and size of materials needed to build your house (with the exception of mechanical system items). Included are framing lumber, windows and doors, kitchen and bath cabinetry, rough and finished hardware, and much more.

Materials List......................................$75 each
Additional Materials Lists (at original time of purchase only).......$20 each

**Plan Your Home-
Building Process – Specification Outline**
Work with your builder on this step-by-step chronicle of 166 stages or items crucial to the building process. It provides a comprehensive review of the construction process and helps you choose materials.
Specification Outline................................$10 each

**Get Accurate Cost Estimates for Your Home –
Quote One® Cost Reports**
The Summary Cost Report, the first element in the Quote One® package, breaks down the cost of your home into various categories based on building materials, labor, and installation, and includes three grades of construction: Budget, Standard, and Custom. Make even more informed decisions about your project with the second element of our package, the Material Cost Report. The material and installation cost is shown for each of more than 1,000 line items provided in the standard-grade Materials List, which is included with this tool. Additional space is included for estimates from contractors and subcontractors, such as for mechanical materials, which are not included in our packages.

Quote One® Summary Cost Report......................................$35
Quote One® Detailed Material Cost Report..........................$140*
*Detailed material cost report includes the Materials List

Learn the Basics of Building – Electrical, Plumbing, Mechanical, Construction Detail Sheets
If you want to know more about building techniques—and deal more confidently with your subcontractors—we offer four useful detail sheets. These sheets provide non-plan-specific general information, but are excellent tools that will add to your understanding of Plumbing Details, Electrical Details, Construction Details, and Mechanical Details.

Electrical Detail Sheet...$14.95
Plumbing Detail Sheet...$14.95
Mechanical Detail Sheet...$14.95
Construction Detail Sheet...$14.95

SUPER VALUE SETS:
Buy any 2: $26.95; Buy any 3: $34.95; Buy All 4: $39.95

GETTY IMAGES (2)

264 HILLSIDE HOME PLANS   ORDER BLUEPRINTS 24 HOURS, 7 DAYS A WEEK, AT 1-800-521-6797 OR EPLANS.COM

MAKE YOUR HOME TECH-READY –
HOME AUTOMATION UPGRADE

Building a new home provides a unique opportunity to wire it with a plan for future needs. A Home Automation-Ready (HA-Ready) home contains the wiring substructure of tomorrow's connected home. It means that every room—from the front porch to the backyard, and from the attic to the basement—is wired for security, lighting, telecommunications, climate control, home computer networking, whole-house audio, home theater, shade control, video surveillance, entry access control, and yes, video gaming electronic solutions.

Along with the conveniences HA-Ready homes provide, they also have a higher resale value. The Consumer Electronics Association (CEA), in conjunction with the Custom Electronic Design and Installation Association (CEDIA), have developed a TechHome™ Rating system that quantifies the value of HA-Ready homes. The rating system is gaining widespread recognition in the real estate industry.

Developed by CEDIA-certified installers, our Home Automation Upgrade package includes everything you need to work with an installer during the construction of your home. It provides a short explanation of the various subsystems, a wiring floor plan for each level of your home, a detailed materials list with estimated costs, and a list of CEDIA-certified installers in your local area.

Home Automation Upgrade..$250

DESIGN YOUR HOME –
INTERIOR AND EXTERIOR FINISHING TOUCHES

Be Your Own Interior Designer! –
Home Furniture Planner

Effectively plan the space in your home using our Hands-On Home Furniture Planner. It's fun and easy—no more moving heavy pieces of furniture to see how the room will go together. The kit includes reusable peel-and-stick furniture templates that fit on a 12"x18" laminated layout board—enough space to lay out every room in your house.

Home Furniture Planning Kit..$15.95

Enjoy the Outdoors! – Deck Plans

Many of our homes have a corresponding deck plan, sold separately, which includes a Deck Plan Frontal Sheet, Deck Framing and Floor Plans, Deck Elevations, and a Deck Materials List. A Standard Deck Details Package, also available, provides all the how-to information necessary for building any deck. Get both the Deck Plan and the Standard Deck Details Package for one low price in our Complete Deck Building Package. See the price tier chart below and call for deck plan availability.

Deck Details (only)..$14.95
Deck Building Package......................................Plan price + $14.95

Create a Professionally Designed Landscape –
Landscape Plans

Many of our homes have a front-yard Landscape Plan that is complementary in design to the house plan. These comprehensive Landscape Blueprint Packages include a Frontal Sheet, Plan View, Regionalized Plant & Materials List, a sheet on Planting and Maintaining Your Landscape, Zone Maps, and a Plant Size and Description Guide. Each set of blueprints is a full 18" x 24" with clear, complete instructions in easy-to-read type. Our Landscape Plans are available with a Plant & Materials List adapted by horticultural experts to eight regions of the country. Please specify your region when ordering your plan—see region map below. Call for more information about landscape plan availability and applicable regions.

LANDSCAPE & DECK PRICE SCHEDULE

PRICE TIERS	1-SET STUDY PACKAGE	5-SET BUILDING PACKAGE	8-SET BUILDING PACKAGE	1-SET REPRODUCIBLE*
P1	$25	$55	$95	$145
P2	$45	$75	$115	$165
P3	$75	$105	$145	$195
P4	$105	$135	$175	$225
P5	$145	$175	$215	$275
P6	$185	$215	$255	$315

TERMS & CONDITIONS

OUR 90-DAY EXCHANGE POLICY

Hanley Wood is committed to ensuring your satisfaction with your blueprint order, which is why we offer a 90-day exchange policy. With the exception of Reproducible Plan Package orders, we will exchange your entire first order for an equal or greater number of blueprints from our plan collection within 90 days of the original order. The entire content of your original order must be returned before an exchange will be processed. Please call our customer service department at 1-888-690-1116 for your return authorization number and shipping instructions. If the returned blueprints look used, redlined, or copied, we will not honor your exchange. Fees for exchanging your blueprints are as follows: 20% of the amount of the original order, plus the difference in cost if exchanging for a design in a higher price bracket or less the difference in cost if exchanging for a design in a lower price bracket. (Because they can be copied, Reproducible blueprints are not exchangeable or refundable.) Please call for current postage and handling prices. Shipping and handling charges are not refundable.

ARCHITECTURAL AND ENGINEERING SEALS

Some cities and states now require that a licensed architect or engineer review and "seal" a blueprint, or officially approve it, prior to construction. Prior to application for a building permit or the start of actual construction, we strongly advise that you consult your local building official who can tell you if such a review is required.

LOCAL BUILDING CODES AND ZONING REQUIREMENTS

Each plan was designed to meet or exceed the requirements of a nationally recognized model building code in effect at the time and place the plan was drawn. Typically plans designed after the year 2000 conform to the International Residential Building Code (IRC 2000 or 2003). The IRC is comprised of portions of the three major codes below. Plans drawn before 2000 conform to one of the three recognized building codes in effect at the time: Building Officials and Code Administrators (BOCA) International, Inc.; the Southern Building Code Congress International, (SBCCI) Inc.; the International Conference of Building Officials (ICBO); or the Council of American Building Officials (CABO).

Because of the great differences in geography and climate throughout the United States and Canada, each state, county, and municipality has its own building codes, zone requirements, ordinances, and building regulations. Your plan may need to be modified to comply with local requirements. In addition, you may need to obtain permits or inspections from local governments before and in the course of construction. We authorize the use of the blueprints on the express condition that you consult a local licensed architect or engineer of your choice prior to beginning construction and strictly comply with all local building codes, zoning requirements, and other applicable laws, regulations, ordinances, and requirements. Notice: Plans for homes to be built in Nevada must be redrawn by a Nevada-registered professional. Consult your local building official for more information on this subject.

TERMS AND CONDITIONS

These designs are protected under the terms of United States Copyright Law and may not be copied or reproduced in any way, by any means, unless you have purchased a Reproducible Plan Package and signed the accompanying license to modify and copy the plan, which clearly indicates your right to modify, copy, or reproduce. We authorize the use of your chosen design as an aid in the construction of ONE (1) single- or multifamily home only. You may not use this design to build a second dwelling or multiple dwellings without purchasing another blueprint or blueprints or paying additional design fees. Multi-use fees vary by designer—please call one of experienced sales representatives for a quote.

DISCLAIMER

The designers we work with have put substantial care and effort into the creation of their blueprints. However, because we cannot provide on-site consultation, supervision, and control over actual construction, and because of the great variance in local building requirements, building practices, and soil, seismic, weather, and other conditions, WE MAKE NO WARRANTY OF ANY KIND, EXPRESS OR IMPLIED, WITH RESPECT TO THE CONTENT OR USE OF THE BLUEPRINTS, INCLUDING BUT NOT LIMITED TO ANY WARRANTY OF MERCHANTABILITY OR OF FITNESS FOR A PARTICULAR PURPOSE. ITEMS, PRICES, TERMS, AND CONDITIONS ARE SUBJECT TO CHANGE WITHOUT NOTICE.

BUY WITH CONFIDENCE!

CALL TOLL-FREE 1-800-521-6797 OR VISIT EPLANS.COM

IMPORTANT COPYRIGHT NOTICE

From the Council of Publishing Home Designers

Blueprints for residential construction (or working drawings, as they are often called in the industry) are copyrighted intellectual property, protected under the terms of the United States Copyright Law and, therefore, cannot be copied legally for use in building. The following are some guidelines to help you get what you need to build your home, without violating copyright law:

1. HOME PLANS ARE COPYRIGHTED

Just like books, movies, and songs, home plans receive protection under the federal copyright laws. The copyright laws prevent anyone, other than the copyright owner, from reproducing, modifying, or reusing the plans or design without permission of the copyright owner.

2. DO NOT COPY DESIGNS OR FLOOR PLANS FROM ANY PUBLICATION, ELECTRONIC MEDIA, OR EXISTING HOME

It is illegal to copy, change, or redraw home designs found in a plan book, CD-ROM, or on the Internet. The right to modify plans is one of the exclusive rights of copyright. It is also illegal to copy or redraw a constructed home that is protected by copyright, even if you have never seen the plans for the home. If you find a plan or home that you like, you must purchase a set of plans from an authorized source. The plans may not be lent, given away, or sold by the purchaser.

3. DO NOT USE PLANS TO BUILD MORE THAN ONE HOUSE

The original purchaser of house plans is typically licensed to build a single home from the plans. Building more than one home from the plans without permission is an infringement of the home designer's copyright. The purchase of a multiple-set package of plans is for the construction of a single home only. The purchase of additional sets of plans does not grant the right to construct more than one home.

4. HOUSE PLANS IN THE FORM OF BLUEPRINTS OR BLACKLINES CANNOT BE COPIED OR REPRODUCED

Plans, blueprints, or blacklines, unless they are reproducibles, cannot be copied or reproduced without prior written consent of the copyright owner. Copy shops and blueprinters are prohibited from making copies of these plans without the copyright release letter you receive with reproducible plans.

5. HOUSE PLANS IN THE FORM OF BLUEPRINTS OR BLACKLINES CANNOT BE REDRAWN

Plans cannot be modified or redrawn without first obtaining the copyright owner's permission. With your purchase of plans, you are licensed to make non-structural changes by "red-lining" the purchased plans. If you need to make structural changes or need to redraw the plans for any reason, you must purchase a reproducible set of plans (see topic 6) which includes a license to modify the plans. Blueprints do not come with a license to make structural changes or to redraw the plans. You may not reuse or sell the modified design.

6. REPRODUCIBILE HOME PLANS

Reproducible plans (for example sepias, mylars, CAD files, electronic files, and vellums) come with a license to make modifications to the plans. Once modified, the plans can be taken to a local copy shop or blueprinter to make up to 10 or 12 copies of the plans to use in the construction of a single home. Only one home can be constructed from any single purchased set of reproducible plans either in original form or as modified. The license to modify and copy must be completed and returned before the plan will be shipped.

7. MODIFIED DESIGNS CANNOT BE REUSED

Even if you are licensed to make modifications to a copyrighted design, the modified design is not free from the original designer's copyright. The sale or reuse of the modified design is prohibited. Also, be aware that any modification to plans relieves the original designer from liability for design defects and voids all warranties expressed or implied.

8. WHO IS RESPONSIBLE FOR COPYRIGHT INFRINGEMENT?

Any party who participates in a copyright violation may be responsible including the purchaser, designers, architects, engineers, drafters, homeowners, builders, contractors, sub-contractors, copy shops, blueprinters, developers, and real estate agencies. It does not matter whether or not the individual knows that a violation is being committed. Ignorance of the law is not a valid defense.

9. PLEASE RESPECT HOME DESIGN COPYRIGHTS

In the event of any suspected violation of a copyright, or if there is any uncertainty about the plans purchased, the publisher, architect, designer, or the Council of Publishing Home Designers (www.cphd.org) should be contacted before proceeding. Awards are sometimes offered for information about home design copyright infringement.

10. PENALTIES FOR INFRINGEMENT

Penalties for violating a copyright may be severe. The responsible parties are required to pay actual damages caused by the infringement (which may be substantial), plus any profits made by the infringer commissions to include all profits from the sale of any home built from an infringing design. The copyright law also allows for the recovery of statutory damages, which may be as high as $150,000 for each infringement. Finally, the infringer may be required to pay legal fees which often exceed the damages.

BLUEPRINT PRICE SCHEDULE

PRICE TIERS	1-SET STUDY PACKAGE	5-SET BUILDING PACKAGE	8-SET BUILDING PACKAGE	1-SET REPRODUCIBLE*
A1	$450	$500	$555	$675
A2	$490	$545	$595	$735
A3	$540	$605	$665	$820
A4	$590	$660	$725	$895
C1	$640	$715	$775	$950
C2	$690	$760	$820	$1025
C3	$735	$810	$875	$1100
C4	$785	$860	$925	$1175
L1	$895	$990	$1075	$1335
L2	$970	$1065	$1150	$1455
L3	$1075	$1175	$1270	$1600
L4	$1185	$1295	$1385	$1775
SQ1				.40/SQ. FT.
SQ3				.55/SQ. FT.
SQ5				.80/SQ. FT.

PRICES SUBJECT TO CHANGE * REQUIRES A FAX NUMBER

PLAN #	PRICE TIER	PAGE	MATERIALS LIST	QUOTE ONE	DECK	DECK PRICE	LANDSCAPE	LANDSCAPE PRICE	REGIONS
HPK1400006	SQ1	8							
HPK1400007	C1	10							
HPK1400008	SQ1	12	Y						
HPK1400009	C1	13	Y	Y			OLA038	P3	7
HPK1400010	C1	14	Y						
HPK1400011	SQ1	15	Y						
HPK1400012	A4	16							
HPK1400013	SQ1	17	Y						
HPK1400014	SQ1	18	Y	Y					
HPK1400015	C1	19	Y						
HPK1400016	C2	20	Y				OLA001	P3	123568
HPK1400017	C1	21							
HPK1400018	C2	22	Y						
HPK1400019	SQ1	23	Y						
HPK1400020	C3	24	Y						
HPK1400021	A4	25							
HPK1400022	A3	26	Y				OLA004	P3	123568
HPK1400023	C1	27							
HPK1400024	C2	28	Y						
HPK1400025	A3	29	Y						
HPK1400026	A3	30							
HPK1400027	A3	31							
HPK1400028	A2	32	Y						
HPK1400029	C2	33							
HPK1400030	A2	34	Y						
HPK1400031	A4	35							
HPK1400032	SQ1	36							
HPK1400033	A3	37							
HPK1400034	A3	38	Y						
HPK1400035	C3	39							
HPK1400036	C1	40							
HPK1400037	A3	41							
HPK1400038	A4	42							
HPK1400039	C1	43							
HPK1400234	C2	44							
HPK1400235	C2	45							
HPK1400040	C2	46	Y						
HPK1400041	C2	47							
HPK1400042	A3	48	Y						
HPK1400043	A3	49							
HPK1400044	A3	50	Y						
HPK1400045	C4	51							
HPK1400046	A3	52							
HPK1400047	C2	53							
HPK1400048	A3	54	Y						
HPK1400049	C2	55							
HPK1400050	L2	58							
HPK1400051	SQ1	60							
HPK1400052	SQ1	62							
HPK1400053	SQ1	63	Y	Y					
HPK1400054	A3	64							
HPK1400236	C2	65							
HPK1400055	C4	66	Y						
HPK1400056	C1	67	Y						
HPK1400057	L2	68							
HPK1400058	C3	69	Y						
HPK1400004	C1	70							
HPK1400059	SQ1	71							
HPK1400060	A3	72	Y						
HPK1400061	C3	73	Y						
HPK1400062	C1	74	Y						
HPK1400063	SQ1	75	Y						
HPK1400002	A2	76	Y						
HPK1400064	L1	77							
HPK1400065	A3	78	Y						
HPK1400066	A1	79	Y						
HPK1400067	A2	80	Y						
HPK1400068	A3	81	Y						
HPK1400069	L2	82							
HPK1400070	SQ1	83	Y						
HPK1400071	C1	84							
HPK1400072	C2	85							
HPK1400073	SQ1	86							
HPK1400074	SQ1	87	Y						
HPK1400075	C4	88	Y						
HPK1400003	C2	89	Y	Y					
HPK1400076	C2	90	Y	Y					
HPK1400077	A3	91							
HPK1400078	A4	92							
HPK1400079	SQ1	93	Y						
HPK1400080	C2	94	Y	Y					
HPK1400081	SQ1	95	Y	Y					
HPK1400082	C2	96	Y	Y					
HPK1400083	C4	97							

PLAN #	PRICE TIER	PAGE	MATERIALS LIST	QUOTE ONE*	DECK	DECK PRICE	LANDSCAPE	LANDSCAPE PRICE	REGIONS
HPK1400084	C4	98							
HPK1400085	C1	99	Y	Y					
HPK1400086	C3	100	Y	Y					
HPK1400087	SQ1	101							
HPK1400088	C2	102							
HPK1400089	C1	103							
HPK1400090	C3	104							
HPK1400091	C2	105							
HPK1400092	L2	106							
HPK1400093	C3	107	Y						
HPK1400094	SQ1	108							
HPK1400005	L3	109							
HPK1400095	L2	110							
HPK1400096	SQ1	111							
HPK1400097	C4	112							
HPK1400098	C4	113	Y	Y	ODA010	P3	OLA021	P3	123568
HPK1400099	L1	114							
HPK1400100	C3	115	Y				OLA038	P3	7
HPK1400101	L1	116	Y						
HPK1400102	C2	117	Y						
HPK1400103	SQ1	118							
HPK1400104	SQ1	119							
HPK1400105	SQ1	120							
HPK1400106	C2	121	Y	Y			OLA003	P3	123568
HPK1400107	C4	122							
HPK1400108	C2	123	Y	Y					
HPK1400109	C3	124							
HPK1400110	SQ1	125							
HPK1400111	SQ1	126							
HPK1400112	SQ1	127							
HPK1400113	C3	128							
HPK1400114	C1	129							
HPK1400115	L1	130							
HPK1400116	SQ1	131	Y	Y					
HPK1400117	C4	132							
HPK1400118	SQ1	133	Y	Y					
HPK1400119	SQ1	136							
HPK1400120	C2	138	Y						
HPK1400121	A2	140	Y						
HPK1400122	A2	141	Y						
HPK1400123	C1	142							
HPK1400124	C1	143							
HPK1400125	C1	144							
HPK1400126	A2	145	Y						
HPK1400127	C1	146							
HPK1400128	A2	147							
HPK1400129	A4	148	Y						
HPK1400130	C1	149							
HPK1400131	A2	150	Y						
HPK1400132	A3	151							
HPK1400133	A2	152	Y						

PLAN #	PRICE TIER	PAGE	MATERIALS LIST	QUOTE ONE*	DECK	DECK PRICE	LANDSCAPE	LANDSCAPE PRICE	REGIONS
HPK1400134	A2	153	Y						
HPK1400135	A2	154	Y						
HPK1400136	A2	155	Y						
HPK1400137	A2	156	Y						
HPK1400138	A2	157	Y						
HPK1400139	A2	158	Y						
HPK1400140	A2	159	Y						
HPK1400141	A2	160	Y						
HPK1400142	A2	161	Y						
HPK1400143	A2	162	Y						
HPK1400237	C2	163							
HPK1400144	A2	164	Y						
HPK1400145	A2	165	Y						
HPK1400146	A3	166							
HPK1400147	A2	167	Y						
HPK1400148	C3	168	Y	Y			OLA021	P3	123568
HPK1400149	A2	169	Y						
HPK1400150	A2	170	Y						
HPK1400151	A2	171	Y						
HPK1400152	A2	172	Y						
HPK1400153	C2	173	Y				OLA029	P3	12345678
HPK1400154	C4	176							
HPK1400155	C4	178							
HPK1400156	C1	180							
HPK1400157	SQ1	181							
HPK1400158	C4	182							
HPK1400159	SQ1	183							
HPK1400160	C1	184							
HPK1400161	A4	185	Y						
HPK1400162	C3	186	Y						
HPK1400163	SQ1	187							
HPK1400164	SQ1	188							
HPK1400165	L1	189	Y						
HPK1400166	A3	190							
HPK1400167	A3	191							
HPK1400168	C1	192	Y						
HPK1400169	C1	193							
HPK1400170	C2	194	Y						
HPK1400171	C2	195	Y						
HPK1400172	C2	196							
HPK1400173	C1	197							
HPK1400174	L1	198	Y						
HPK1400175	C4	199	Y						
HPK1400176	C1	200							
HPK1400177	SQ3	201							
HPK1400178	L3	202							
HPK1400179	L2	203							
HPK1400180	C3	204							
HPK1400181	SQ1	205							
HPK1400182	SQ1	206							
HPK1400183	L1	207							

PLAN #	PRICE TIER	PAGE	MATERIALS LIST	QUOTE ONE*	DECK	DECK PRICE	LANDSCAPE	LANDSCAPE PRICE	REGIONS
HPK1400184	L2	210							
HPK1400185	SQ1	212							
HPK1400186	C1	214							
HPK1400187	C4	215							
HPK1400188	C3	216	Y						
HPK1400189	L1	217							
HPK1400190	C3	218							
HPK1400191	C4	219							
HPK1400192	C2	220							
HPK1400193	C1	221							
HPK1400194	C3	222	Y						
HPK1400195	A4	223	Y						
HPK1400196	A2	224	Y						
HPK1400197	A4	225							
HPK1400198	C1	226							
HPK1400199	C3	227	Y						
HPK1400200	A4	228							
HPK1400201	L2	229	Y	Y			OLA024	P4	123568
HPK1400202	C1	230					OLA024	P4	123568
HPK1400203	C1	231					OLA024	P4	123568
HPK1400204	A4	232							
HPK1400205	A3	233	Y						
HPK1400206	A3	234	Y						
HPK1400207	C1	235	Y						
HPK1400208	C2	236	Y						
HPK1400209	SQ1	237							
HPK1400210	C4	238	Y						
HPK1400211	C1	239	Y						
HPK1400212	C1	240							
HPK1400213	A3	241							
HPK1400214	C4	242							
HPK1400215	C3	243	Y						
HPK1400216	C4	244							
HPK1400217	L1	245							
HPK1400218	C4	246							
HPK1400219	A4	247	Y						
HPK1400220	L1	248							
HPK1400221	A2	249							
HPK1400222	C2	250	Y	Y					
HPK1400223	SQ1	251							
HPK1400224	C2	252	Y	Y			OLA024	P4	123568
HPK1400225	C4	253							
HPK1400226	SQ1	254							
HPK1400227	C2	255	Y						
HPK1400228	A4	256							
HPK1400229	C2	257	Y						
HPK1400230	A2	258	Y						
HPK1400231	C1	259							
HPK1400232	C2	260	Y						
HPK1400233	C3	261					OLA004	P3	123568

Idyllic Escapes

Take the plunge and start building your perfect vacation home. No matter if you are seeking a breathtaking view, a relaxing retreat or a cozy cabin, HomePlanners has the house plan to fit your every fantasy.

If you are looking to build a vacation home, look to HomePlanners first.

pick up a copy today!

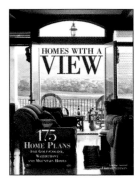

HOMES WITH A VIEW
ISBN 1-931131-25-2

$14.95 (192 PAGES)

175 Plans for Golf-Course, Waterfront and Mountain Homes
This stunning collection features homes as magnificent as the vistas they showcase. A 32-page, full-color gallery showcases the most spectacular homes—all designed specifically to accent the natural beauty of their surrounding landscapes.

COOL COTTAGES
ISBN 1-881955-91-5

$10.95 (256 PAGES)

245 Delightful Retreats 825 to 3,500 square feet
Cozy, inviting house plans designed to provide the ideal escape from the stress of daily life. This charming compilation offers perfect hideaways for every locale: mountaintops to foothills, woodlands to everglades.

VACATION AND SECOND HOMES, 3RD ED.
ISBN 1-881955-97-4

$9.95 (448 PAGES)

430 House Plans for Retreats and Getaways
Visit the cutting edge of home design in this fresh portfolio of getaway plans—ready to build anywhere. From sprawling haciendas to small rustic cabins, this collection takes on your wildest dreams with designs suited for waterfronts, cliffsides, or wide-open spaces.

Toll-Free: **800.322.6797**   Online: **http://books.eplans.com**

GETAWAY HOMES
ISBN 1-931131-37-6
$11.95 (288 PAGES)

250 Home Plans for Cottages, Bungalows & Capes
This is the perfect volume for anyone looking to create their own relaxing place to escape life's pressures—whether it's a vacation home or primary residence! Also included, tips to create a comfortable, yet beautiful atmosphere in a small space.

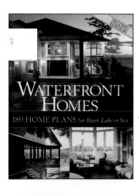

WATERFRONT HOMES
ISBN 1-931131-28-7
$10.95 (208 PAGES)

189 Home Plans for River, Lake or Sea
A beautiful waterfront setting calls for a beautiful home. Whether you are looking for a year-round home or a vacation getaway, this is a fantastic collection of home plans to choose from.

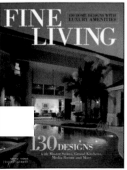

FINE LIVING
ISBN 1-931131-24-4
$17.95 (192 PAGES)

130 Home Designs with Luxury Amenities
The homes in this collection offer lovely exteriors, flowing floor plans and ample interior space, plus a stunning array of amenities that goes above and beyond standard designs. This title features gorgeous full-color photos, tips on furnishing and decorating as well as an extensive reference section packed with inspiring ideas.

HANLEY WOOD CONSUMER GROUP
One Thomas Circle, NW, Suite 600, Washington, DC 20005

A sloping lot allows this home—which strikes an unassuming pose from the front—to make a grand statement in back. Porches on the main level and covered basement both overlook the pool. For details, see page 119.

RUSSELL KINGMAN (2)